GHOST

VOLUME ONE

PROJEKT™

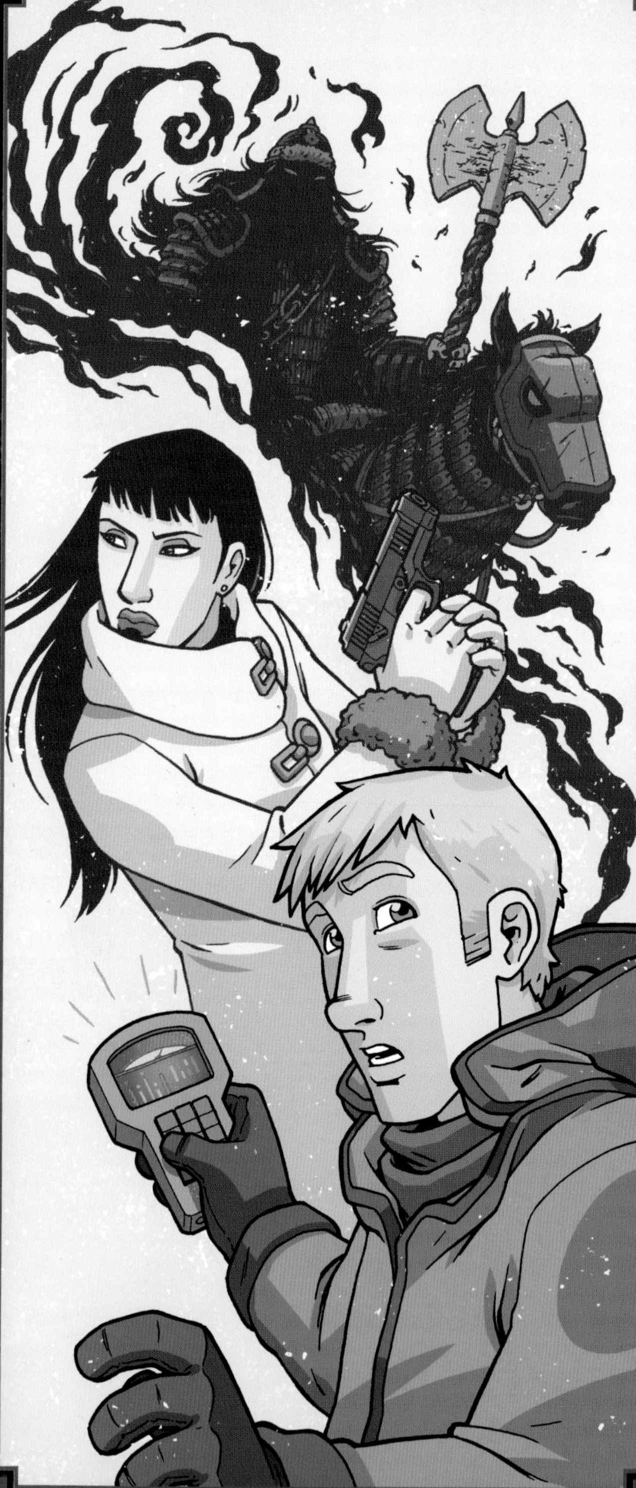

GHOST

VOLUME ONE

PROJEKT

WRITTEN BY
JOE HARRIS

ILLUSTRATED BY
STEVE ROLSTON

COLORED BY
DEAN TRIPPE

LETTERED BY
DOUGLAS E. SHERWOOD

DESIGN BY
KEITH WOOD

SERIES EDITED BY
JAMES LUCAS JONES WITH JILL BEATON

COLLECTION EDITED BY
JILL BEATON

ONI PRESS, INC.
JOE NOZEMACK PUBLISHER
JAMES LUCAS JONES EDITOR IN CHIEF
KEITH WOOD ART DIRECTOR
CORY CASONI MARKETING DIRECTOR
GEORGE ROHAC OPERATIONS DIRECTOR
JILL BEATON ASSOCIATE EDITOR
CHARLIE CHU ASSOCIATE EDITOR
DOUGLAS E. SHERWOOD PRODUCTION ASSISTANT

GHOST PROJEKT™

CREATED BY

JOE HARRIS & STEVE ROLSTON

This volume collects issues #1-5 of the
Oni Press series *Ghost Projekt*.

Oni Press, Inc.
1305 SE Martin Luther King Jr. Blvd.
Suite A
Portland, OR 97214
USA

onipress.com :: joeharris.net :: steverolston.com

First Edition, February 2011

ISBN: 978-1-934964-42-2

1 3 5 7 9 10 8 6 4 2

PRINTED IN CHINA.

CHAPTER 1:

COLD WARRIORS

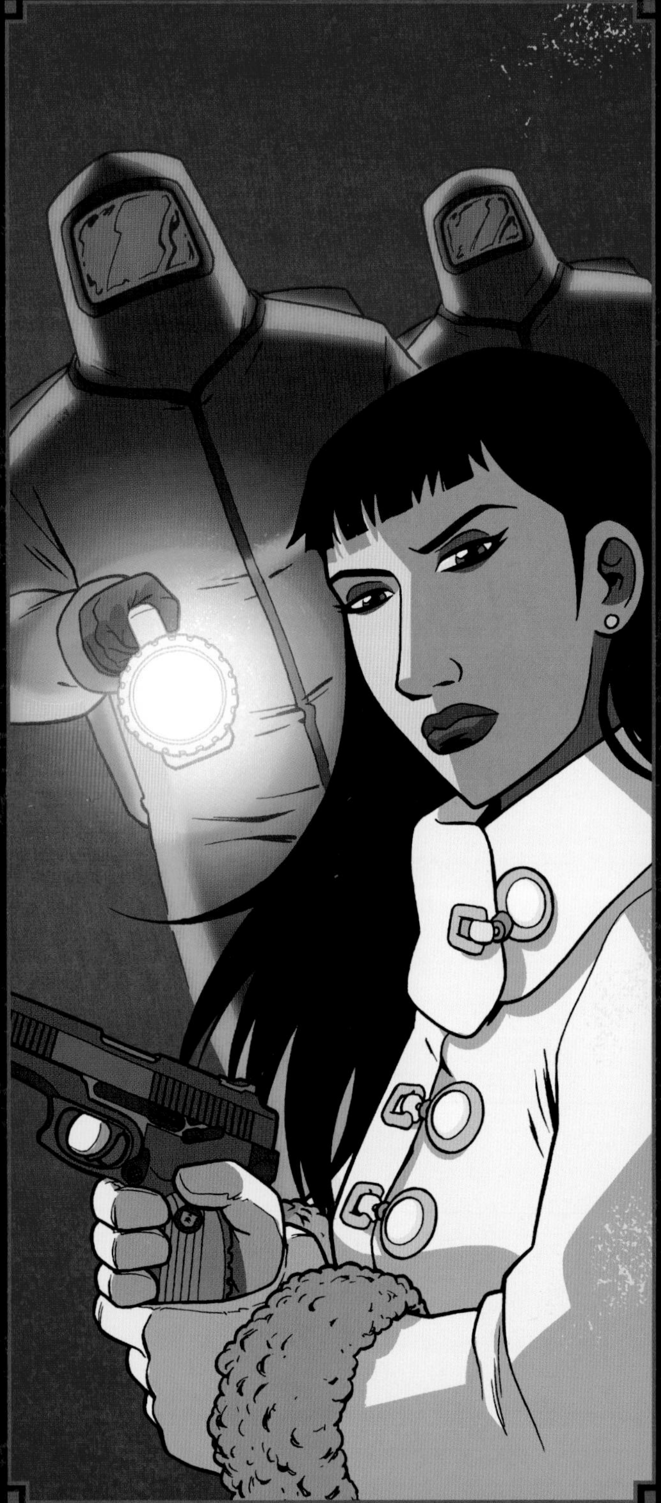

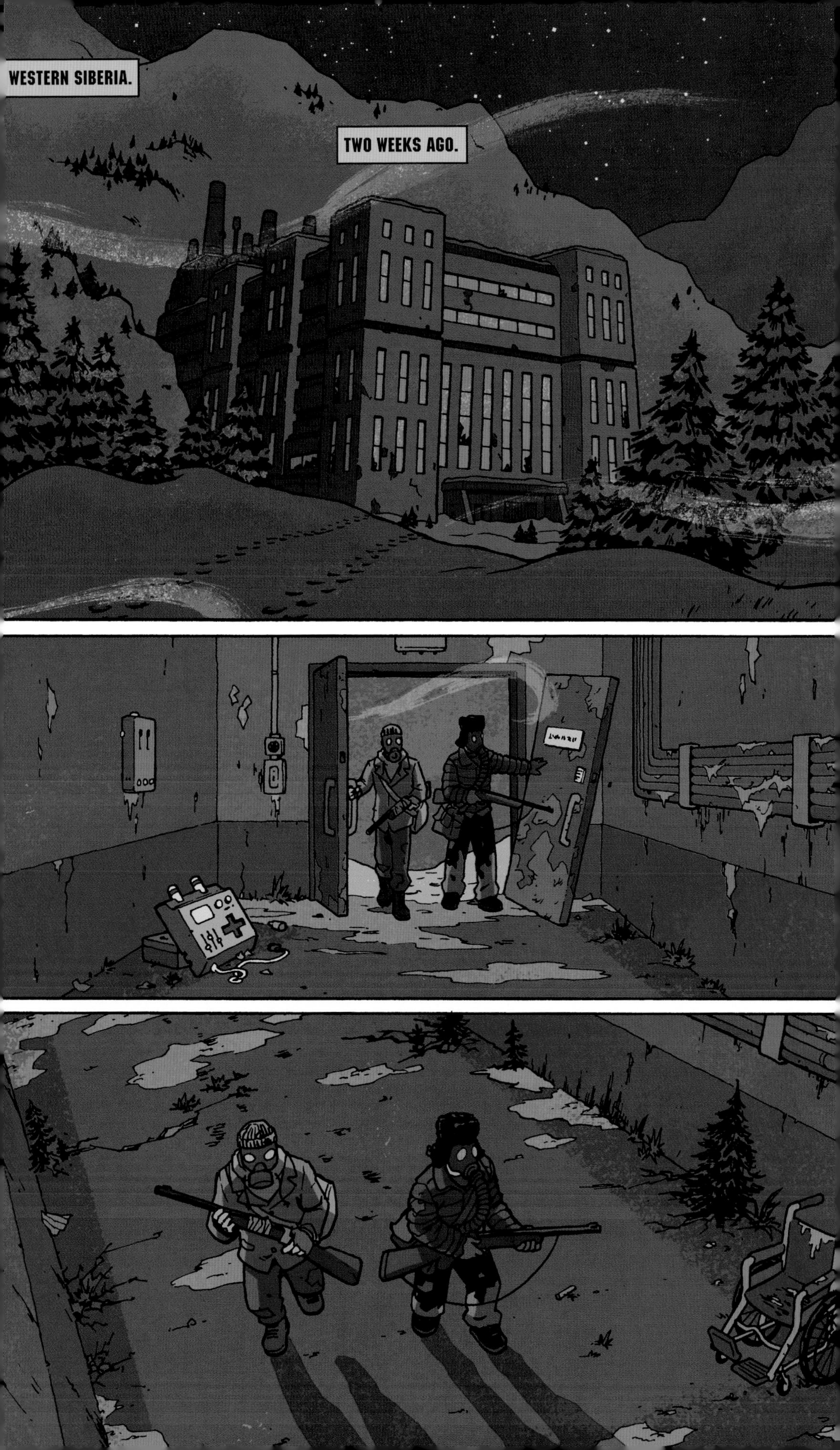
WESTERN SIBERIA.
TWO WEEKS AGO.

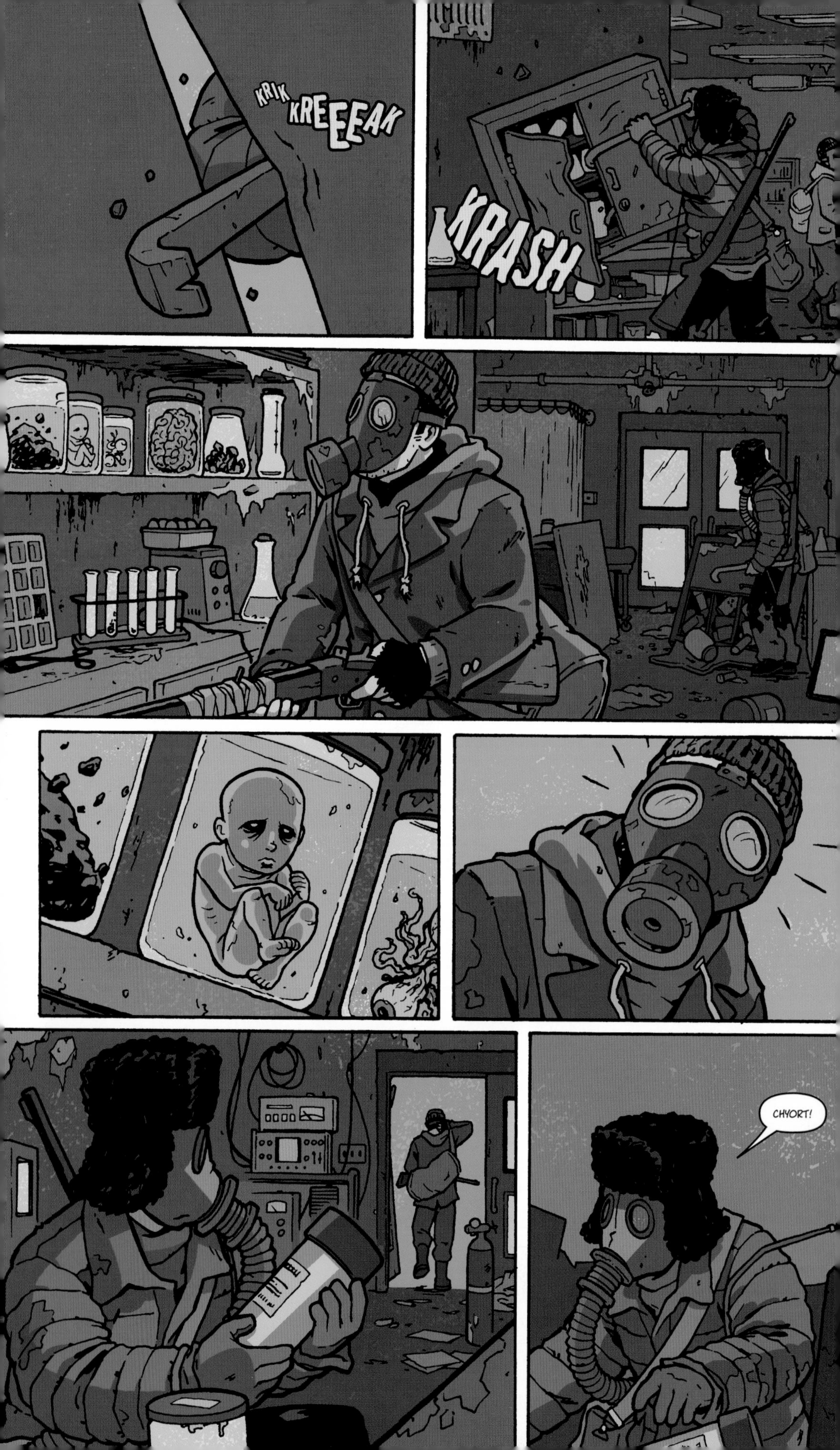
KRIK KREEEEAK
KRASH
CHYORT!

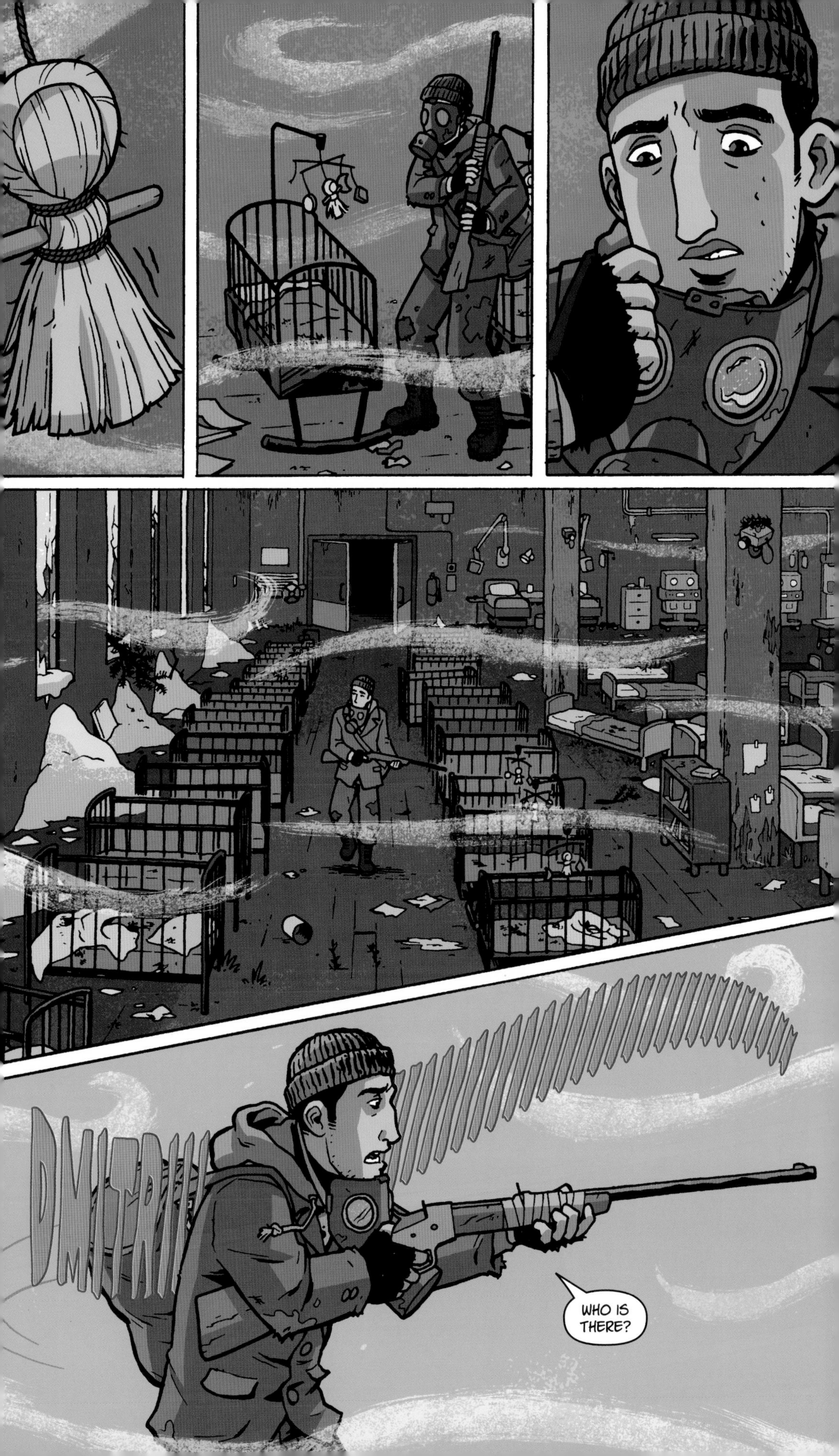
DMITRIII
WHO IS THERE?

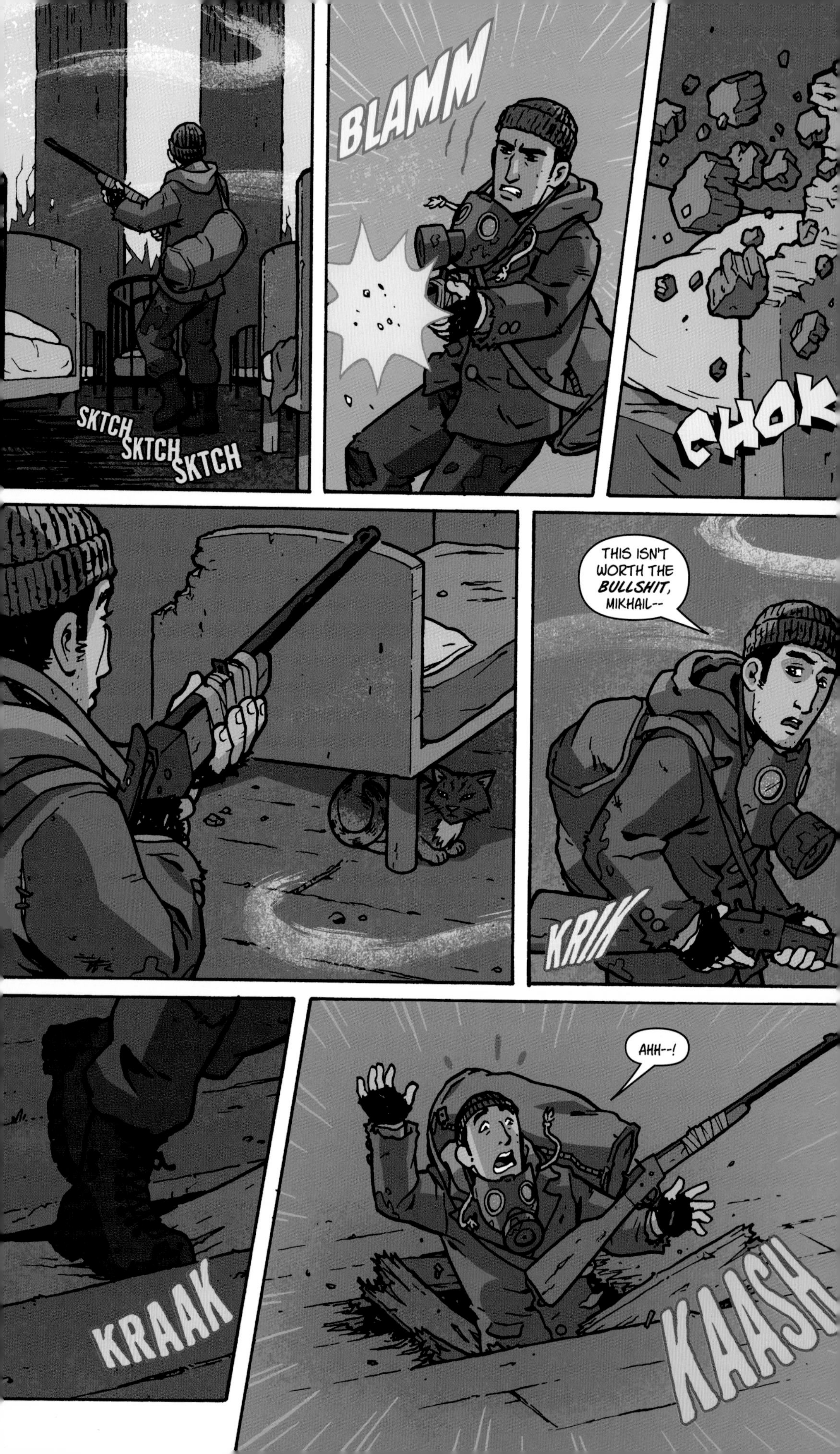
SKTCH
SKTCH
SKTCH
BLAMM
CHOK
THIS ISN'T WORTH THE BULLSHIT, MIKHAIL--
KRIK
KRAAK
AHH--!
KAASH

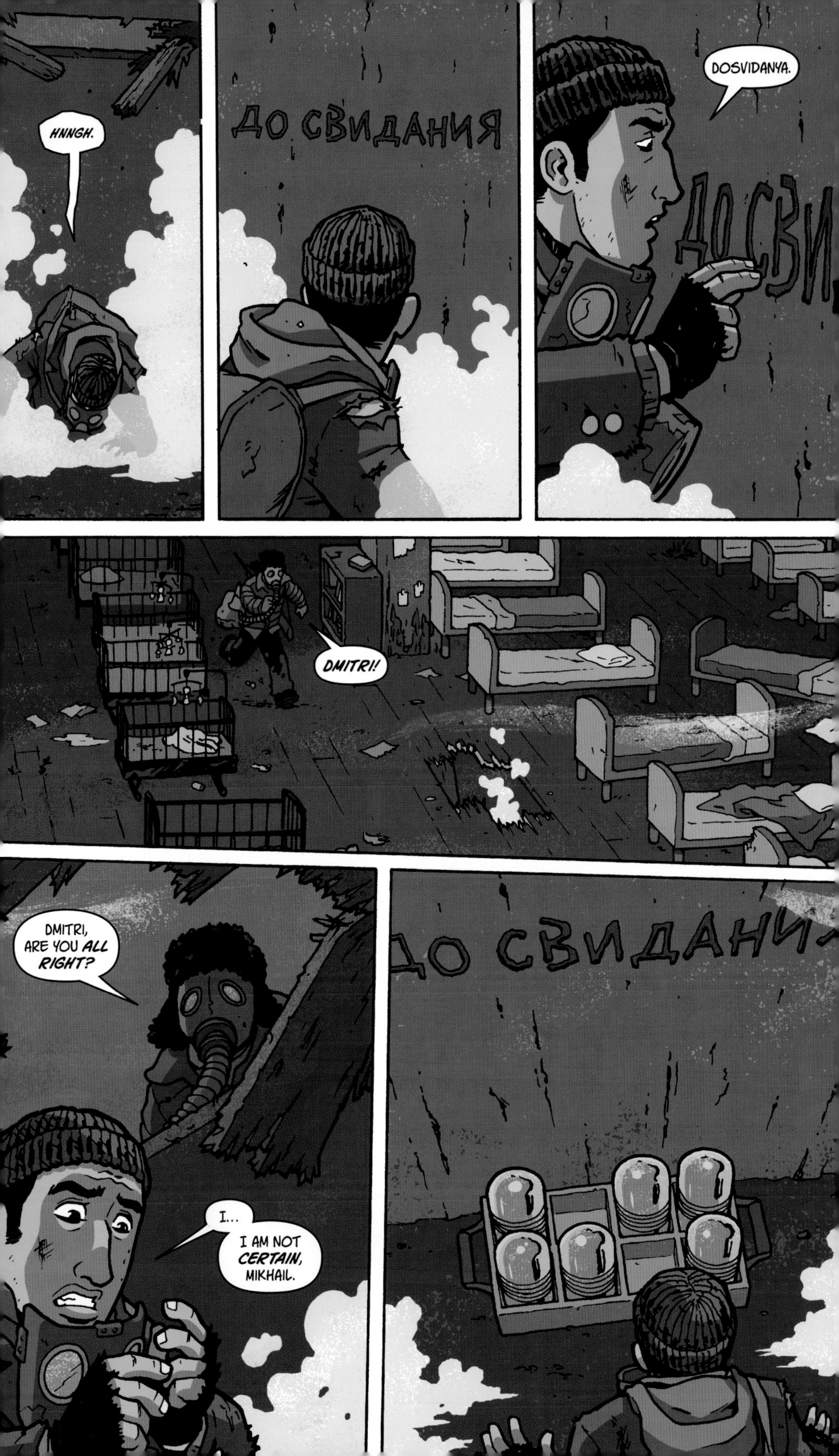
HNNGH.
ДО СВИДАНИЯ
DOSVIDANYA.
ДО СВИ
DMITRI!!
DMITRI, ARE YOU ALL RIGHT?
I... I AM NOT CERTAIN, MIKHAIL.
ДО СВИДАНИ

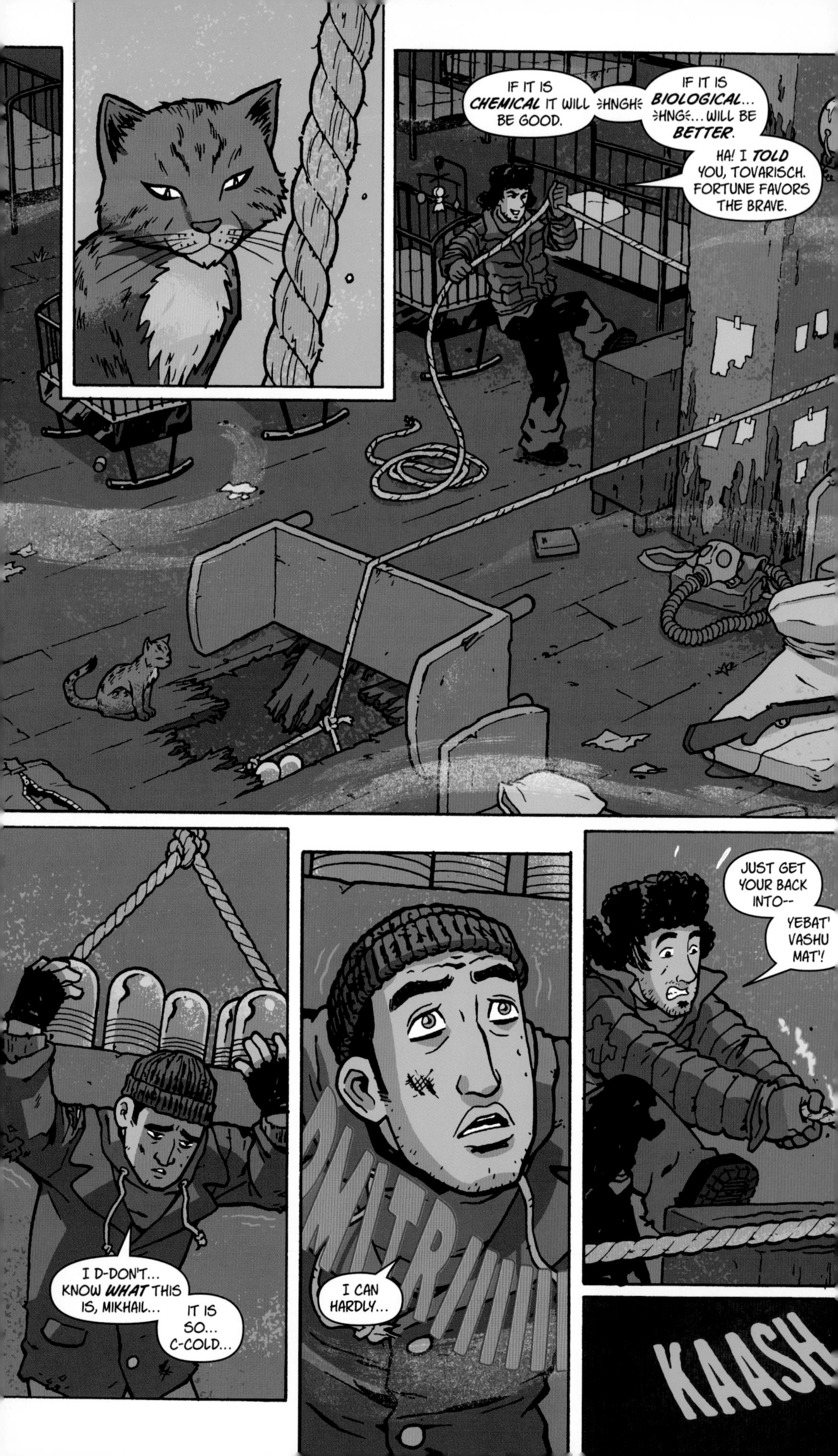
IF IT IS CHEMICAL IT WILL BE GOOD.
≷HNGH≶
IF IT IS BIOLOGICAL... ≷HNG≶... WILL BE BETTER.
HA! I TOLD YOU, TOVARISCH. FORTUNE FAVORS THE BRAVE.
I D-DON'T... KNOW WHAT THIS IS, MIKHAIL...
IT IS SO... C-COLD...
DMITRIIIII
I CAN HARDLY...
JUST GET YOUR BACK INTO--
YEBAT' VASHU MAT'!
KAASH

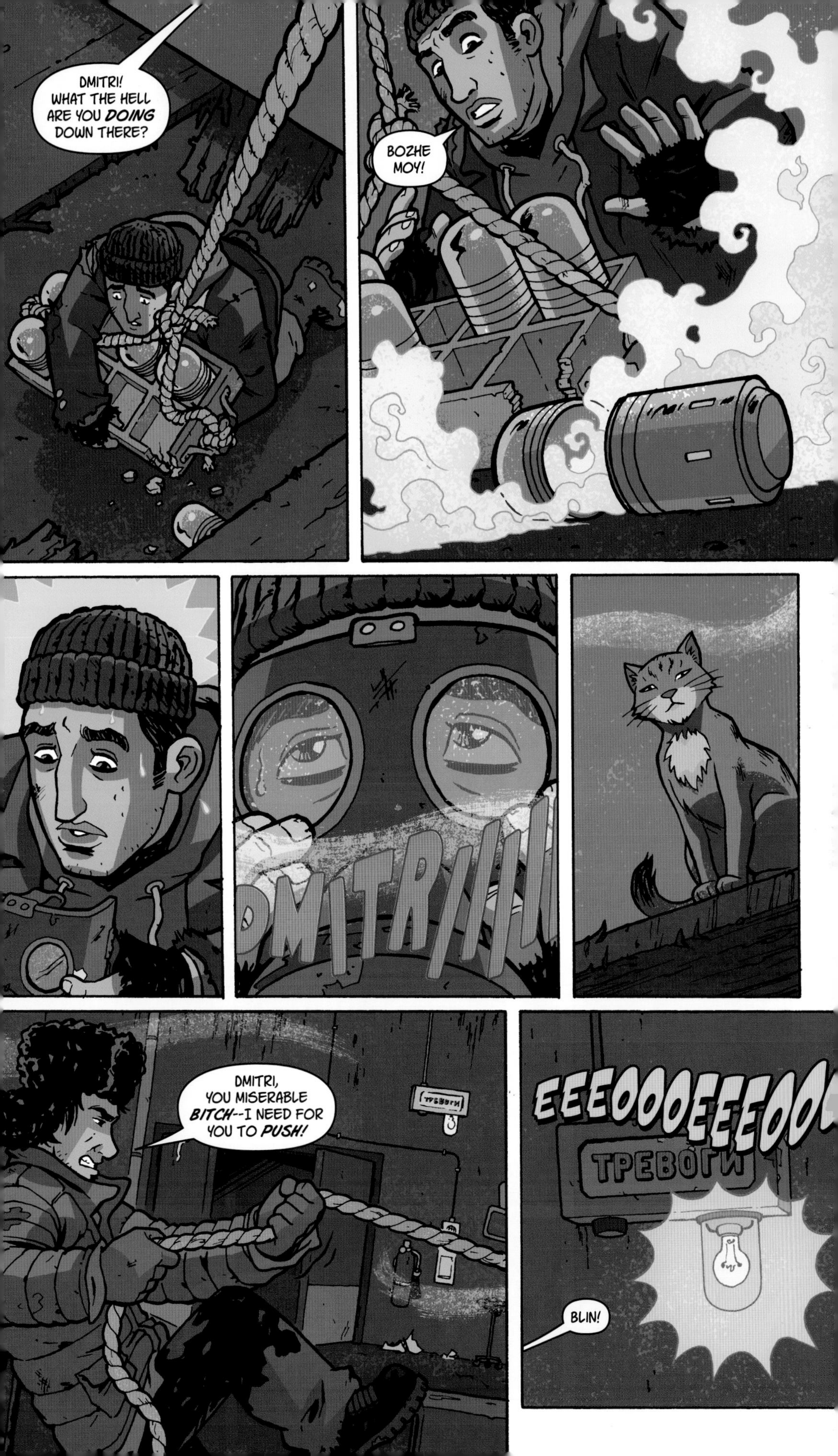
DMITRI! WHAT THE HELL ARE YOU *DOING* DOWN THERE?
BOZHE MOY!
DMITRIIIIII
DMITRI, YOU MISERABLE *BITCH*--I NEED FOR YOU TO *PUSH!*
ТРЕВОГИ
EEEOOOEEEOO
ТРЕВОГИ
BLIN!

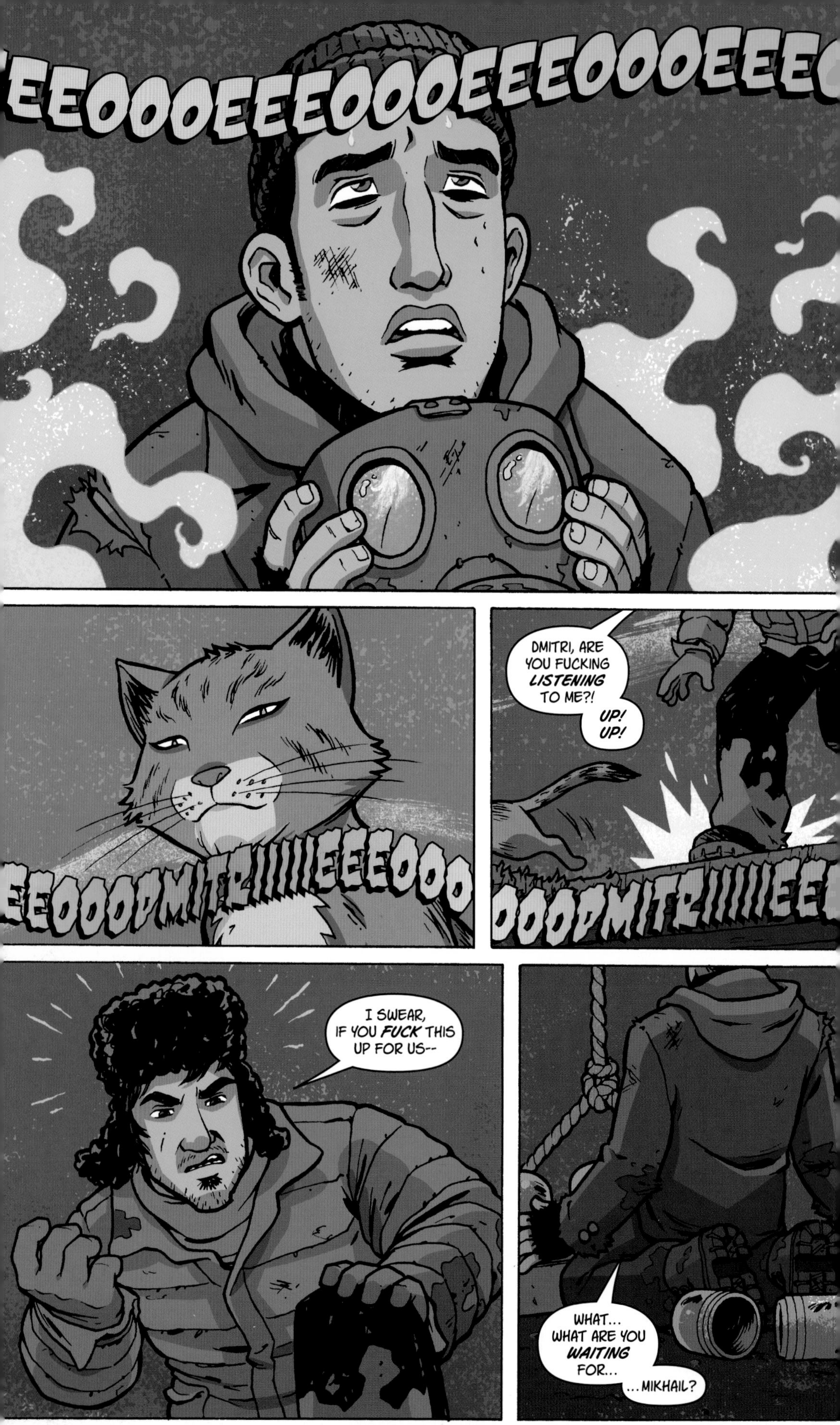
EEOOOOEEEOOOOEEEOOOOEEEO
EEOOOODMITRIIIIIEEEOOO
DMITRI, ARE YOU FUCKING *LISTENING* TO ME?!
UP! UP!
OOOODMITRIIIIIEEE
I SWEAR, IF YOU *FUCK* THIS UP FOR US--
WHAT... WHAT ARE YOU *WAITING* FOR...
...MIKHAIL?

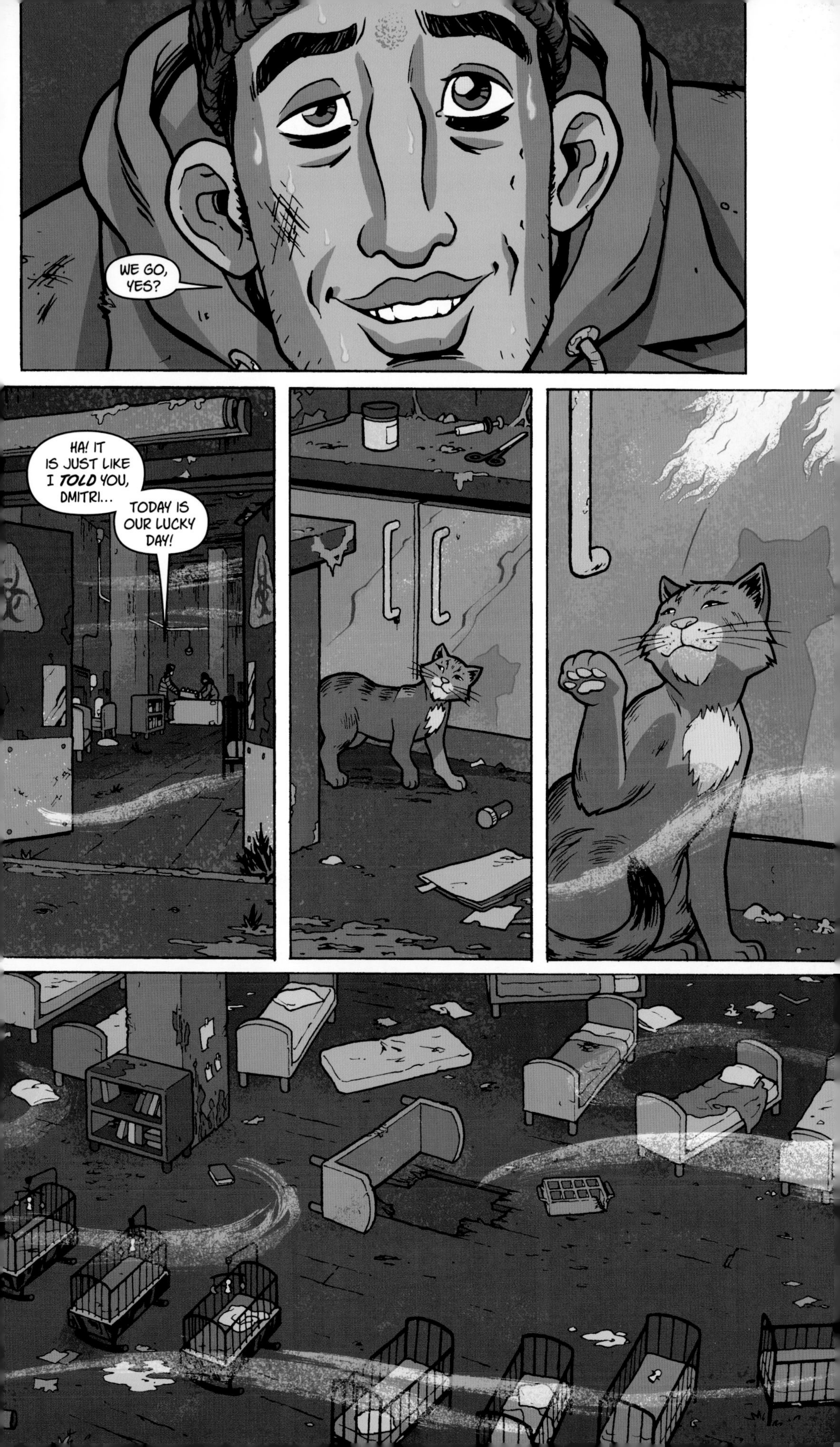
WE GO, YES?
HA! IT IS JUST LIKE I *TOLD* YOU, DMITRI...
TODAY IS OUR LUCKY DAY!

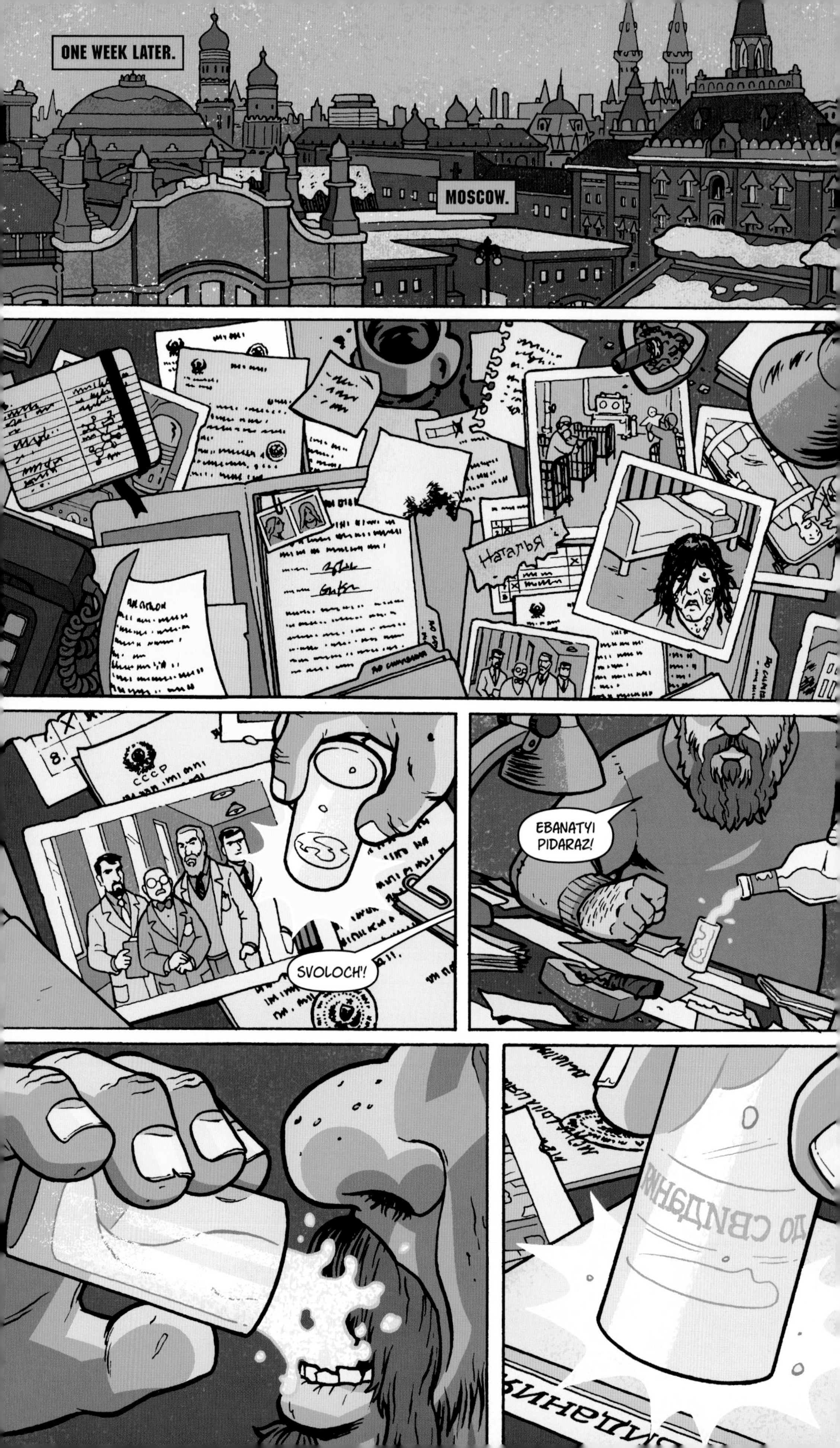
ONE WEEK LATER.
MOSCOW.
Наталья
СССР
SVOLOCH'!
EBANATYI PIDARAZ!
ДО СВИДАНИЯ

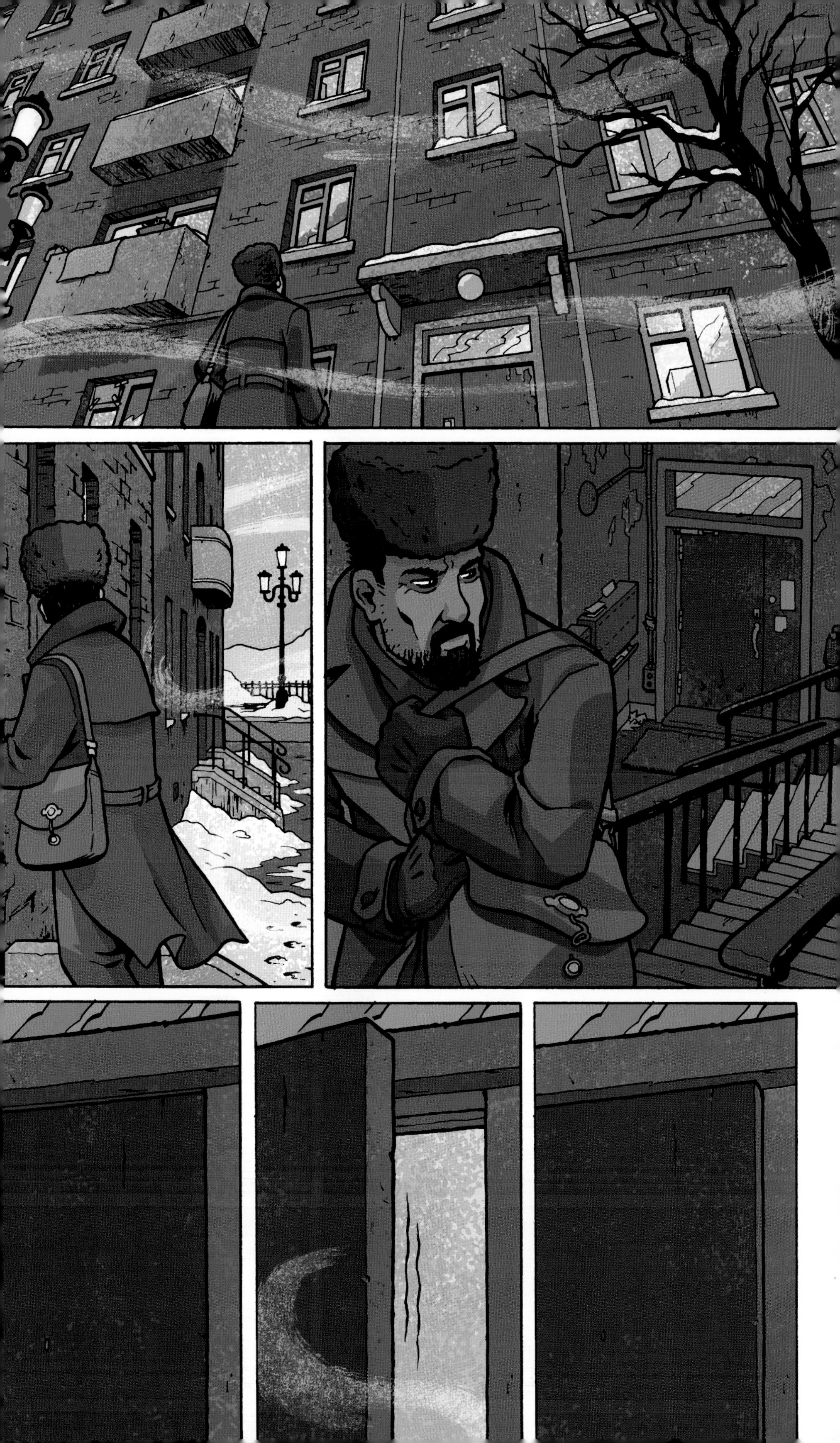

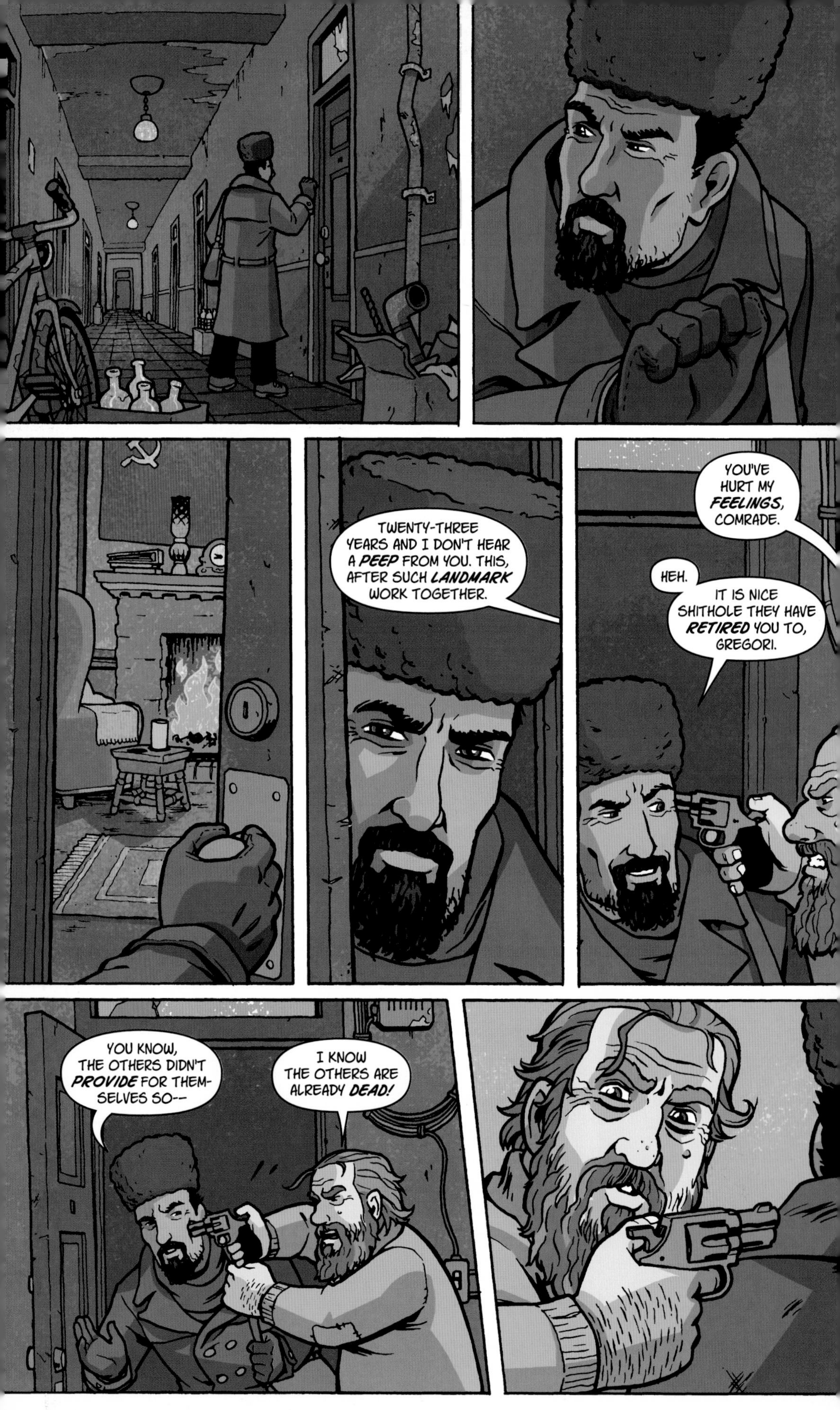
TWENTY-THREE YEARS AND I DON'T HEAR A PEEP FROM YOU. THIS, AFTER SUCH LANDMARK WORK TOGETHER.
YOU'VE HURT MY FEELINGS, COMRADE.
HEH.
IT IS NICE SHITHOLE THEY HAVE RETIRED YOU TO, GREGORI.
YOU KNOW, THE OTHERS DIDN'T PROVIDE FOR THEM-SELVES SO--
I KNOW THE OTHERS ARE ALREADY DEAD!

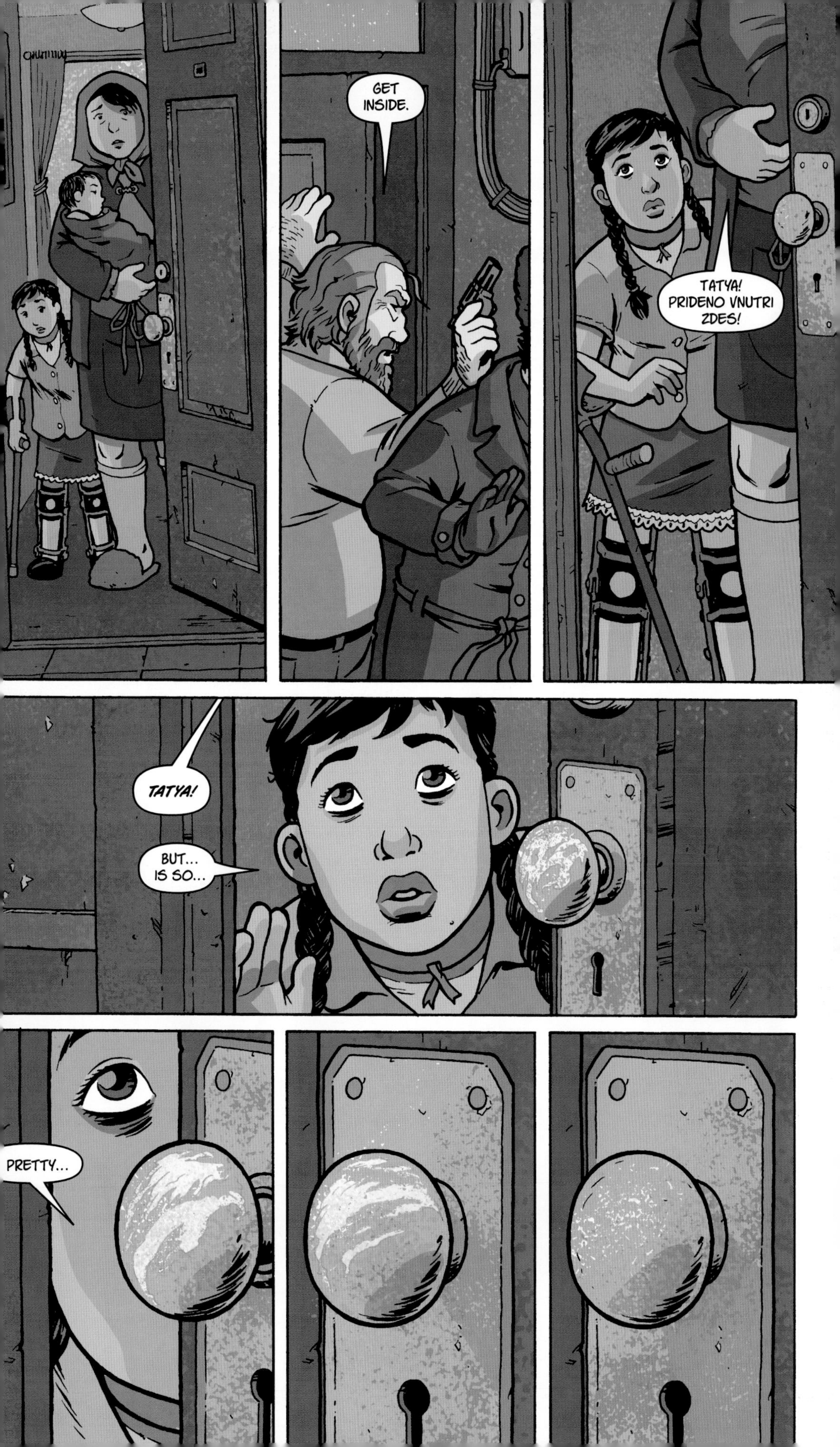
GET INSIDE.
TATYA! PRIDENO VNUTRI ZDES!
TATYA!
BUT... IS SO...
PRETTY...

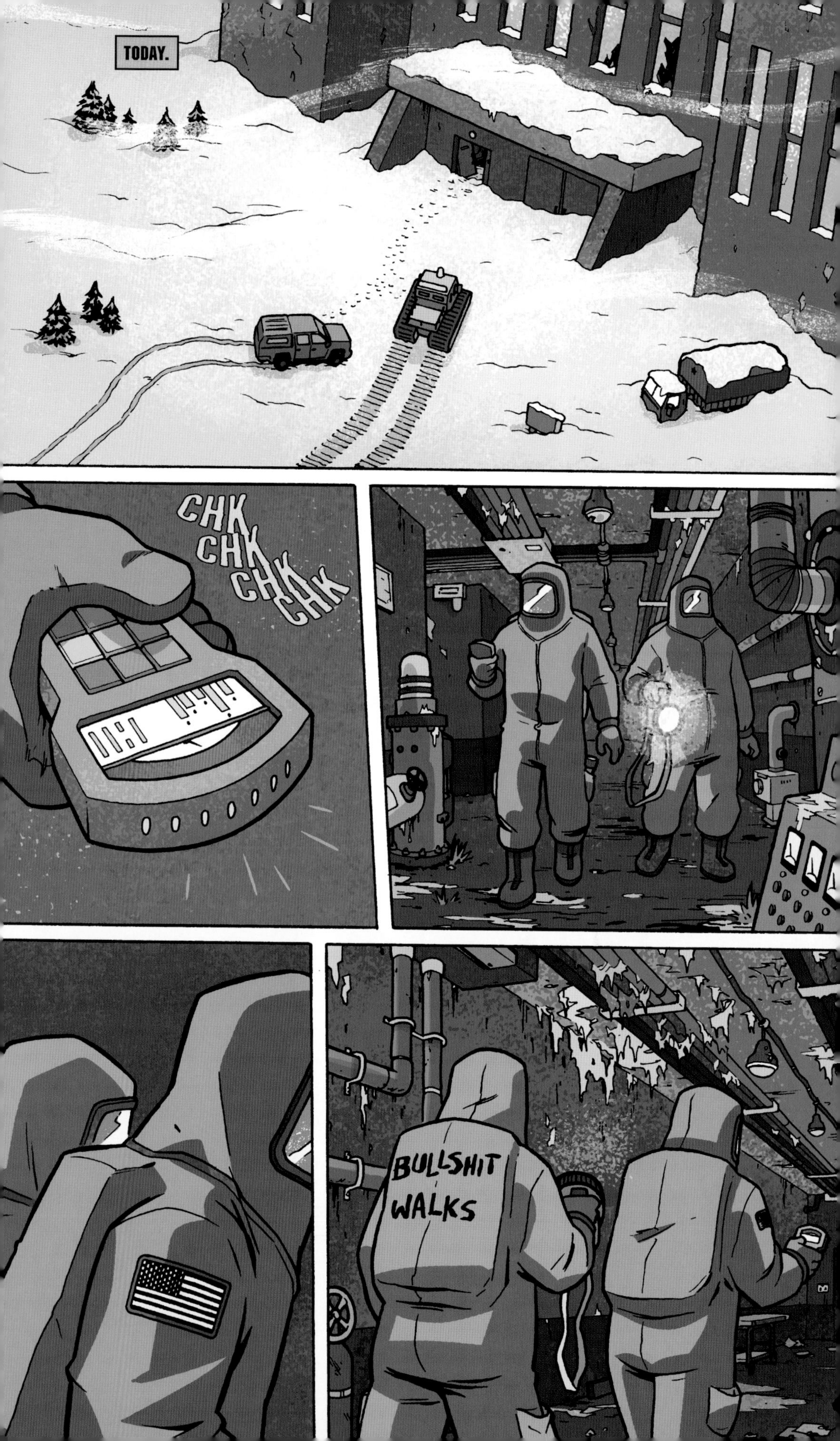
TODAY.
CHK
CHK
CHK
CHK
BULLSHIT
WALKS

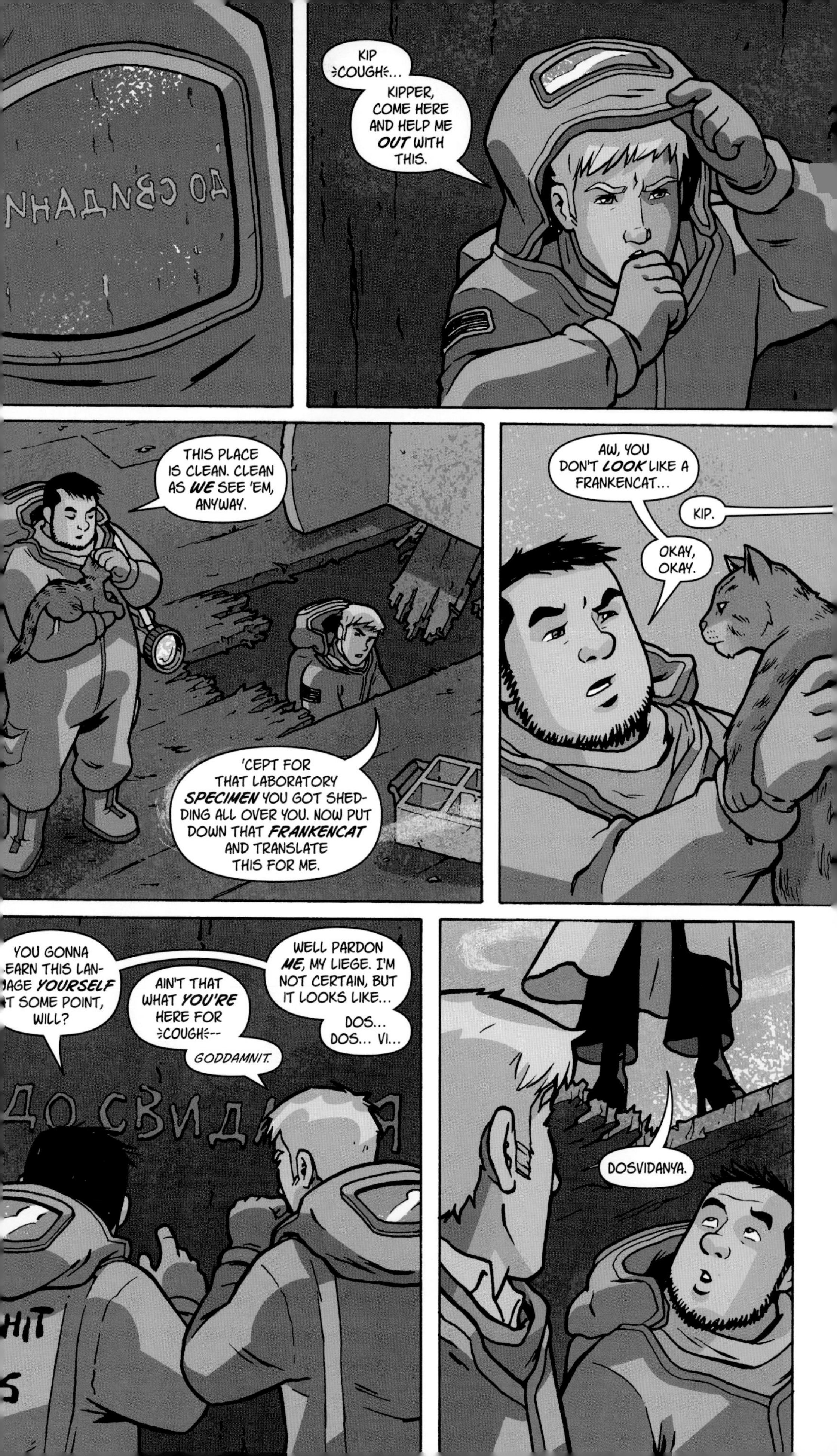

ДО СВИДАНИ
KIP ⁓COUGH⁓...
KIPPER, COME HERE AND HELP ME OUT WITH THIS.
THIS PLACE IS CLEAN. CLEAN AS WE SEE 'EM, ANYWAY.
'CEPT FOR THAT LABORATORY SPECIMEN YOU GOT SHEDDING ALL OVER YOU. NOW PUT DOWN THAT FRANKENCAT AND TRANSLATE THIS FOR ME.
AW, YOU DON'T LOOK LIKE A FRANKENCAT...
KIP.
OKAY, OKAY.
YOU GONNA LEARN THIS LANGUAGE YOURSELF AT SOME POINT, WILL?
AIN'T THAT WHAT YOU'RE HERE FOR ⁓COUGH⁓--
GODDAMNIT.
WELL PARDON ME, MY LIEGE. I'M NOT CERTAIN, BUT IT LOOKS LIKE...
DOS... DOS... VI...
ДО СВИД
DOSVIDANYA.

I AM LIEUTENANT *ANYA ROMANOVA.* OPERA-TIVNIK WITH RUSSIAN *MILITSIYA.*

I COME TO THIS COMPLEX ON *OFFICIAL* BUSINESS.

SHE'S THE *POLICE,* WILL.

I CAN SEE THAT, KIP. THANK YOU.

MY NAME'S *WILL HALEY.*

I'M WITH THE UNITED STATES DEPARTMENT OF DEFENSE CONDUCTING A JOINT EXERCISE WITH *YOUR* DEFENSE MINISTRY.

THAT'S MY PARTNER, KIP.

HELLO.

WE'RE HERE ON

BULLSHIT WALKS

YOU ARE HERE AS PART OF TH *COOPERATIVE THRE REDUCTION* INITIATIVE EFFORT TO CATALOGUE SECURE BIOLOGICAL A CHEMICAL WEAPONS MATERIALS.

YES, I KNOW.

YOU WILL TELL ME EVERYTHING YOU HAVE *LEARNED* ABOUT THIS FACILITY.

AND WHY AM I GOING TO DO *THAT?*

BECAUSE I HAVE A *GUN.*

AND BECAUSE YOUR *SUPERVISOR* HAS ALREADY PROMISED ME YOUR COOPERATION.

WELL, IF YOU'RE GONNA *SHOOT* ME OVER IT...

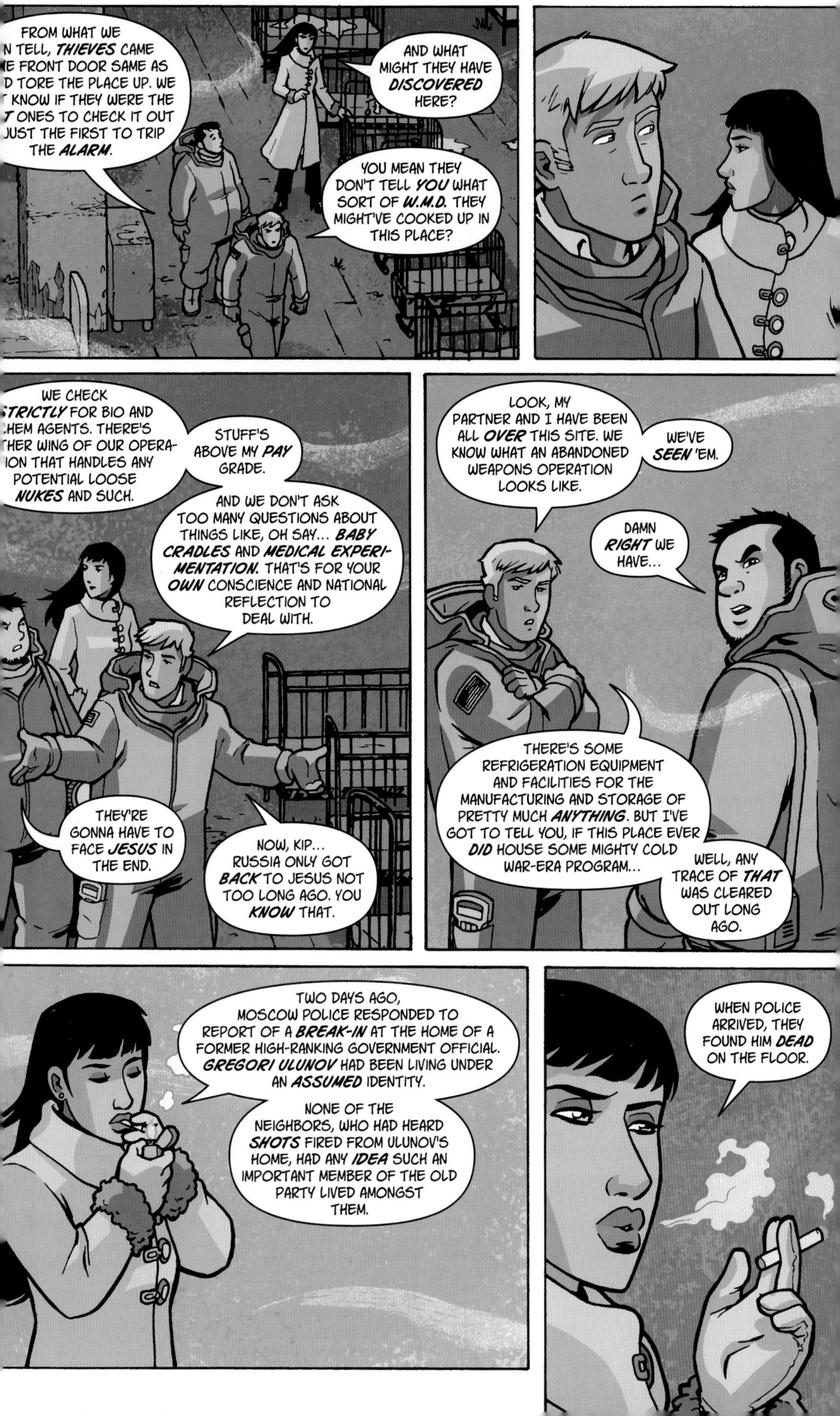

FROM WHAT WE N TELL, THIEVES CAME E FRONT DOOR SAME AS D TORE THE PLACE UP. WE KNOW IF THEY WERE THE T ONES TO CHECK IT OUT JUST THE FIRST TO TRIP THE ALARM.
AND WHAT MIGHT THEY HAVE DISCOVERED HERE?
YOU MEAN THEY DON'T TELL YOU WHAT SORT OF W.M.D. THEY MIGHT'VE COOKED UP IN THIS PLACE?
WE CHECK STRICTLY FOR BIO AND CHEM AGENTS. THERE'S THER WING OF OUR OPERA- ION THAT HANDLES ANY POTENTIAL LOOSE NUKES AND SUCH.
STUFF'S ABOVE MY PAY GRADE.
AND WE DON'T ASK TOO MANY QUESTIONS ABOUT THINGS LIKE, OH SAY... BABY CRADLES AND MEDICAL EXPERI- MENTATION. THAT'S FOR YOUR OWN CONSCIENCE AND NATIONAL REFLECTION TO DEAL WITH.
THEY'RE GONNA HAVE TO FACE JESUS IN THE END.
NOW, KIP... RUSSIA ONLY GOT BACK TO JESUS NOT TOO LONG AGO. YOU KNOW THAT.
LOOK, MY PARTNER AND I HAVE BEEN ALL OVER THIS SITE. WE KNOW WHAT AN ABANDONED WEAPONS OPERATION LOOKS LIKE.
WE'VE SEEN 'EM.
DAMN RIGHT WE HAVE...
THERE'S SOME REFRIGERATION EQUIPMENT AND FACILITIES FOR THE MANUFACTURING AND STORAGE OF PRETTY MUCH ANYTHING. BUT I'VE GOT TO TELL YOU, IF THIS PLACE EVER DID HOUSE SOME MIGHTY COLD WAR-ERA PROGRAM...
WELL, ANY TRACE OF THAT WAS CLEARED OUT LONG AGO.
TWO DAYS AGO, MOSCOW POLICE RESPONDED TO REPORT OF A BREAK-IN AT THE HOME OF A FORMER HIGH-RANKING GOVERNMENT OFFICIAL. GREGORI ULUNOV HAD BEEN LIVING UNDER AN ASSUMED IDENTITY.
NONE OF THE NEIGHBORS, WHO HAD HEARD SHOTS FIRED FROM ULUNOV'S HOME, HAD ANY IDEA SUCH AN IMPORTANT MEMBER OF THE OLD PARTY LIVED AMONGST THEM.
WHEN POLICE ARRIVED, THEY FOUND HIM DEAD ON THE FLOOR.

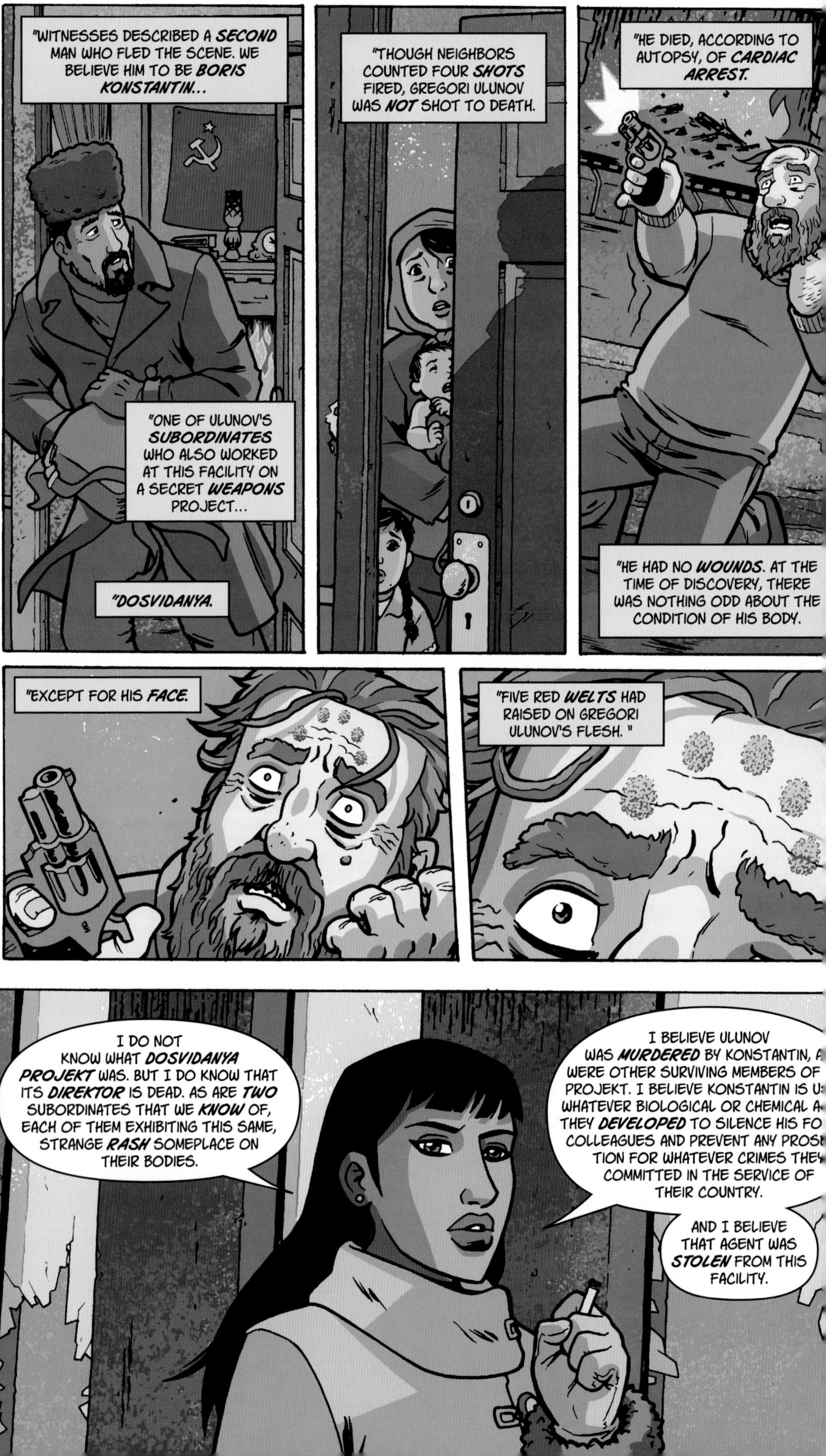
"WITNESSES DESCRIBED A SECOND MAN WHO FLED THE SCENE. WE BELIEVE HIM TO BE BORIS KONSTANTIN...
"ONE OF ULUNOV'S SUBORDINATES WHO ALSO WORKED AT THIS FACILITY ON A SECRET WEAPONS PROJECT...
"DOSVIDANYA.
"THOUGH NEIGHBORS COUNTED FOUR SHOTS FIRED, GREGORI ULUNOV WAS NOT SHOT TO DEATH.
"HE DIED, ACCORDING TO AUTOPSY, OF CARDIAC ARREST.
"HE HAD NO WOUNDS. AT THE TIME OF DISCOVERY, THERE WAS NOTHING ODD ABOUT THE CONDITION OF HIS BODY.
"EXCEPT FOR HIS FACE.
"FIVE RED WELTS HAD RAISED ON GREGORI ULUNOV'S FLESH."
I DO NOT KNOW WHAT DOSVIDANYA PROJEKT WAS. BUT I DO KNOW THAT ITS DIREKTOR IS DEAD. AS ARE TWO SUBORDINATES THAT WE KNOW OF, EACH OF THEM EXHIBITING THIS SAME, STRANGE RASH SOMEPLACE ON THEIR BODIES.
I BELIEVE ULUNOV WAS MURDERED BY KONSTANTIN, A WERE OTHER SURVIVING MEMBERS OF PROJEKT. I BELIEVE KONSTANTIN IS U WHATEVER BIOLOGICAL OR CHEMICAL A THEY DEVELOPED TO SILENCE HIS FO COLLEAGUES AND PREVENT ANY PROS TION FOR WHATEVER CRIMES THE COMMITTED IN THE SERVICE OF THEIR COUNTRY.
AND I BELIEVE THAT AGENT WAS STOLEN FROM THIS FACILITY.

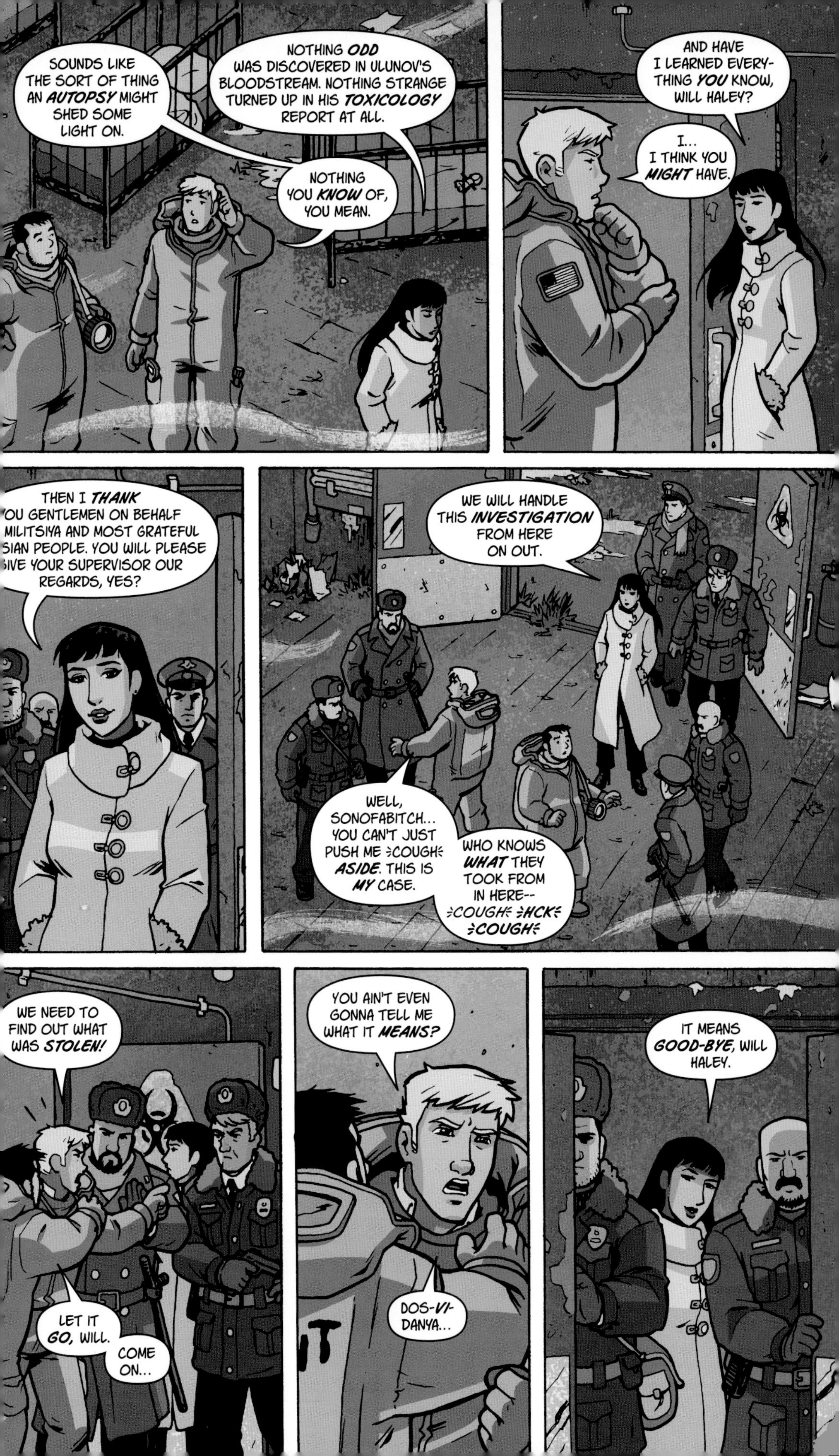
SOUNDS LIKE THE SORT OF THING AN AUTOPSY MIGHT SHED SOME LIGHT ON.
NOTHING ODD WAS DISCOVERED IN ULUNOV'S BLOODSTREAM. NOTHING STRANGE TURNED UP IN HIS TOXICOLOGY REPORT AT ALL.
NOTHING YOU KNOW OF, YOU MEAN.
AND HAVE I LEARNED EVERY-THING YOU KNOW, WILL HALEY?
I... I THINK YOU MIGHT HAVE.
THEN I THANK YOU GENTLEMEN ON BEHALF MILITSIYA AND MOST GRATEFUL SIAN PEOPLE. YOU WILL PLEASE GIVE YOUR SUPERVISOR OUR REGARDS, YES?
WE WILL HANDLE THIS INVESTIGATION FROM HERE ON OUT.
WELL, SONOFABITCH... YOU CAN'T JUST PUSH ME *COUGH* ASIDE. THIS IS MY CASE.
WHO KNOWS WHAT THEY TOOK FROM IN HERE-- *COUGH* *HCK* *COUGH*
WE NEED TO FIND OUT WHAT WAS STOLEN!
LET IT GO, WILL.
COME ON...
YOU AIN'T EVEN GONNA TELL ME WHAT IT MEANS?
DOS-VI-DANYA...
IT MEANS GOOD-BYE, WILL HALEY.

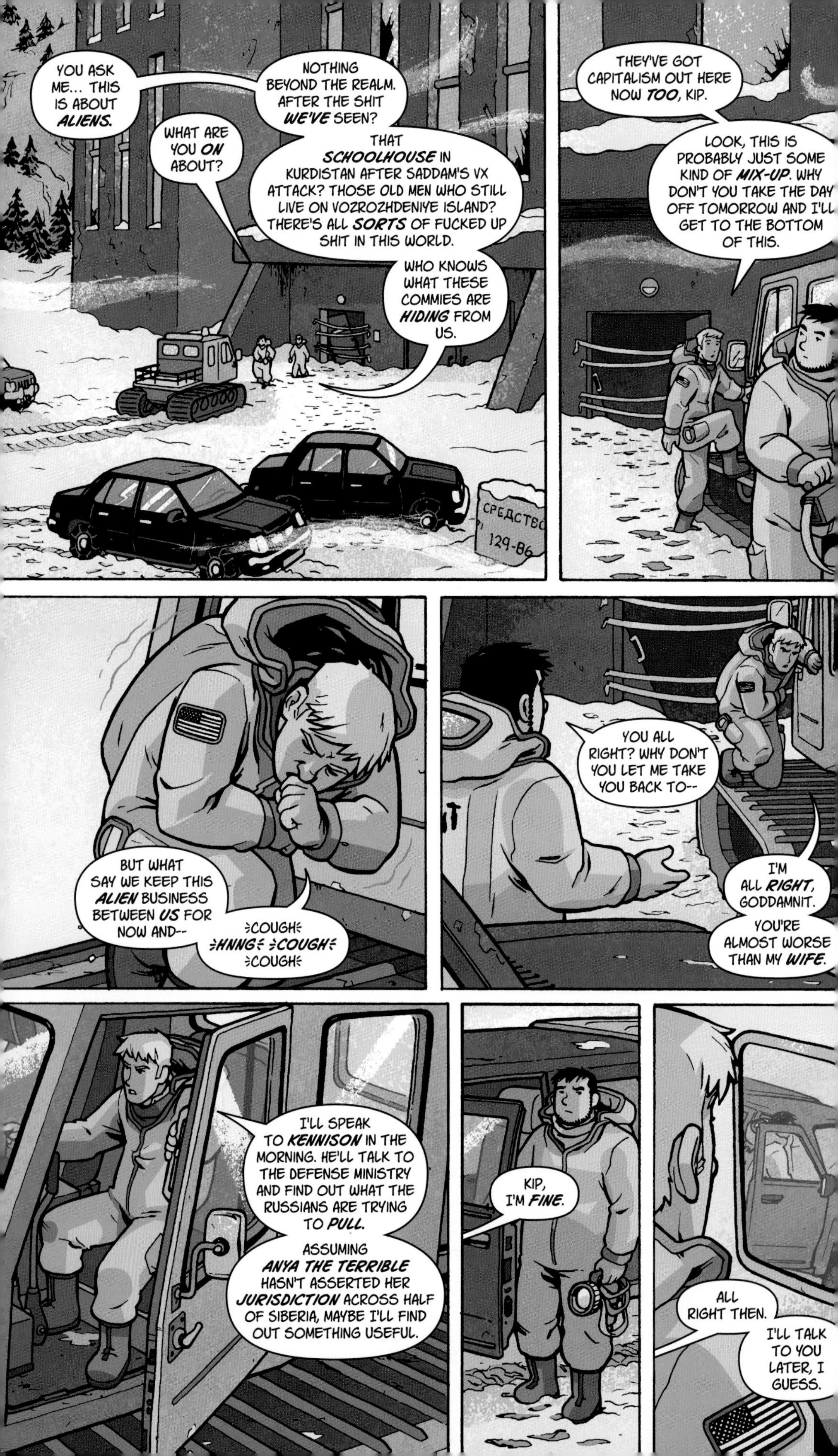
YOU ASK ME... THIS IS ABOUT ALIENS.
NOTHING BEYOND THE REALM. AFTER THE SHIT WE'VE SEEN?
WHAT ARE YOU ON ABOUT?
THAT SCHOOLHOUSE IN KURDISTAN AFTER SADDAM'S VX ATTACK? THOSE OLD MEN WHO STILL LIVE ON VOZROZHDENIYE ISLAND? THERE'S ALL SORTS OF FUCKED UP SHIT IN THIS WORLD.
WHO KNOWS WHAT THESE COMMIES ARE HIDING FROM US.
СРЕДСТВО 129-В6
THEY'VE GOT CAPITALISM OUT HERE NOW TOO, KIP.
LOOK, THIS IS PROBABLY JUST SOME KIND OF MIX-UP. WHY DON'T YOU TAKE THE DAY OFF TOMORROW AND I'LL GET TO THE BOTTOM OF THIS.
BUT WHAT SAY WE KEEP THIS ALIEN BUSINESS BETWEEN US FOR NOW AND--
COUGH HNNG COUGH COUGH
YOU ALL RIGHT? WHY DON'T YOU LET ME TAKE YOU BACK TO--
I'M ALL RIGHT, GODDAMNIT.
YOU'RE ALMOST WORSE THAN MY WIFE.
I'LL SPEAK TO KENNISON IN THE MORNING. HE'LL TALK TO THE DEFENSE MINISTRY AND FIND OUT WHAT THE RUSSIANS ARE TRYING TO PULL.
ASSUMING ANYA THE TERRIBLE HASN'T ASSERTED HER JURISDICTION ACROSS HALF OF SIBERIA, MAYBE I'LL FIND OUT SOMETHING USEFUL.
KIP, I'M FINE.
ALL RIGHT THEN.
I'LL TALK TO YOU LATER, I GUESS.

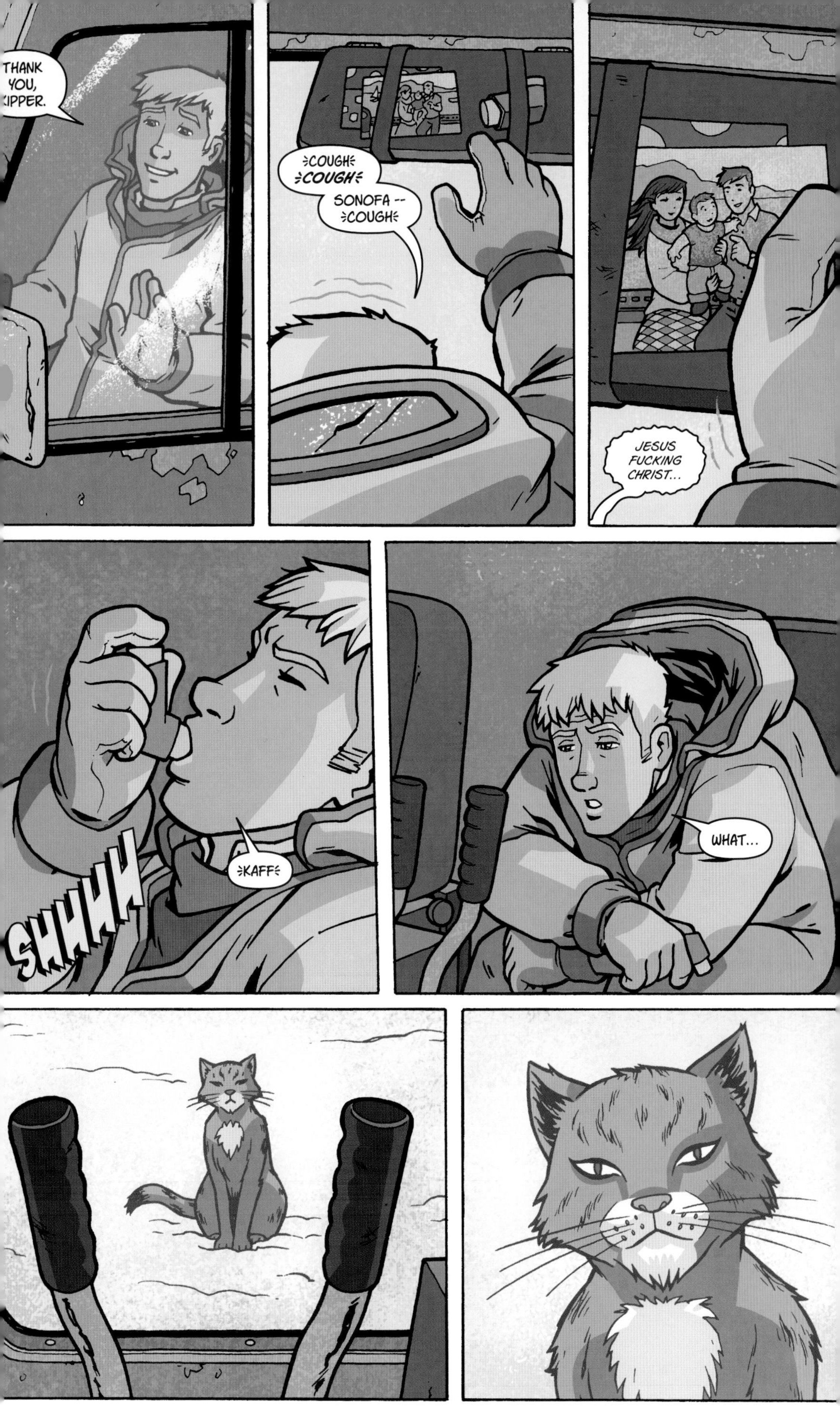
THANK YOU, KIPPER.
COUGH COUGH
SONOFA -- COUGH
JESUS FUCKING CHRIST...
SHHHH
KAFF
WHAT...

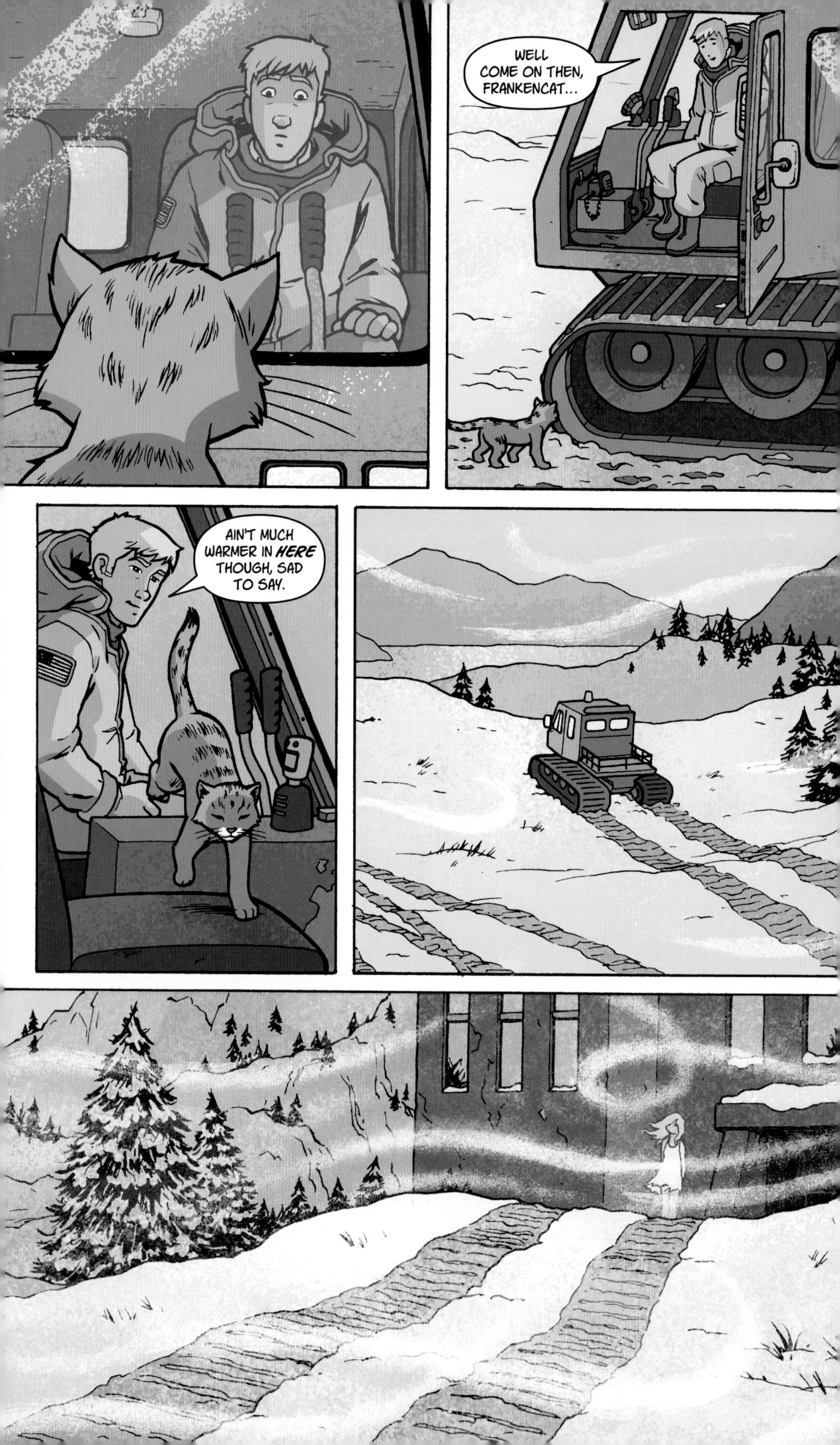
WELL COME ON THEN, FRANKENCAT...
AIN'T MUCH WARMER IN ***HERE*** THOUGH, SAD TO SAY.

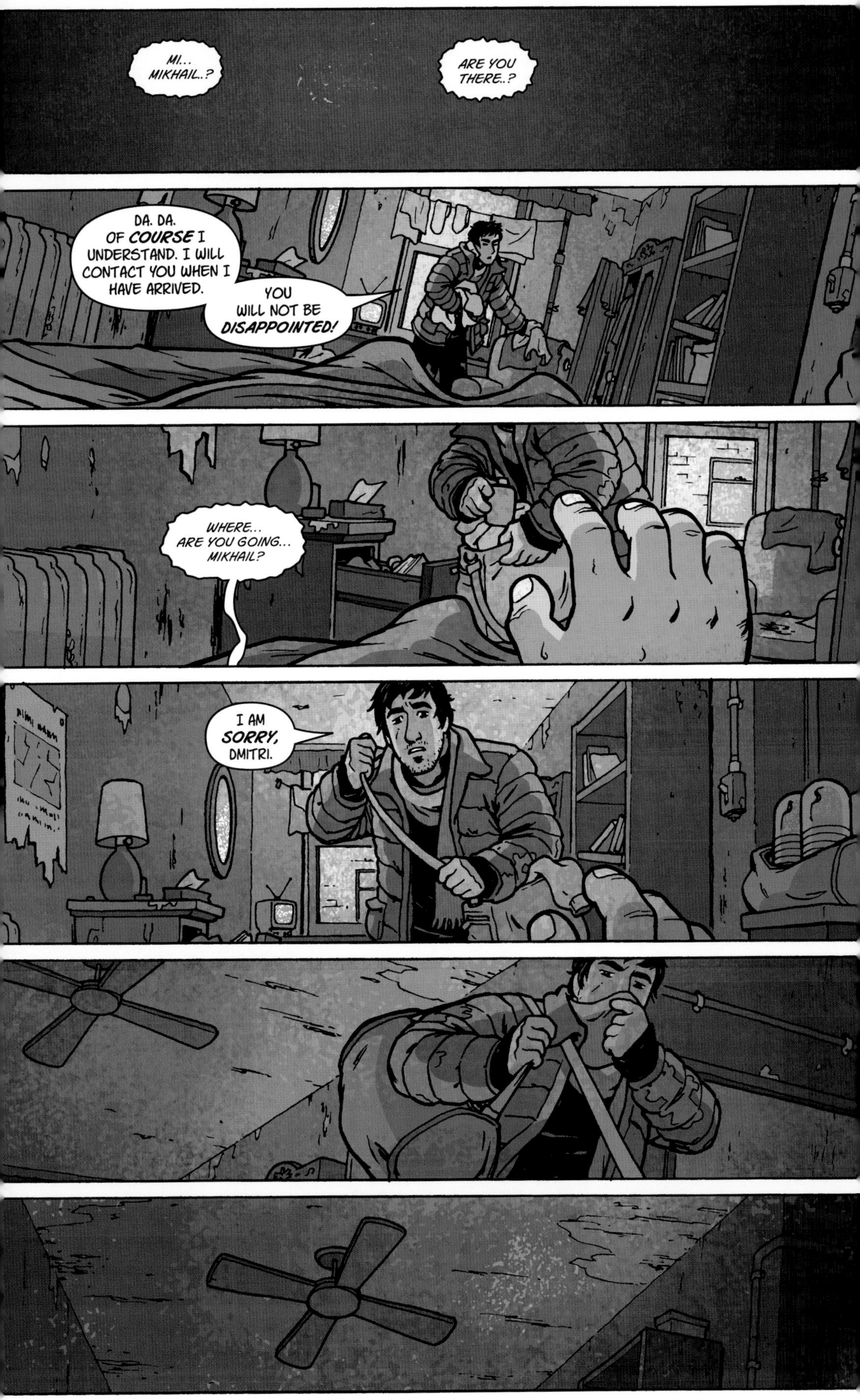
MI... MIKHAIL..?
ARE YOU THERE..?
DA. DA. OF COURSE I UNDERSTAND. I WILL CONTACT YOU WHEN I HAVE ARRIVED.
YOU WILL NOT BE DISAPPOINTED!
WHERE... ARE YOU GOING... MIKHAIL?
I AM SORRY, DMITRI.

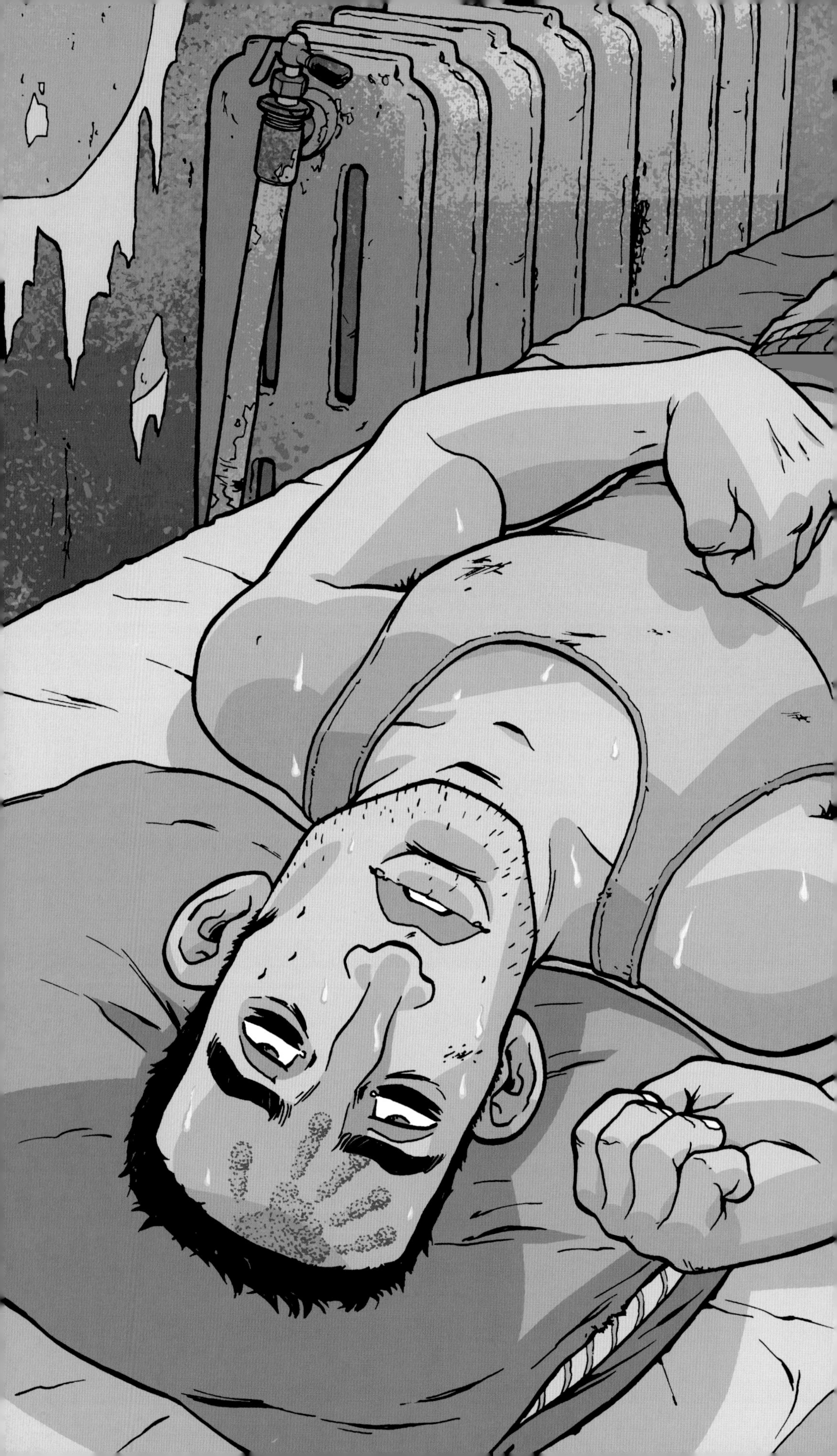

CHAPTER 2:

SNOW GHOSTS

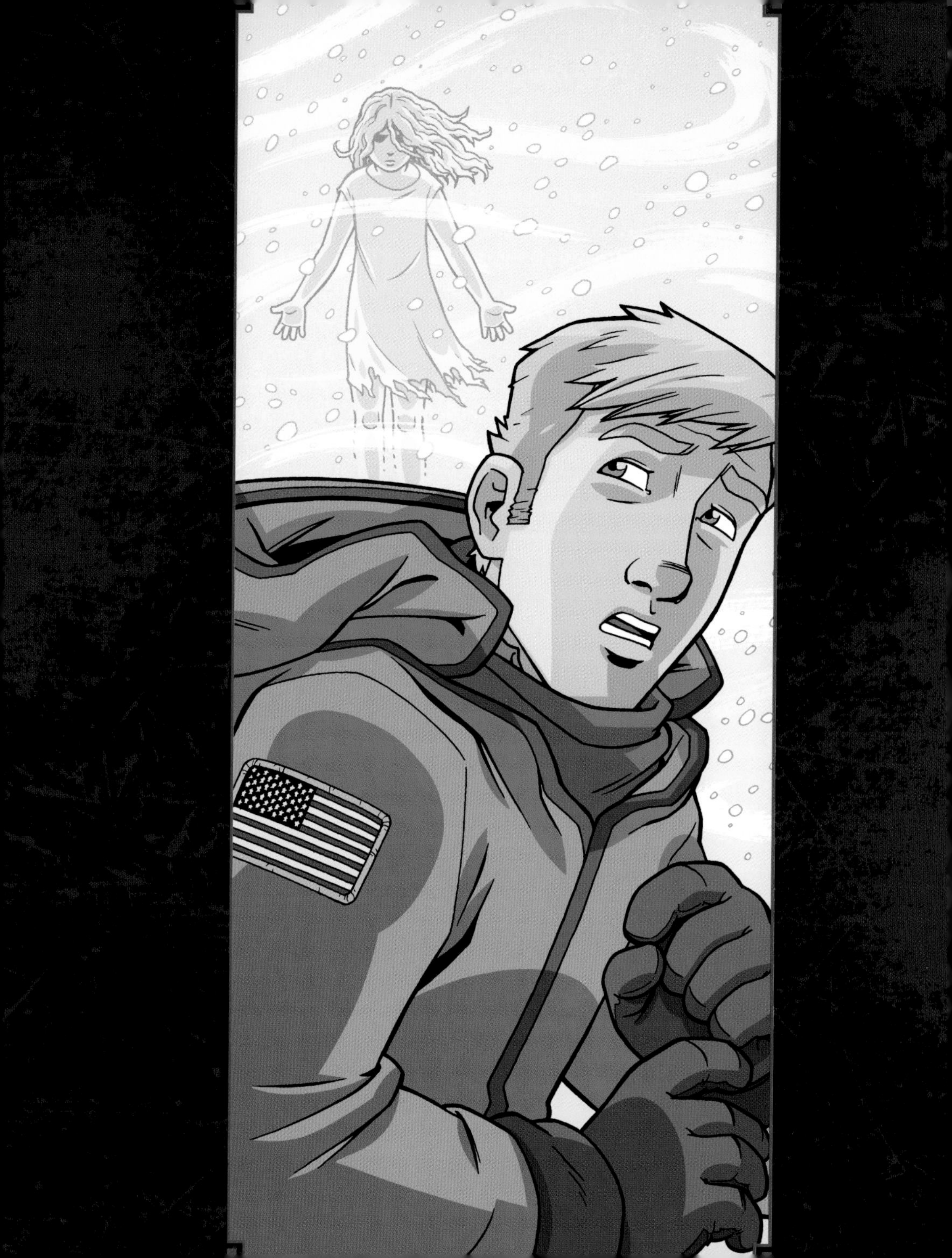

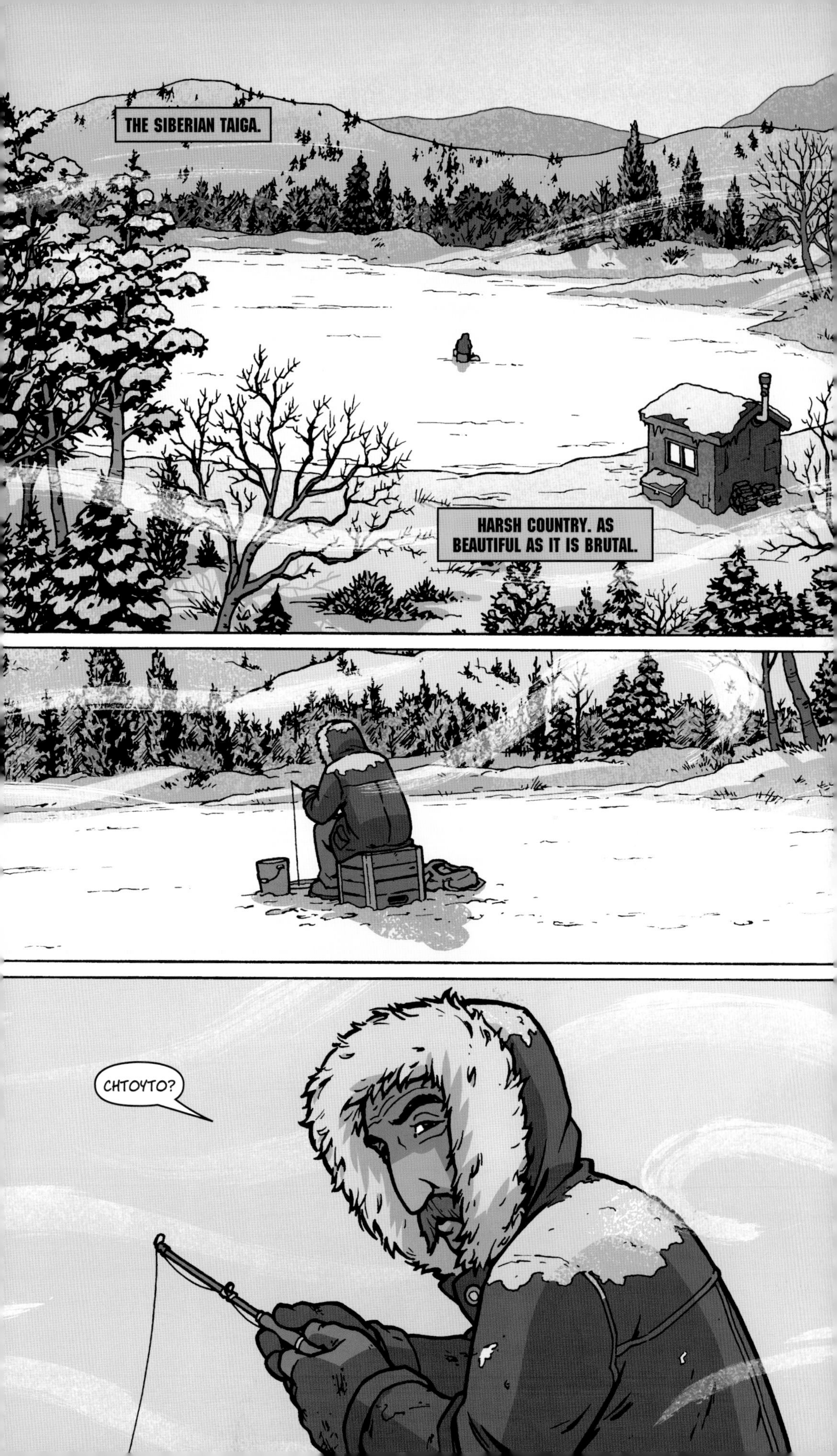
THE SIBERIAN TAIGA.
HARSH COUNTRY. AS BEAUTIFUL AS IT IS BRUTAL.
CHTOYTO?

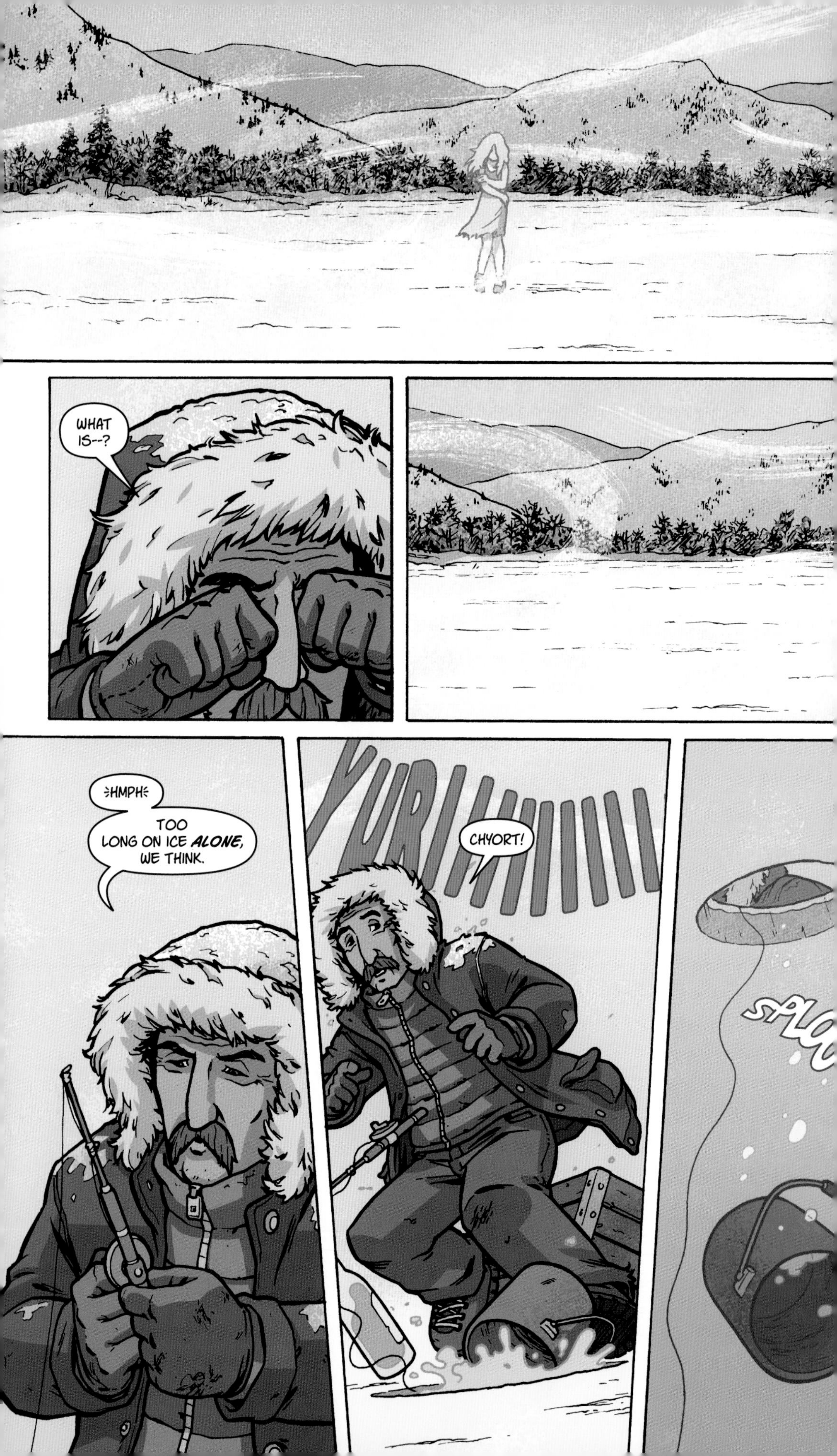
WHAT IS--?
≷HMPH≶
TOO LONG ON ICE *ALONE*, WE THINK.
YURIIIIIIII
CHYORT!
SPLO

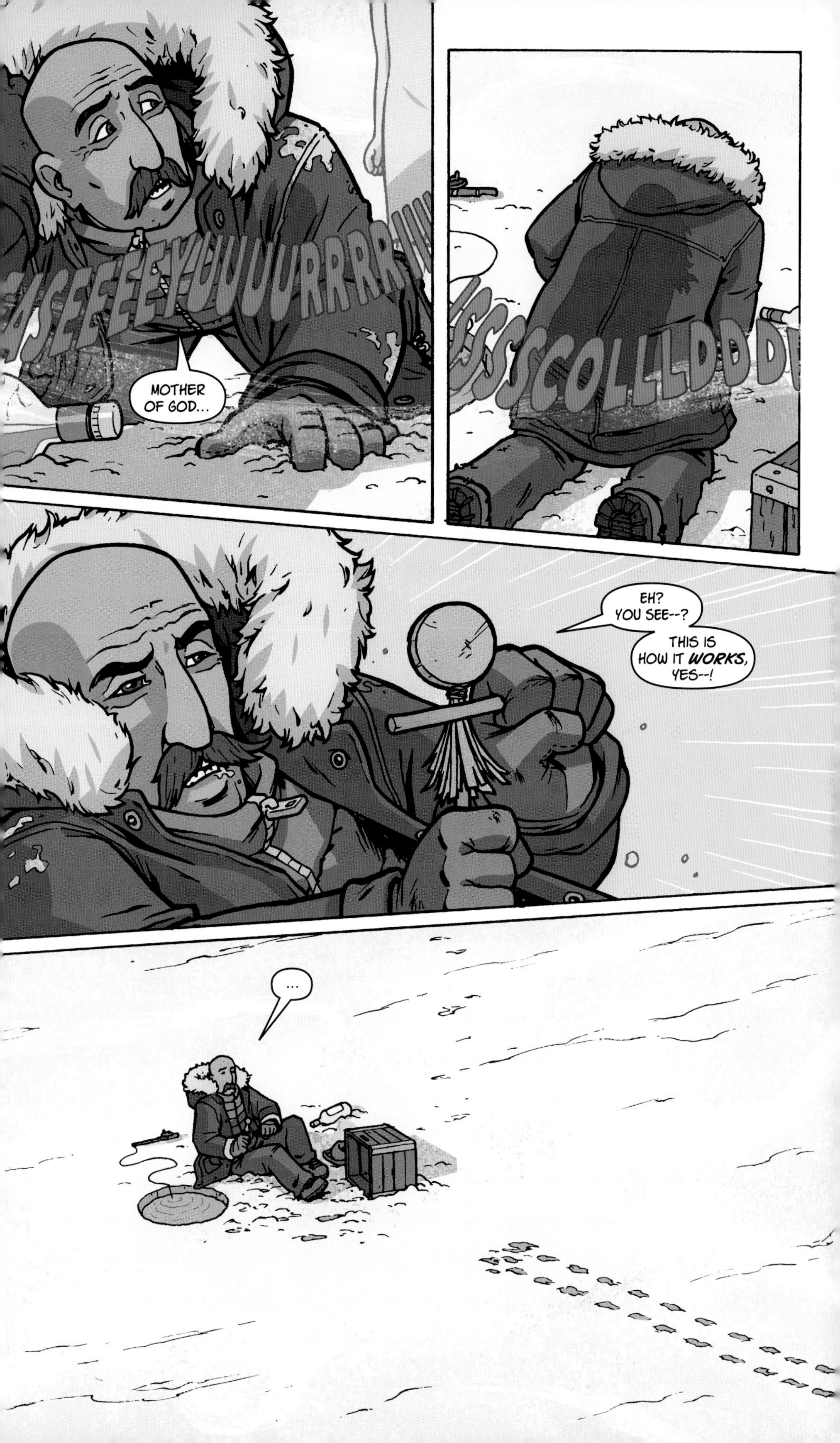
ASEEEEEYUUUUURRRRR-
MOTHER OF GOD...
SSSCOLLLDDD
EH? YOU SEE--?
THIS IS HOW IT ***WORKS***, YES--!
...

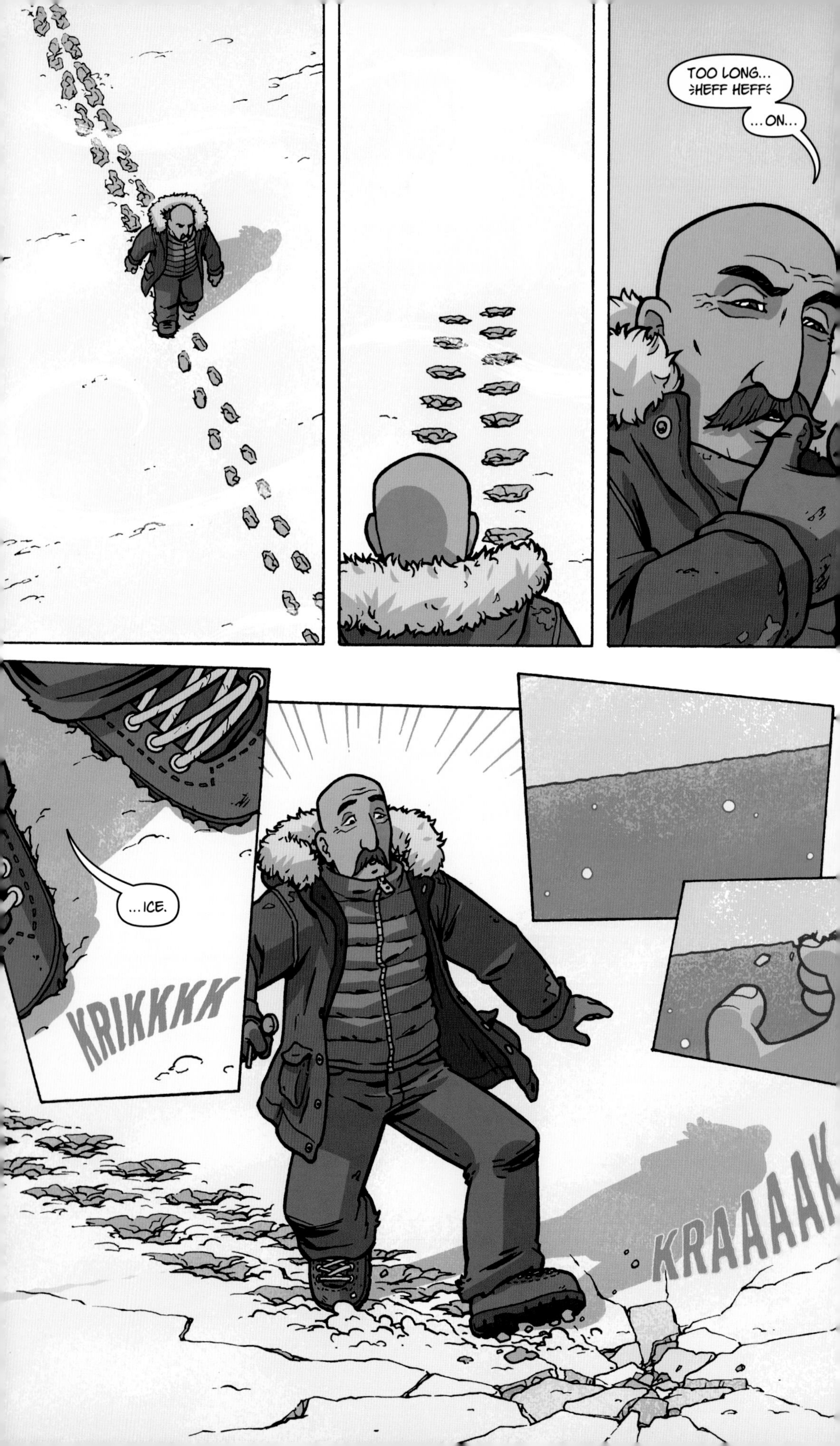
TOO LONG...
HEFF HEFF
...ON...
...ICE.
KRIKKKK
KRAAAAK

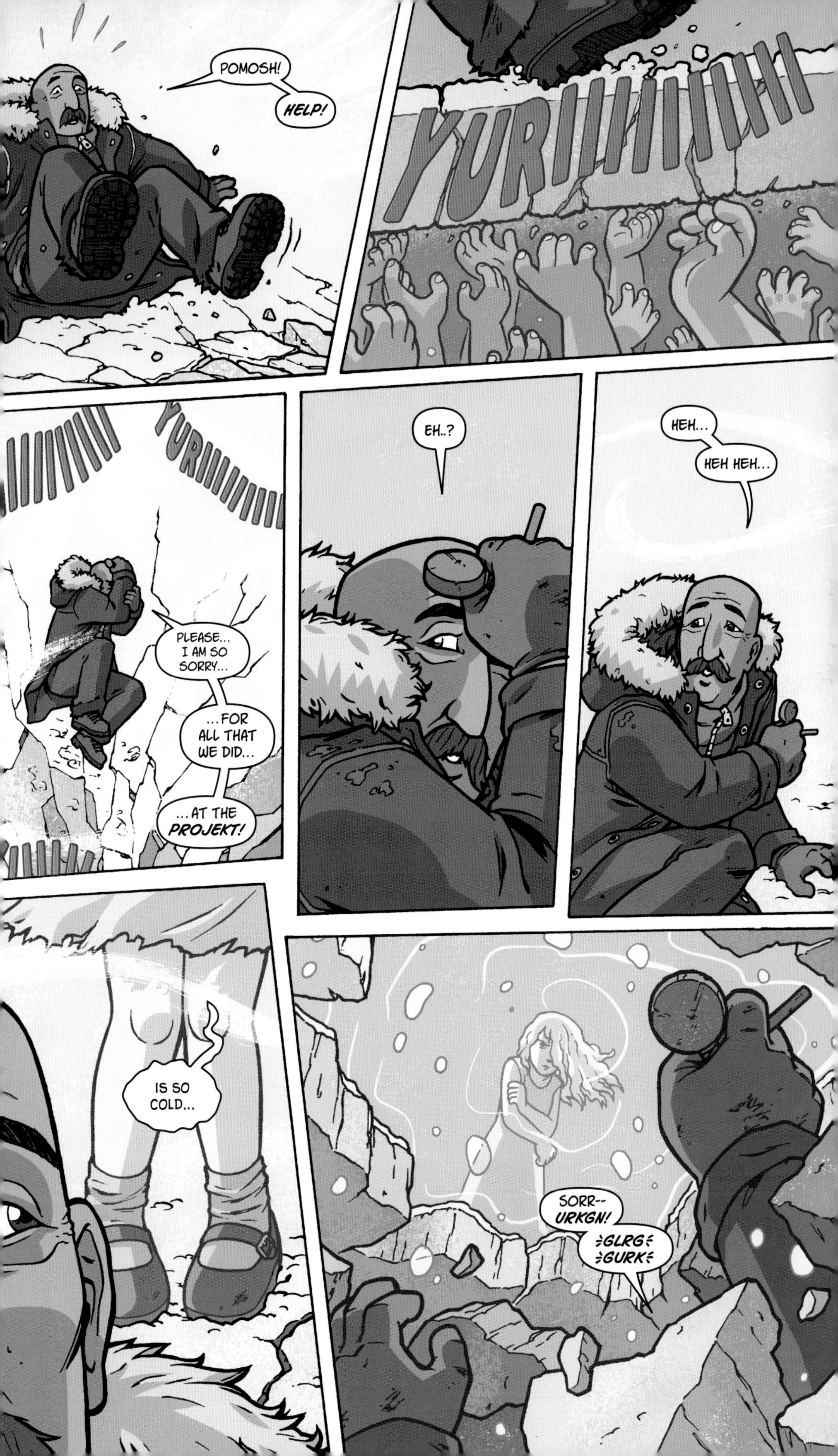
POMOSH!
HELP!
YURIIIIIIIIIII
YURIIIIIIIIIIIII
PLEASE... I AM SO SORRY...
...FOR ALL THAT WE DID...
...AT THE PROJEKT!
EH..?
HEH...
HEH HEH...
IS SO COLD...
SORR-- URKGN!
GLRG GURK

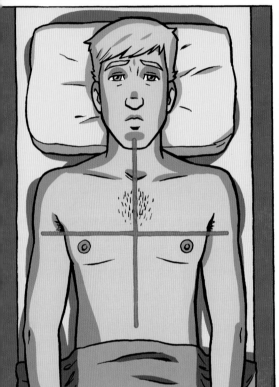

KAK PAZHIVAYESH?

YOU ARE GOO MR. HALE

I'VE BEEN BETTER.

"THIS COUNTRY'S ABOUT TEN YEARS EVOLVED FROM SHITTING IN A FROZEN HOLE OUTSIDE THE BACK DOOR. DON'T KNOW HOW MUCH *I'D* TRUST THESE MEDICAL FACILITIES.

"YOU LOOK LIKE *SHIT*, WILL."

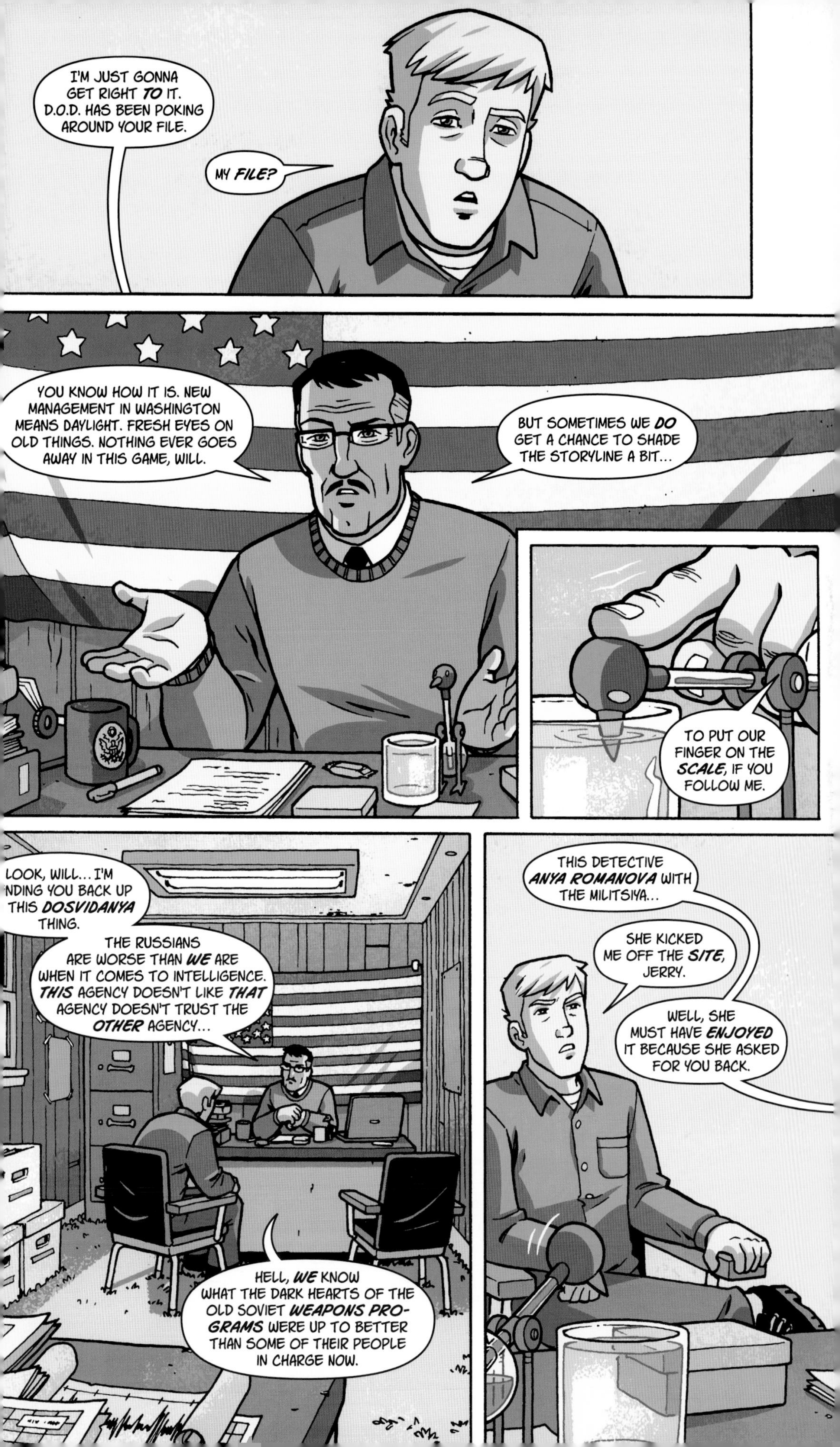
I'M JUST GONNA GET RIGHT *TO* IT. D.O.D. HAS BEEN POKING AROUND YOUR FILE.
MY *FILE?*
YOU KNOW HOW IT IS. NEW MANAGEMENT IN WASHINGTON MEANS DAYLIGHT. FRESH EYES ON OLD THINGS. NOTHING EVER GOES AWAY IN THIS GAME, WILL.
BUT SOMETIMES WE *DO* GET A CHANCE TO SHADE THE STORYLINE A BIT...
TO PUT OUR FINGER ON THE *SCALE,* IF YOU FOLLOW ME.
LOOK, WILL... I'M
NDING YOU BACK UP
THIS *DOSVIDANYA* THING.
THE RUSSIANS ARE WORSE THAN *WE* ARE WHEN IT COMES TO INTELLIGENCE. *THIS* AGENCY DOESN'T LIKE *THAT* AGENCY DOESN'T TRUST THE *OTHER* AGENCY...
HELL, *WE* KNOW WHAT THE DARK HEARTS OF THE OLD SOVIET *WEAPONS PROGRAMS* WERE UP TO BETTER THAN SOME OF THEIR PEOPLE IN CHARGE NOW.
THIS DETECTIVE *ANYA ROMANOVA* WITH THE MILITSIYA...
SHE KICKED ME OFF THE *SITE,* JERRY.
WELL, SHE MUST HAVE *ENJOYED* IT BECAUSE SHE ASKED FOR YOU BACK.

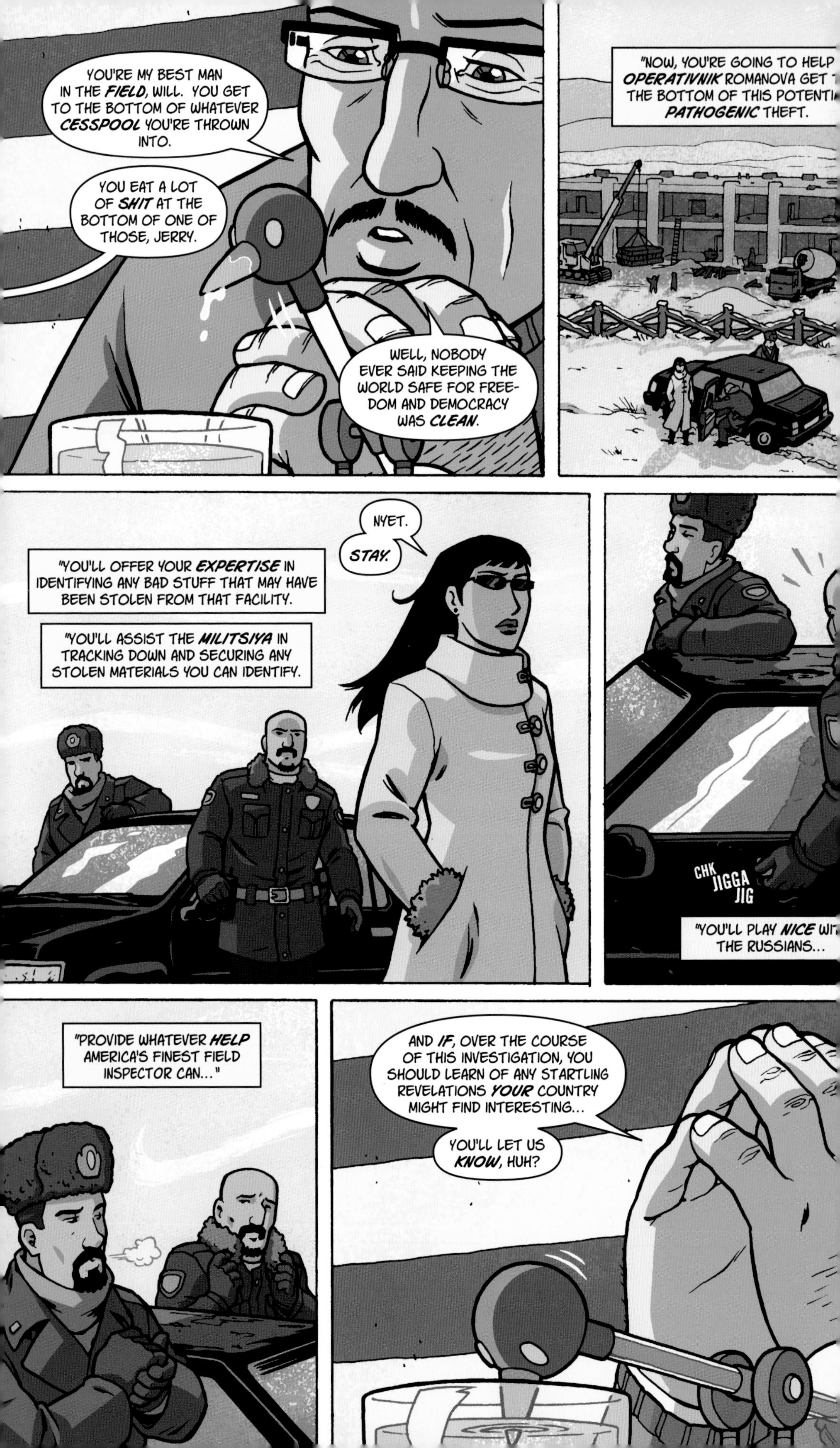
YOU'RE MY BEST MAN IN THE *FIELD*, WILL. YOU GET TO THE BOTTOM OF WHATEVER *CESSPOOL* YOU'RE THROWN INTO.
YOU EAT A LOT OF *SHIT* AT THE BOTTOM OF ONE OF THOSE, JERRY.
WELL, NOBODY EVER SAID KEEPING THE WORLD SAFE FOR FREE-DOM AND DEMOCRACY WAS *CLEAN*.
"NOW, YOU'RE GOING TO HELP *OPERATIVNIK* ROMANOVA GET T THE BOTTOM OF THIS POTENTI *PATHOGENIC* THEFT.
"YOU'LL OFFER YOUR *EXPERTISE* IN IDENTIFYING ANY BAD STUFF THAT MAY HAVE BEEN STOLEN FROM THAT FACILITY.
"YOU'LL ASSIST THE *MILITSIYA* IN TRACKING DOWN AND SECURING ANY STOLEN MATERIALS YOU CAN IDENTIFY.
NYET. *STAY.*
CHK JIGGA JIG
"YOU'LL PLAY *NICE* WIT THE RUSSIANS...
"PROVIDE WHATEVER *HELP* AMERICA'S FINEST FIELD INSPECTOR CAN..."
AND *IF*, OVER THE COURSE OF THIS INVESTIGATION, YOU SHOULD LEARN OF ANY STARTLING REVELATIONS *YOUR* COUNTRY MIGHT FIND INTERESTING...
YOU'LL LET US *KNOW*, HUH?

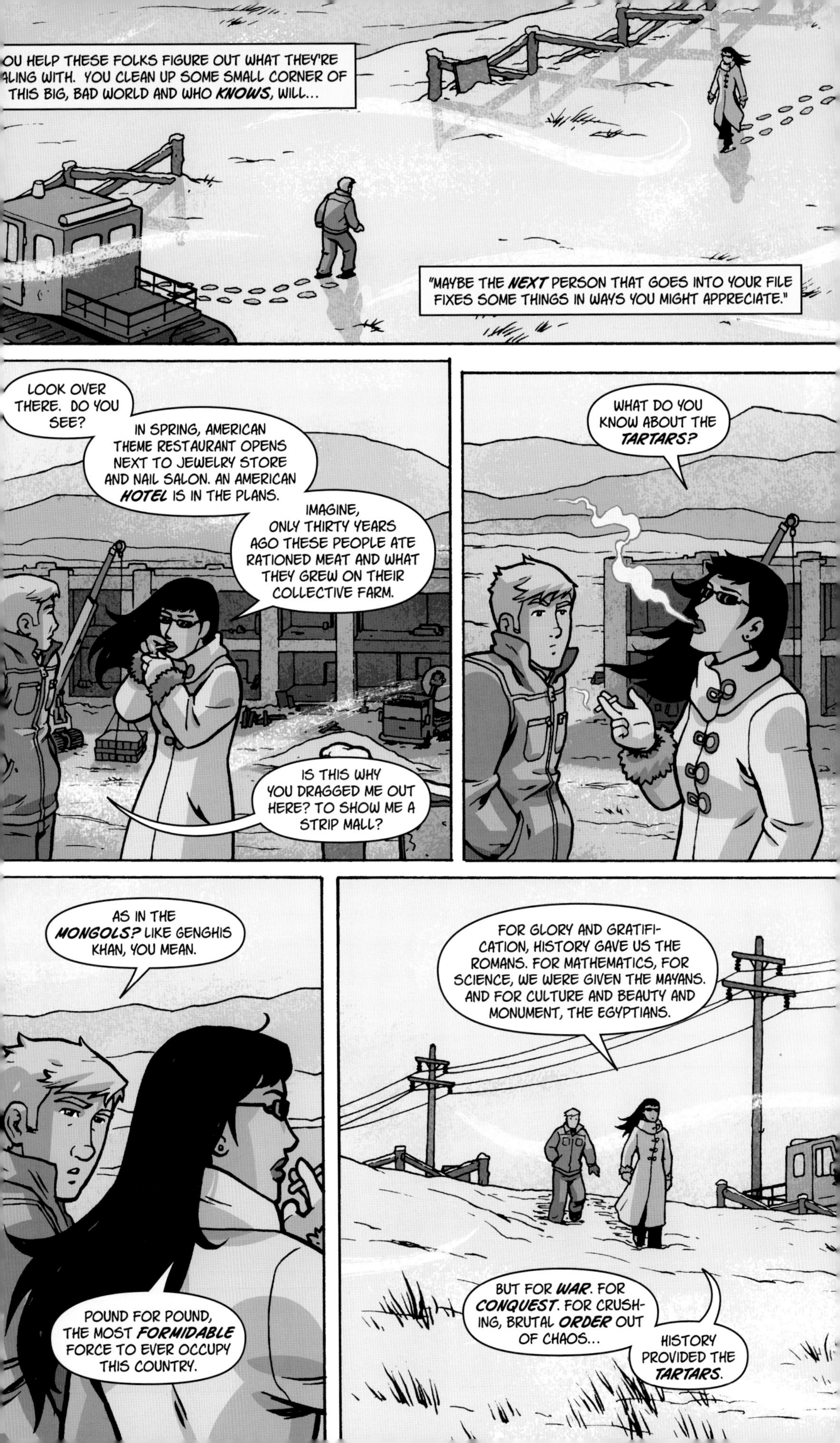
OU HELP THESE FOLKS FIGURE OUT WHAT THEY'RE
ALING WITH. YOU CLEAN UP SOME SMALL CORNER OF
THIS BIG, BAD WORLD AND WHO KNOWS, WILL...
"MAYBE THE NEXT PERSON THAT GOES INTO YOUR FILE FIXES SOME THINGS IN WAYS YOU MIGHT APPRECIATE."
LOOK OVER THERE. DO YOU SEE?
IN SPRING, AMERICAN THEME RESTAURANT OPENS NEXT TO JEWELRY STORE AND NAIL SALON. AN AMERICAN HOTEL IS IN THE PLANS.
IMAGINE, ONLY THIRTY YEARS AGO THESE PEOPLE ATE RATIONED MEAT AND WHAT THEY GREW ON THEIR COLLECTIVE FARM.
IS THIS WHY YOU DRAGGED ME OUT HERE? TO SHOW ME A STRIP MALL?
WHAT DO YOU KNOW ABOUT THE TARTARS?
AS IN THE MONGOLS? LIKE GENGHIS KHAN, YOU MEAN.
POUND FOR POUND, THE MOST FORMIDABLE FORCE TO EVER OCCUPY THIS COUNTRY.
FOR GLORY AND GRATIFI-CATION, HISTORY GAVE US THE ROMANS. FOR MATHEMATICS, FOR SCIENCE, WE WERE GIVEN THE MAYANS. AND FOR CULTURE AND BEAUTY AND MONUMENT, THE EGYPTIANS.
BUT FOR WAR. FOR CONQUEST. FOR CRUSH-ING, BRUTAL ORDER OUT OF CHAOS...
HISTORY PROVIDED THE TARTARS.

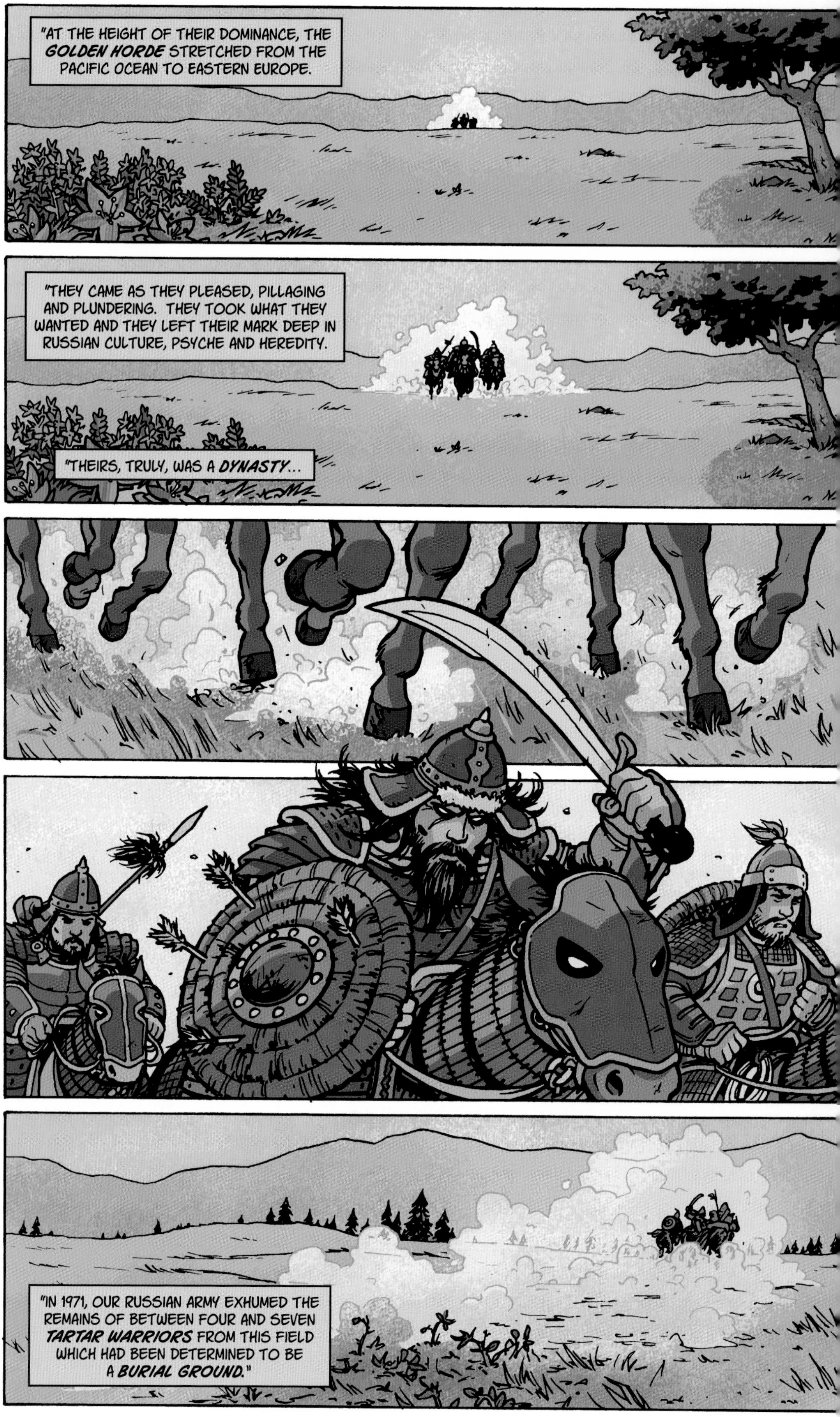
"AT THE HEIGHT OF THEIR DOMINANCE, THE GOLDEN HORDE STRETCHED FROM THE PACIFIC OCEAN TO EASTERN EUROPE.
"THEY CAME AS THEY PLEASED, PILLAGING AND PLUNDERING. THEY TOOK WHAT THEY WANTED AND THEY LEFT THEIR MARK DEEP IN RUSSIAN CULTURE, PSYCHE AND HEREDITY.
"THEIRS, TRULY, WAS A DYNASTY...
"IN 1971, OUR RUSSIAN ARMY EXHUMED THE REMAINS OF BETWEEN FOUR AND SEVEN TARTAR WARRIORS FROM THIS FIELD WHICH HAD BEEN DETERMINED TO BE A BURIAL GROUND."

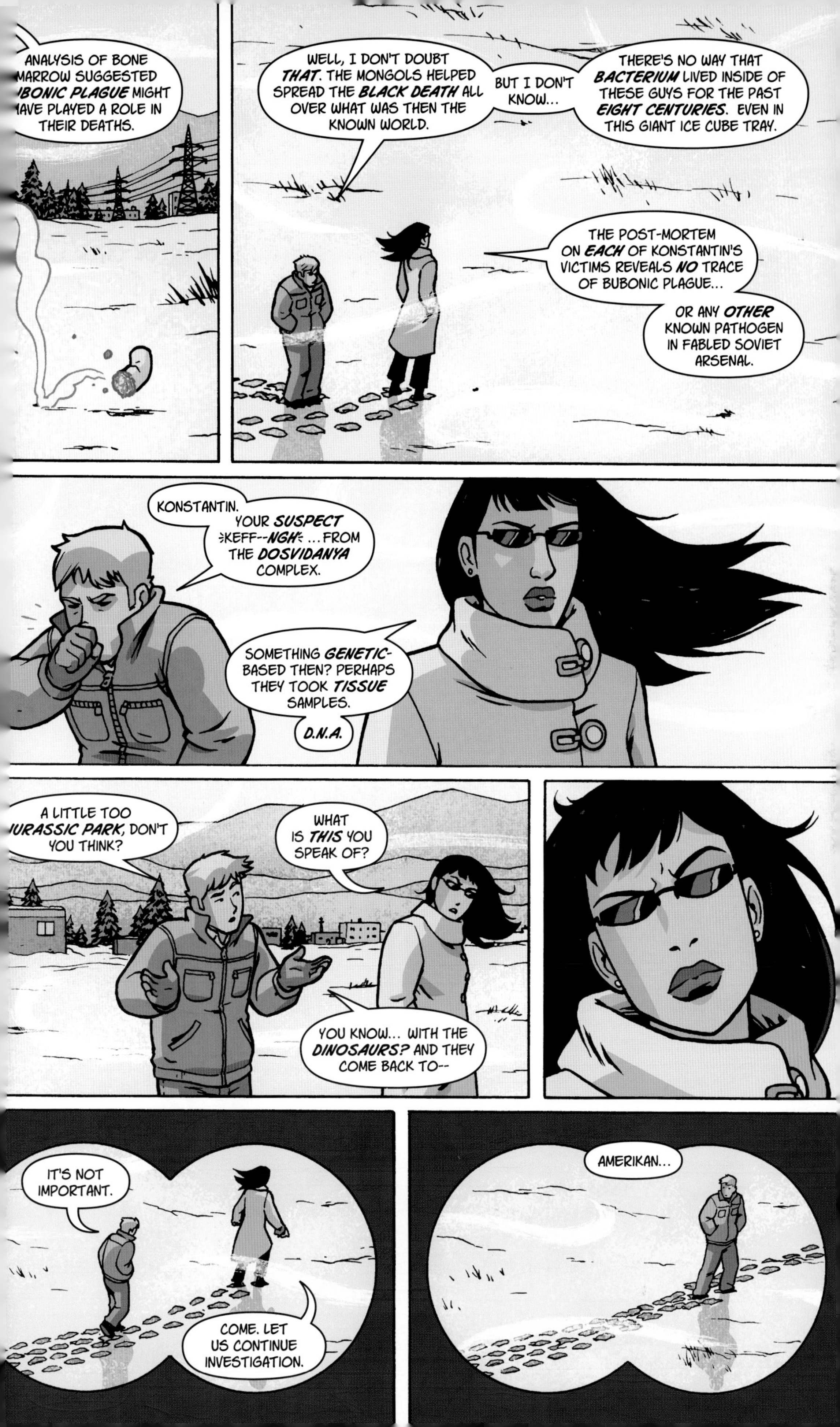
ANALYSIS OF BONE MARROW SUGGESTED UBONIC PLAGUE MIGHT AVE PLAYED A ROLE IN THEIR DEATHS.
WELL, I DON'T DOUBT THAT. THE MONGOLS HELPED SPREAD THE BLACK DEATH ALL OVER WHAT WAS THEN THE KNOWN WORLD.
BUT I DON'T KNOW...
THERE'S NO WAY THAT BACTERIUM LIVED INSIDE OF THESE GUYS FOR THE PAST EIGHT CENTURIES. EVEN IN THIS GIANT ICE CUBE TRAY.
THE POST-MORTEM ON EACH OF KONSTANTIN'S VICTIMS REVEALS NO TRACE OF BUBONIC PLAGUE...
OR ANY OTHER KNOWN PATHOGEN IN FABLED SOVIET ARSENAL.
KONSTANTIN.
YOUR SUSPECT *KEFF--NGH* ...FROM THE DOSVIDANYA COMPLEX.
SOMETHING GENETIC-BASED THEN? PERHAPS THEY TOOK TISSUE SAMPLES.
D.N.A.
A LITTLE TOO URASSIC PARK, DON'T YOU THINK?
WHAT IS THIS YOU SPEAK OF?
YOU KNOW... WITH THE DINOSAURS? AND THEY COME BACK TO--
IT'S NOT IMPORTANT.
COME. LET US CONTINUE INVESTIGATION.
AMERIKAN...

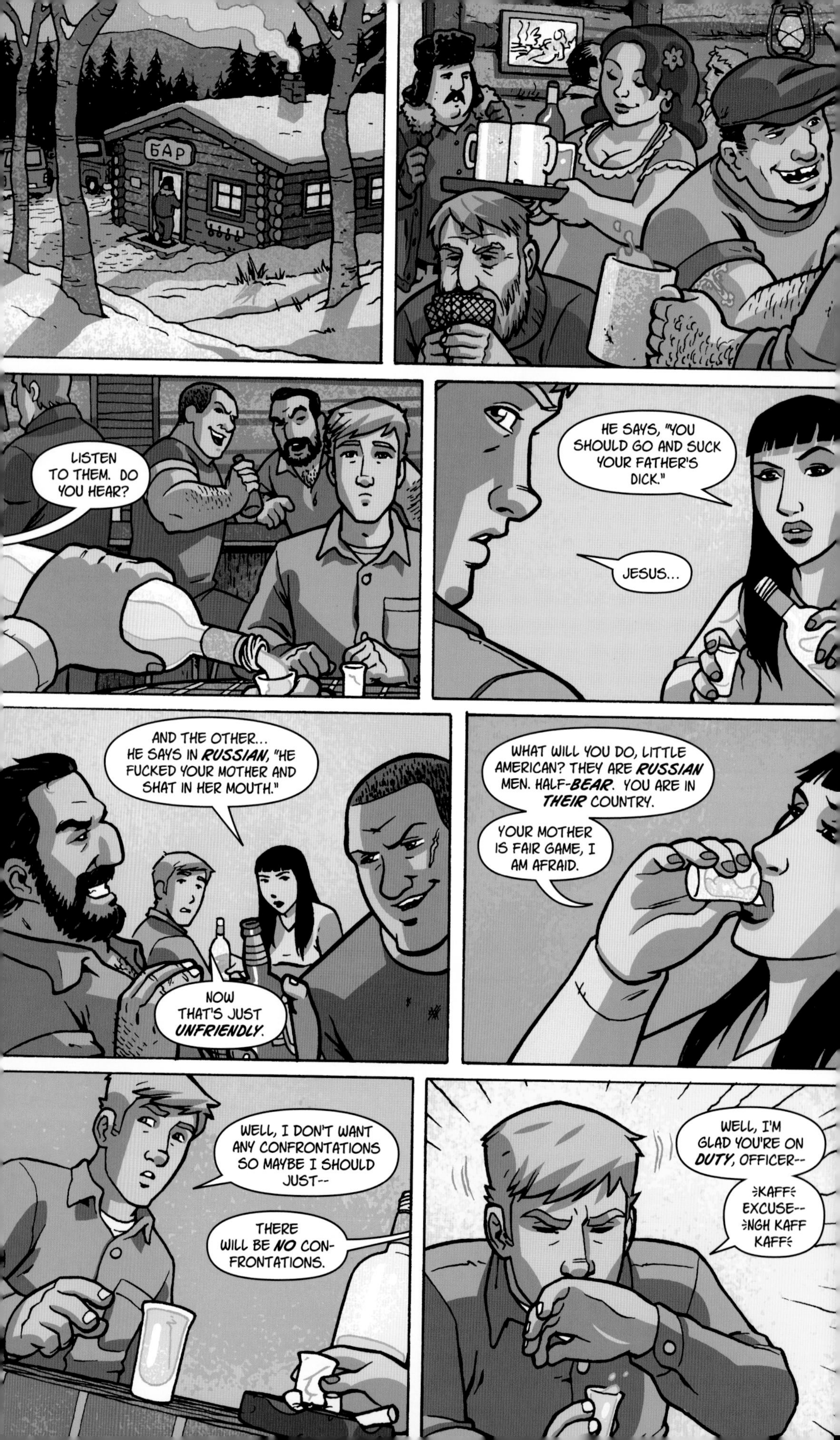
БАР
LISTEN TO THEM. DO YOU HEAR?
HE SAYS, "YOU SHOULD GO AND SUCK YOUR FATHER'S DICK."
JESUS...
AND THE OTHER... HE SAYS IN *RUSSIAN*, "HE FUCKED YOUR MOTHER AND SHAT IN HER MOUTH."
NOW THAT'S JUST *UNFRIENDLY*.
WHAT WILL YOU DO, LITTLE AMERICAN? THEY ARE *RUSSIAN* MEN. HALF-*BEAR*. YOU ARE IN *THEIR* COUNTRY.
YOUR MOTHER IS FAIR GAME, I AM AFRAID.
WELL, I DON'T WANT ANY CONFRONTATIONS SO MAYBE I SHOULD JUST--
THERE WILL BE *NO* CONFRONTATIONS.
WELL, I'M GLAD YOU'RE ON *DUTY*, OFFICER--
KAFF EXCUSE-- NGH KAFF KAFF

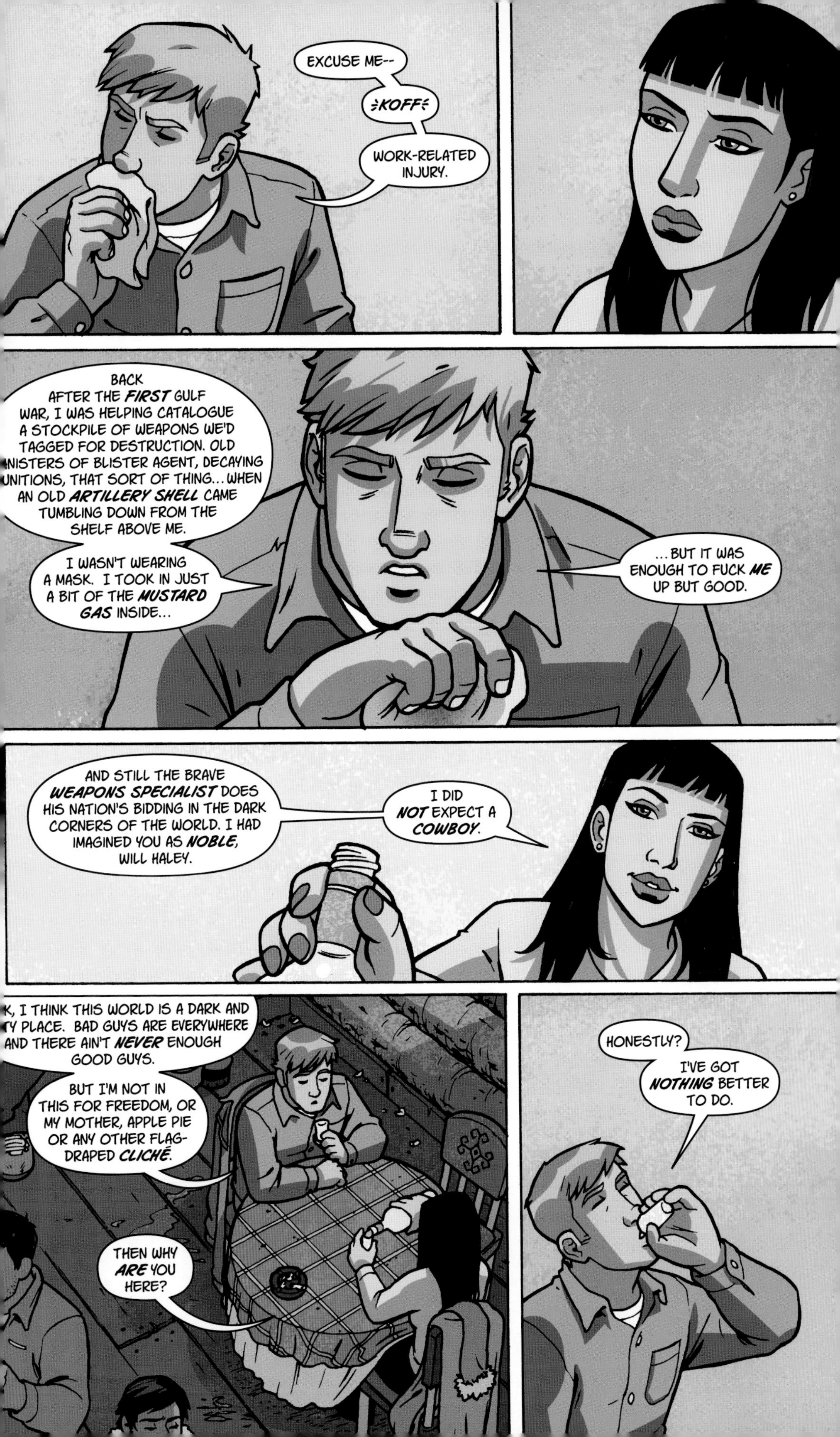
EXCUSE ME--
KOFF
WORK-RELATED INJURY.
BACK AFTER THE FIRST GULF WAR, I WAS HELPING CATALOGUE A STOCKPILE OF WEAPONS WE'D TAGGED FOR DESTRUCTION. OLD ANISTERS OF BLISTER AGENT, DECAYING UNITIONS, THAT SORT OF THING... WHEN AN OLD ARTILLERY SHELL CAME TUMBLING DOWN FROM THE SHELF ABOVE ME.
I WASN'T WEARING A MASK. I TOOK IN JUST A BIT OF THE MUSTARD GAS INSIDE...
...BUT IT WAS ENOUGH TO FUCK ME UP BUT GOOD.
AND STILL THE BRAVE WEAPONS SPECIALIST DOES HIS NATION'S BIDDING IN THE DARK CORNERS OF THE WORLD. I HAD IMAGINED YOU AS NOBLE, WILL HALEY.
I DID NOT EXPECT A COWBOY.
K, I THINK THIS WORLD IS A DARK AND TY PLACE. BAD GUYS ARE EVERYWHERE AND THERE AIN'T NEVER ENOUGH GOOD GUYS.
BUT I'M NOT IN THIS FOR FREEDOM, OR MY MOTHER, APPLE PIE OR ANY OTHER FLAG-DRAPED CLICHÉ.
THEN WHY ARE YOU HERE?
HONESTLY?
I'VE GOT NOTHING BETTER TO DO.

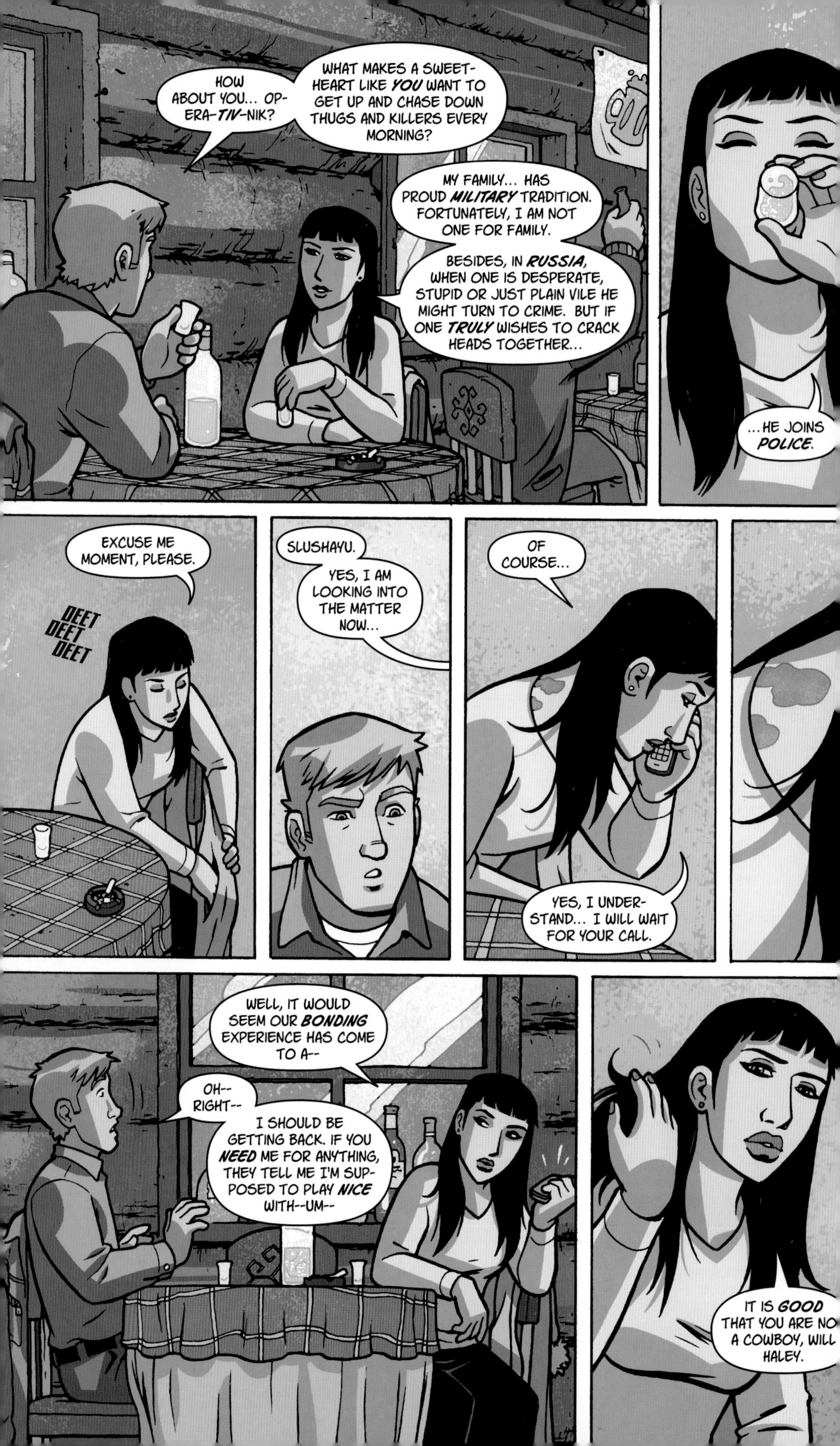

HOW ABOUT YOU... OP-ERA-TIV-NIK?
WHAT MAKES A SWEET-HEART LIKE YOU WANT TO GET UP AND CHASE DOWN THUGS AND KILLERS EVERY MORNING?
MY FAMILY... HAS PROUD MILITARY TRADITION. FORTUNATELY, I AM NOT ONE FOR FAMILY.
BESIDES, IN RUSSIA, WHEN ONE IS DESPERATE, STUPID OR JUST PLAIN VILE HE MIGHT TURN TO CRIME. BUT IF ONE TRULY WISHES TO CRACK HEADS TOGETHER...
...HE JOINS POLICE.
EXCUSE ME MOMENT, PLEASE.
DEET DEET DEET
SLUSHAYU.
YES, I AM LOOKING INTO THE MATTER NOW...
OF COURSE...
YES, I UNDER-STAND... I WILL WAIT FOR YOUR CALL.
WELL, IT WOULD SEEM OUR BONDING EXPERIENCE HAS COME TO A--
OH-- RIGHT--
I SHOULD BE GETTING BACK. IF YOU NEED ME FOR ANYTHING, THEY TELL ME I'M SUP-POSED TO PLAY NICE WITH--UM--
IT IS GOOD THAT YOU ARE NO A COWBOY, WILL HALEY.

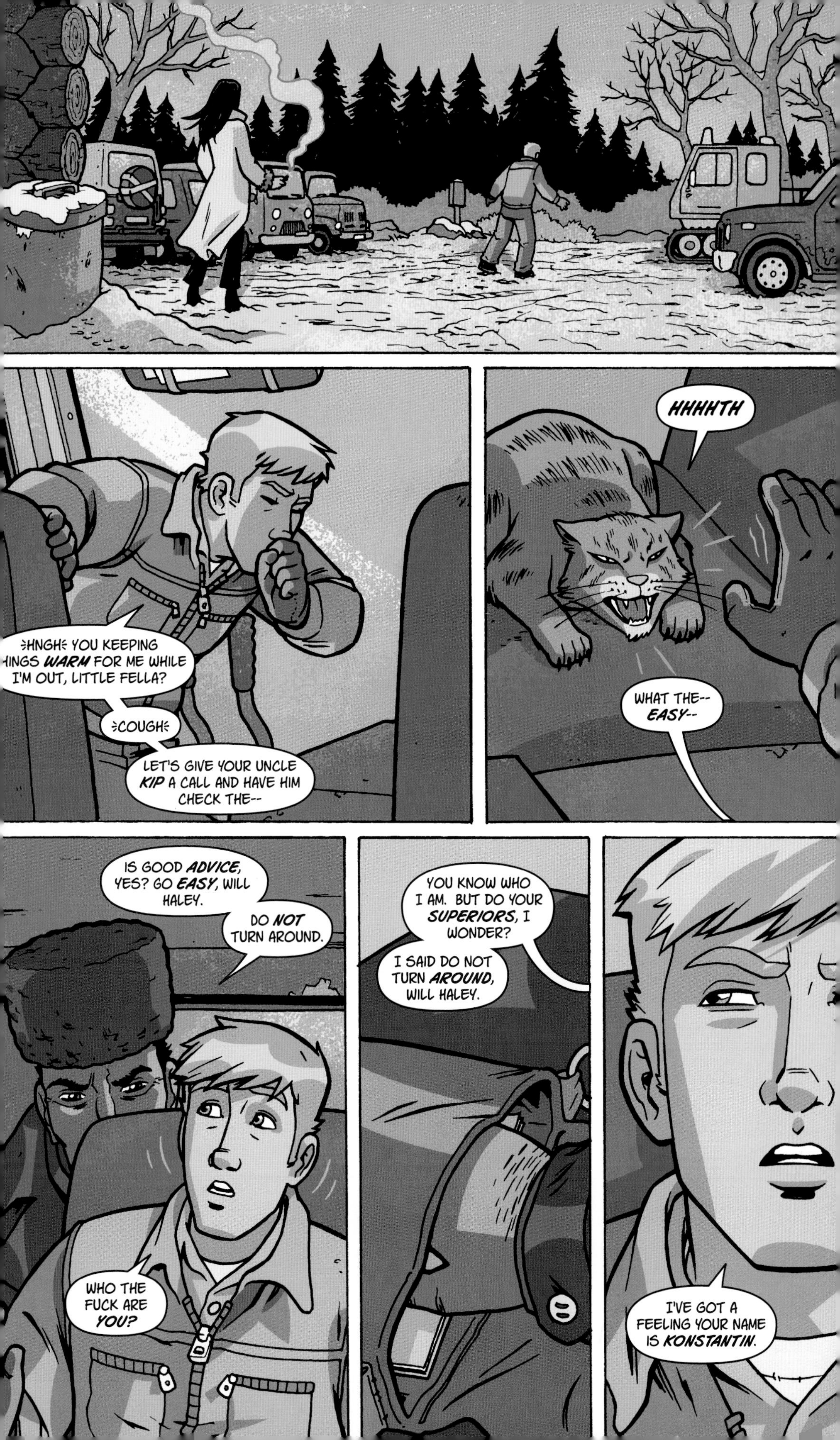

HNGH YOU KEEPING THINGS WARM FOR ME WHILE I'M OUT, LITTLE FELLA?
COUGH
LET'S GIVE YOUR UNCLE KIP A CALL AND HAVE HIM CHECK THE--
HHHHTH
WHAT THE-- EASY--
IS GOOD ADVICE, YES? GO EASY, WILL HALEY.
DO NOT TURN AROUND.
WHO THE FUCK ARE YOU?
YOU KNOW WHO I AM. BUT DO YOUR SUPERIORS, I WONDER?
I SAID DO NOT TURN AROUND, WILL HALEY.
I'VE GOT A FEELING YOUR NAME IS KONSTANTIN.

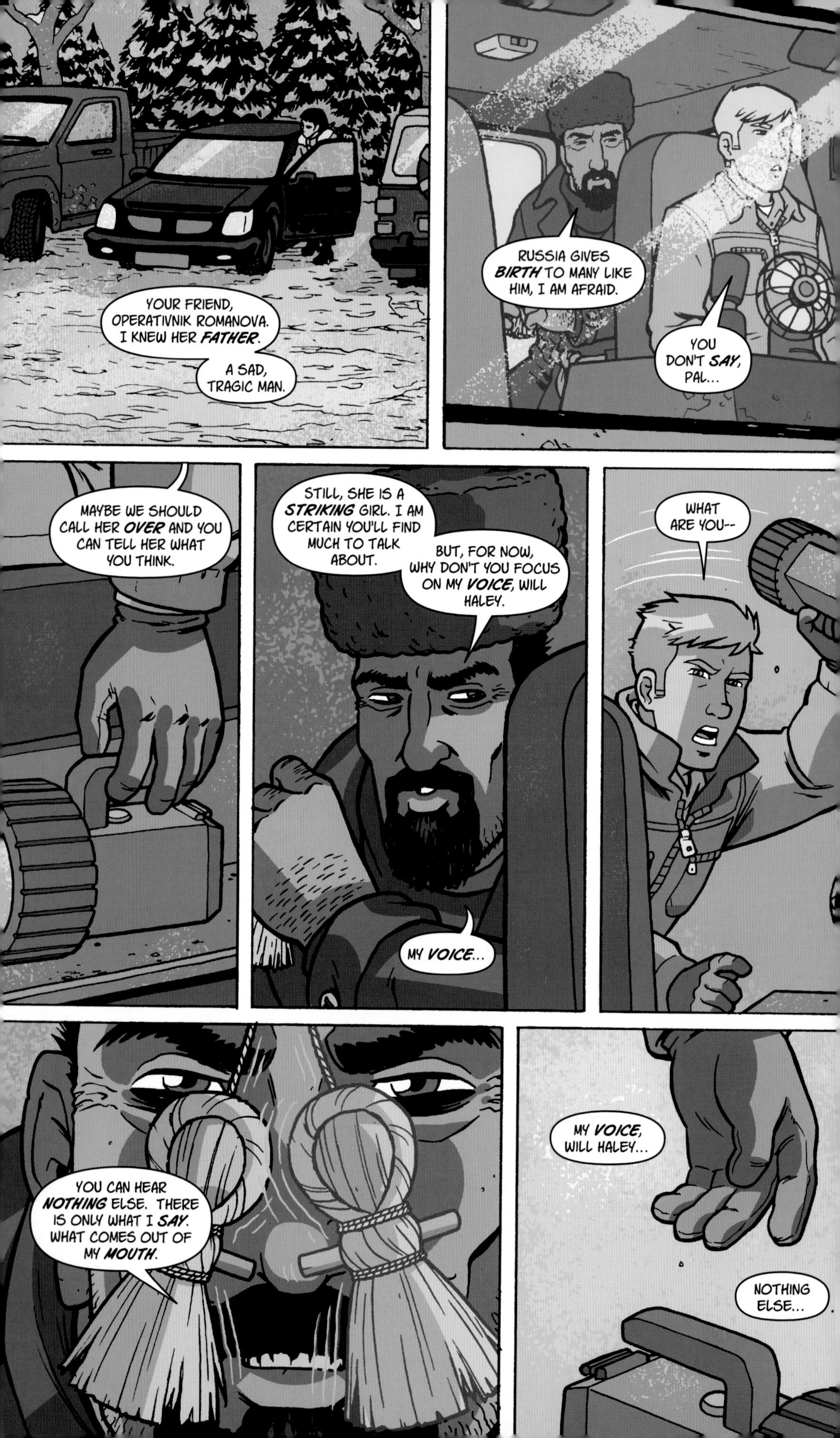
YOUR FRIEND, OPERATIVNIK ROMANOVA. I KNEW HER FATHER.
A SAD, TRAGIC MAN.
RUSSIA GIVES BIRTH TO MANY LIKE HIM, I AM AFRAID.
YOU DON'T SAY, PAL...
MAYBE WE SHOULD CALL HER OVER AND YOU CAN TELL HER WHAT YOU THINK.
STILL, SHE IS A STRIKING GIRL. I AM CERTAIN YOU'LL FIND MUCH TO TALK ABOUT.
BUT, FOR NOW, WHY DON'T YOU FOCUS ON MY VOICE, WILL HALEY.
MY VOICE...
WHAT ARE YOU--
YOU CAN HEAR NOTHING ELSE. THERE IS ONLY WHAT I SAY. WHAT COMES OUT OF MY MOUTH.
MY VOICE, WILL HALEY...
NOTHING ELSE...

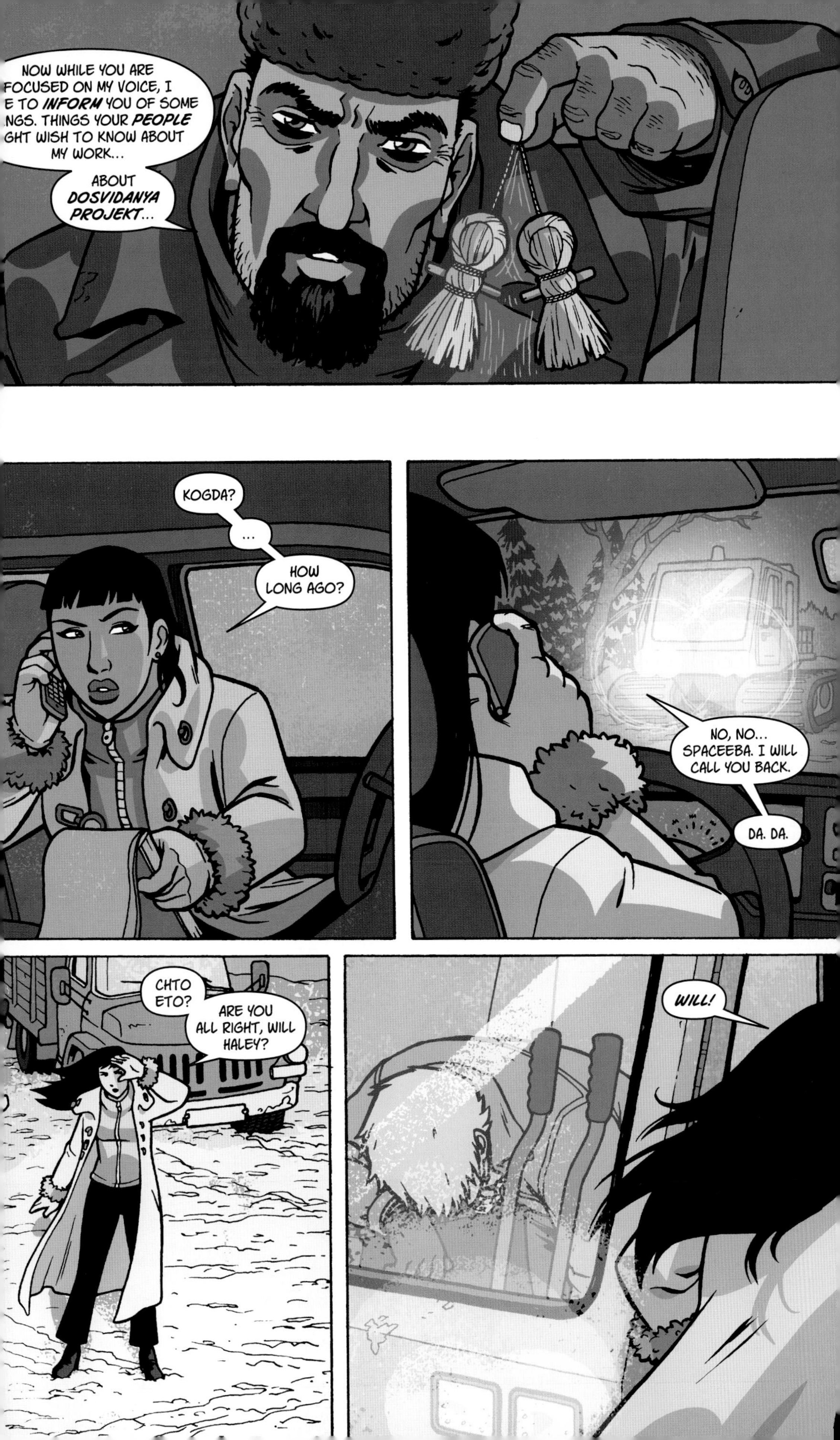
NOW WHILE YOU ARE
FOCUSED ON MY VOICE, I
E TO *INFORM* YOU OF SOME
NGS. THINGS YOUR *PEOPLE*
GHT WISH TO KNOW ABOUT
MY WORK...
ABOUT *DOSVIDANYA PROJEKT*...
KOGDA?
...
HOW LONG AGO?
NO, NO... SPACEEBA. I WILL CALL YOU BACK.
DA. DA.
CHTO ETO?
ARE YOU ALL RIGHT, WILL HALEY?
WILL!

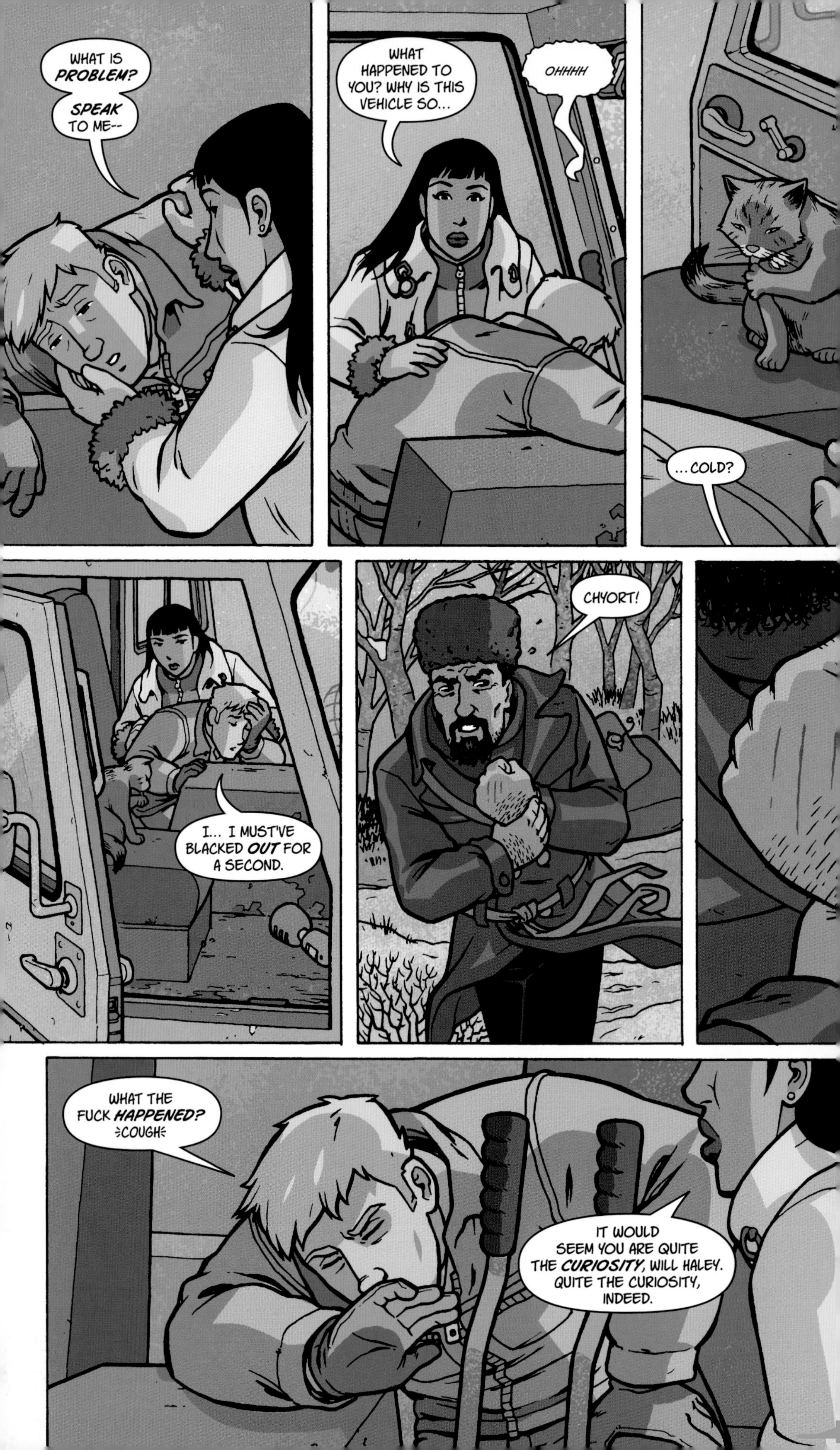
WHAT IS PROBLEM?
SPEAK TO ME--
WHAT HAPPENED TO YOU? WHY IS THIS VEHICLE SO...
OHHHH
...COLD?
I... I MUST'VE BLACKED OUT FOR A SECOND.
CHYORT!
WHAT THE FUCK HAPPENED? COUGH
IT WOULD SEEM YOU ARE QUITE THE CURIOSITY, WILL HALEY. QUITE THE CURIOSITY, INDEED.

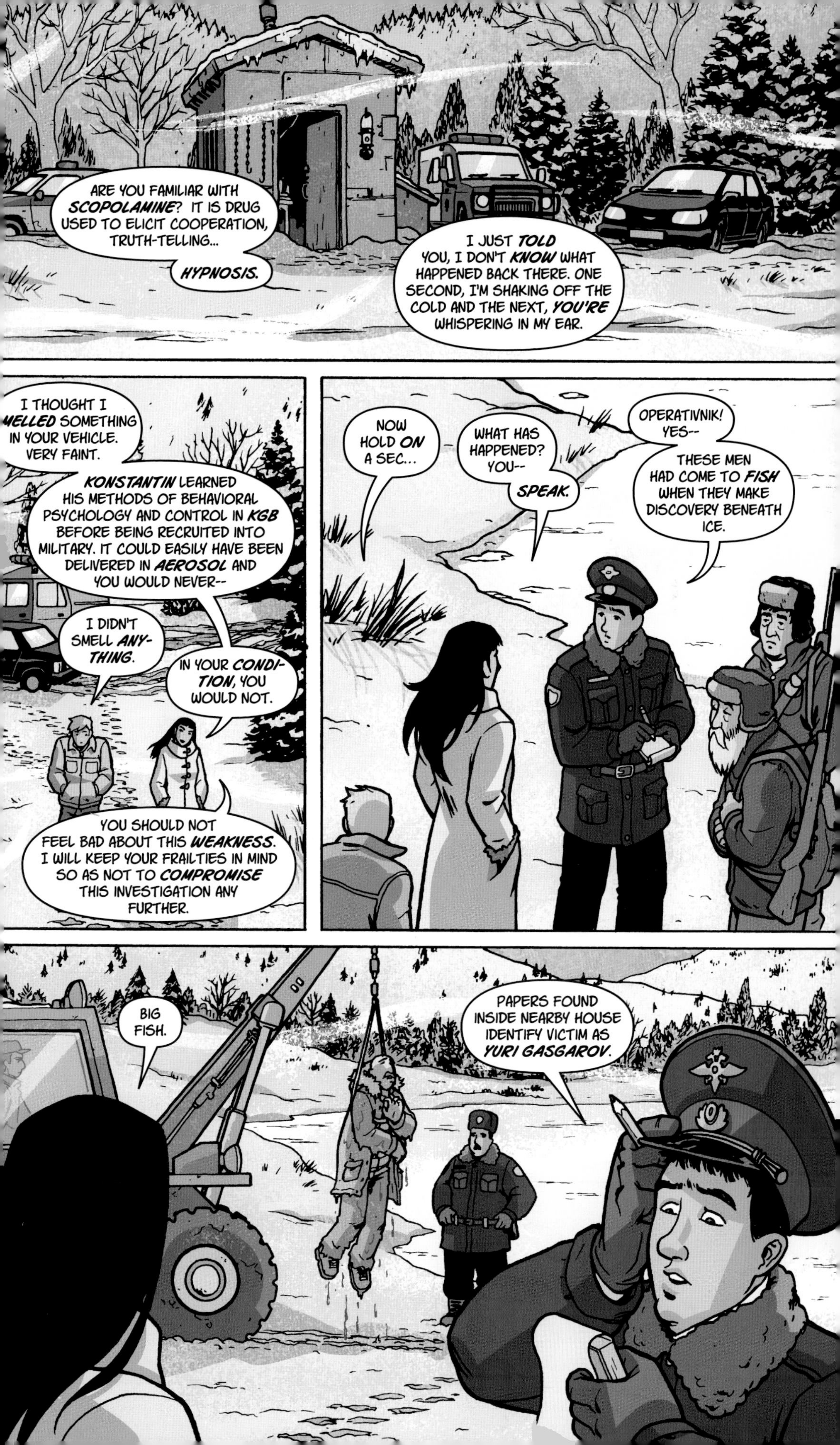
ARE YOU FAMILIAR WITH SCOPOLAMINE? IT IS DRUG USED TO ELICIT COOPERATION, TRUTH-TELLING...
HYPNOSIS.
I JUST TOLD YOU, I DON'T KNOW WHAT HAPPENED BACK THERE. ONE SECOND, I'M SHAKING OFF THE COLD AND THE NEXT, YOU'RE WHISPERING IN MY EAR.
I THOUGHT I MELLED SOMETHING IN YOUR VEHICLE. VERY FAINT.
KONSTANTIN LEARNED HIS METHODS OF BEHAVIORAL PSYCHOLOGY AND CONTROL IN KGB BEFORE BEING RECRUITED INTO MILITARY. IT COULD EASILY HAVE BEEN DELIVERED IN AEROSOL AND YOU WOULD NEVER--
I DIDN'T SMELL ANYTHING.
IN YOUR CONDITION, YOU WOULD NOT.
YOU SHOULD NOT FEEL BAD ABOUT THIS WEAKNESS. I WILL KEEP YOUR FRAILTIES IN MIND SO AS NOT TO COMPROMISE THIS INVESTIGATION ANY FURTHER.
NOW HOLD ON A SEC...
WHAT HAS HAPPENED? YOU--
SPEAK.
OPERATIVNIK! YES--
THESE MEN HAD COME TO FISH WHEN THEY MAKE DISCOVERY BENEATH ICE.
BIG FISH.
PAPERS FOUND INSIDE NEARBY HOUSE IDENTIFY VICTIM AS YURI GASGAROV.

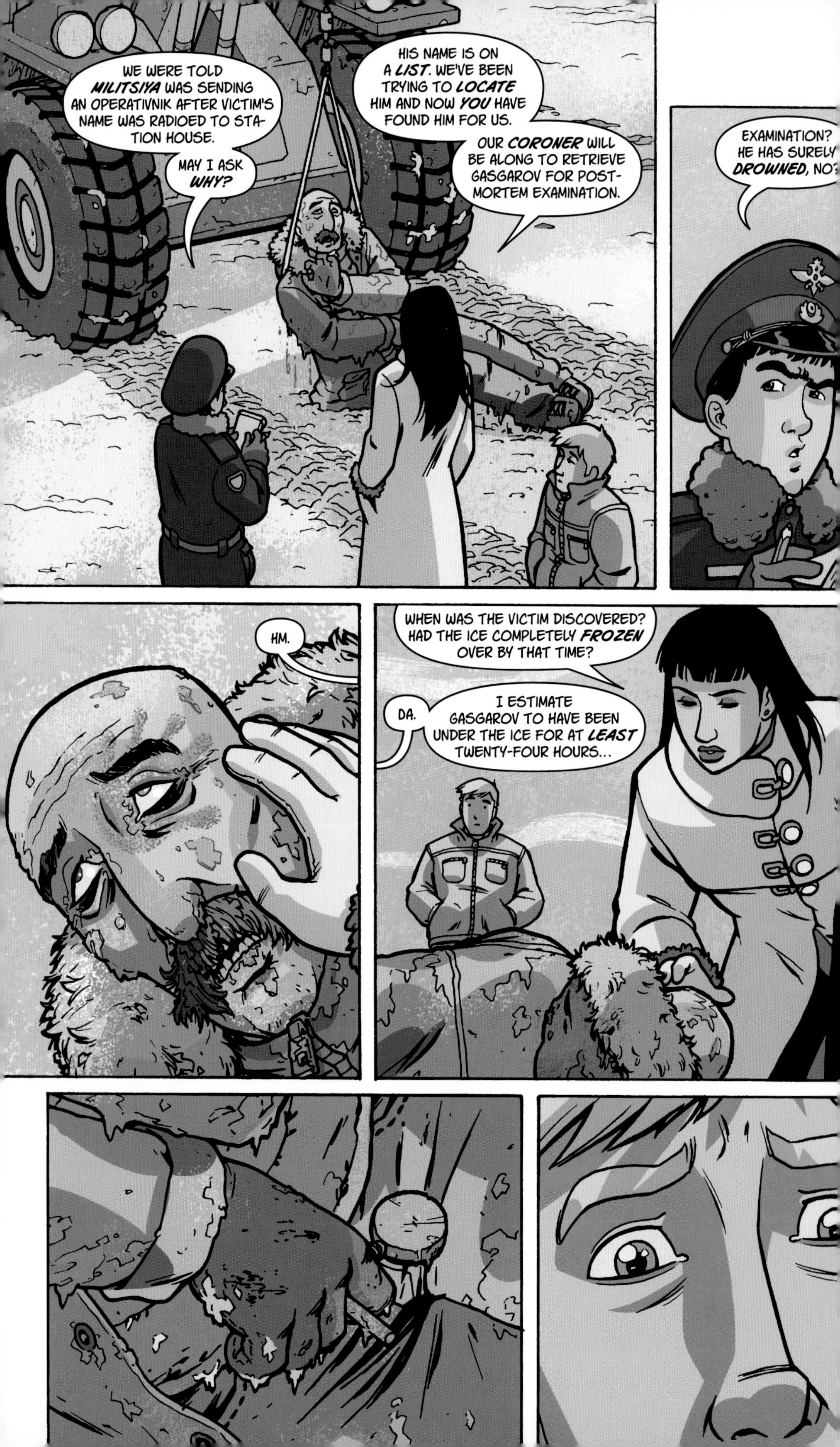
WE WERE TOLD MILITSIYA WAS SENDING AN OPERATIVNIK AFTER VICTIM'S NAME WAS RADIOED TO STATION HOUSE.
MAY I ASK WHY?
HIS NAME IS ON A LIST. WE'VE BEEN TRYING TO LOCATE HIM AND NOW YOU HAVE FOUND HIM FOR US.
OUR CORONER WILL BE ALONG TO RETRIEVE GASGAROV FOR POST-MORTEM EXAMINATION.
EXAMINATION? HE HAS SURELY DROWNED, NO?
HM.
WHEN WAS THE VICTIM DISCOVERED? HAD THE ICE COMPLETELY FROZEN OVER BY THAT TIME?
DA.
I ESTIMATE GASGAROV TO HAVE BEEN UNDER THE ICE FOR AT LEAST TWENTY-FOUR HOURS...

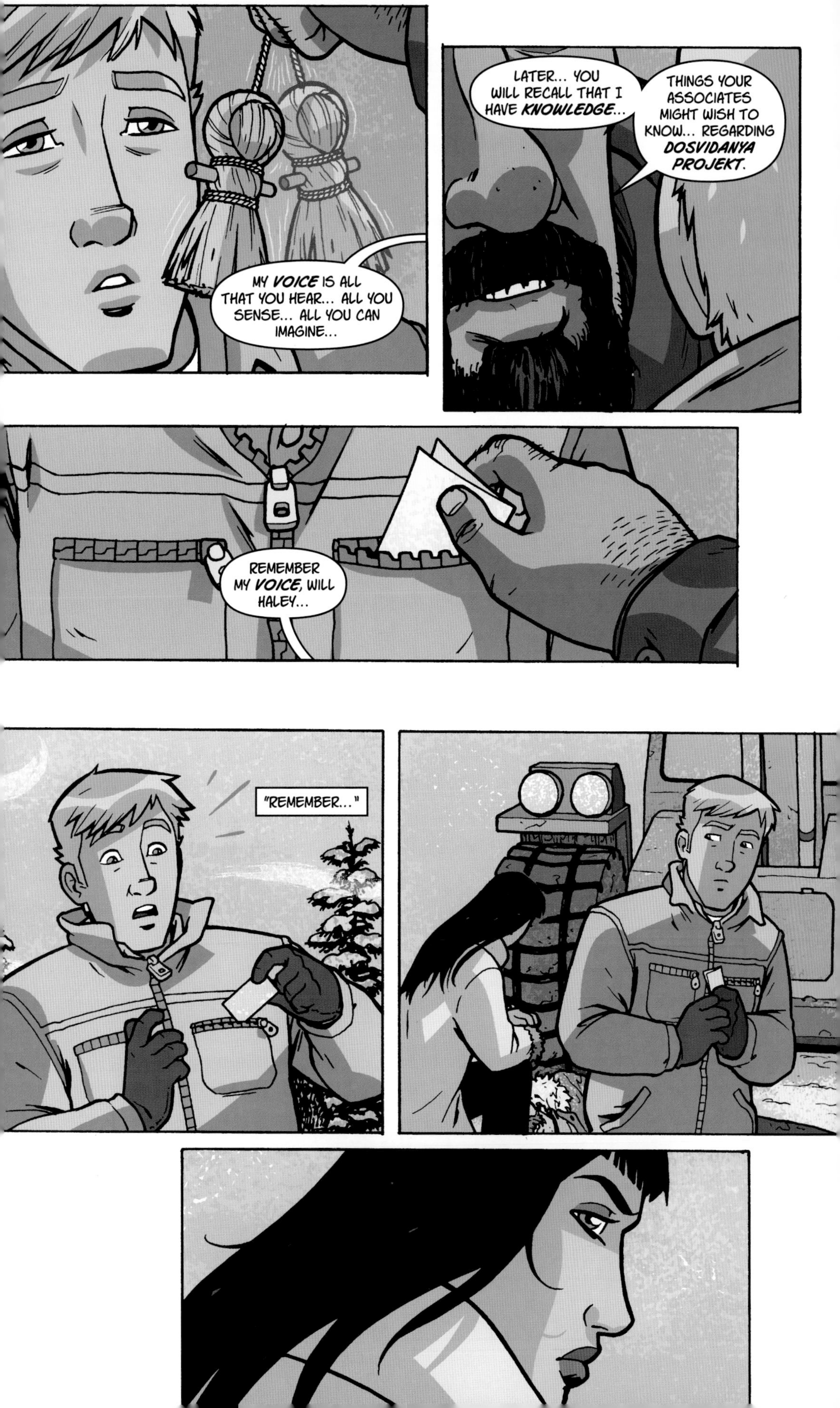
MY *VOICE* IS ALL THAT YOU HEAR... ALL YOU SENSE... ALL YOU CAN IMAGINE...
LATER... YOU WILL RECALL THAT I HAVE *KNOWLEDGE*...
THINGS YOUR ASSOCIATES MIGHT WISH TO KNOW... REGARDING *DOSVIDANYA PROJEKT*.
REMEMBER MY *VOICE*, WILL HALEY...
"REMEMBER..."

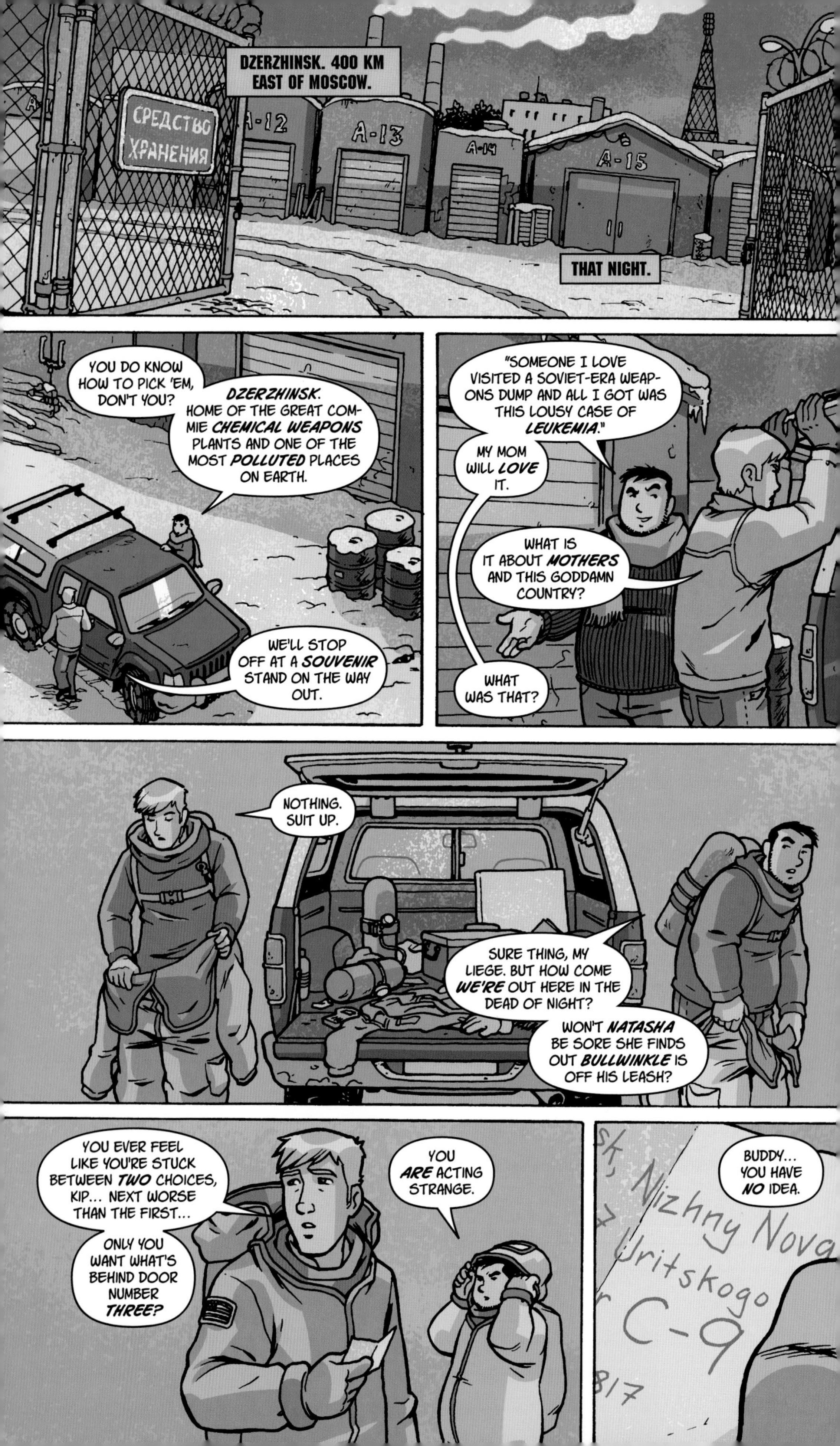
DZERZHINSK. 400 KM EAST OF MOSCOW.
СРЕДСТВО ХРАНЕНИЯ
A-12
A-13
A-14
A-15
THAT NIGHT.
YOU DO KNOW HOW TO PICK 'EM, DON'T YOU?
DZERZHINSK. HOME OF THE GREAT COMMIE CHEMICAL WEAPONS PLANTS AND ONE OF THE MOST POLLUTED PLACES ON EARTH.
WE'LL STOP OFF AT A SOUVENIR STAND ON THE WAY OUT.
"SOMEONE I LOVE VISITED A SOVIET-ERA WEAPONS DUMP AND ALL I GOT WAS THIS LOUSY CASE OF LEUKEMIA."
MY MOM WILL LOVE IT.
WHAT IS IT ABOUT MOTHERS AND THIS GODDAMN COUNTRY?
WHAT WAS THAT?
NOTHING. SUIT UP.
SURE THING, MY LIEGE. BUT HOW COME WE'RE OUT HERE IN THE DEAD OF NIGHT?
WON'T NATASHA BE SORE SHE FINDS OUT BULLWINKLE IS OFF HIS LEASH?
YOU EVER FEEL LIKE YOU'RE STUCK BETWEEN TWO CHOICES, KIP... NEXT WORSE THAN THE FIRST...
ONLY YOU WANT WHAT'S BEHIND DOOR NUMBER THREE?
YOU ARE ACTING STRANGE.
Nizhny Nova
Uritskogo
C-9
BUDDY... YOU HAVE NO IDEA.

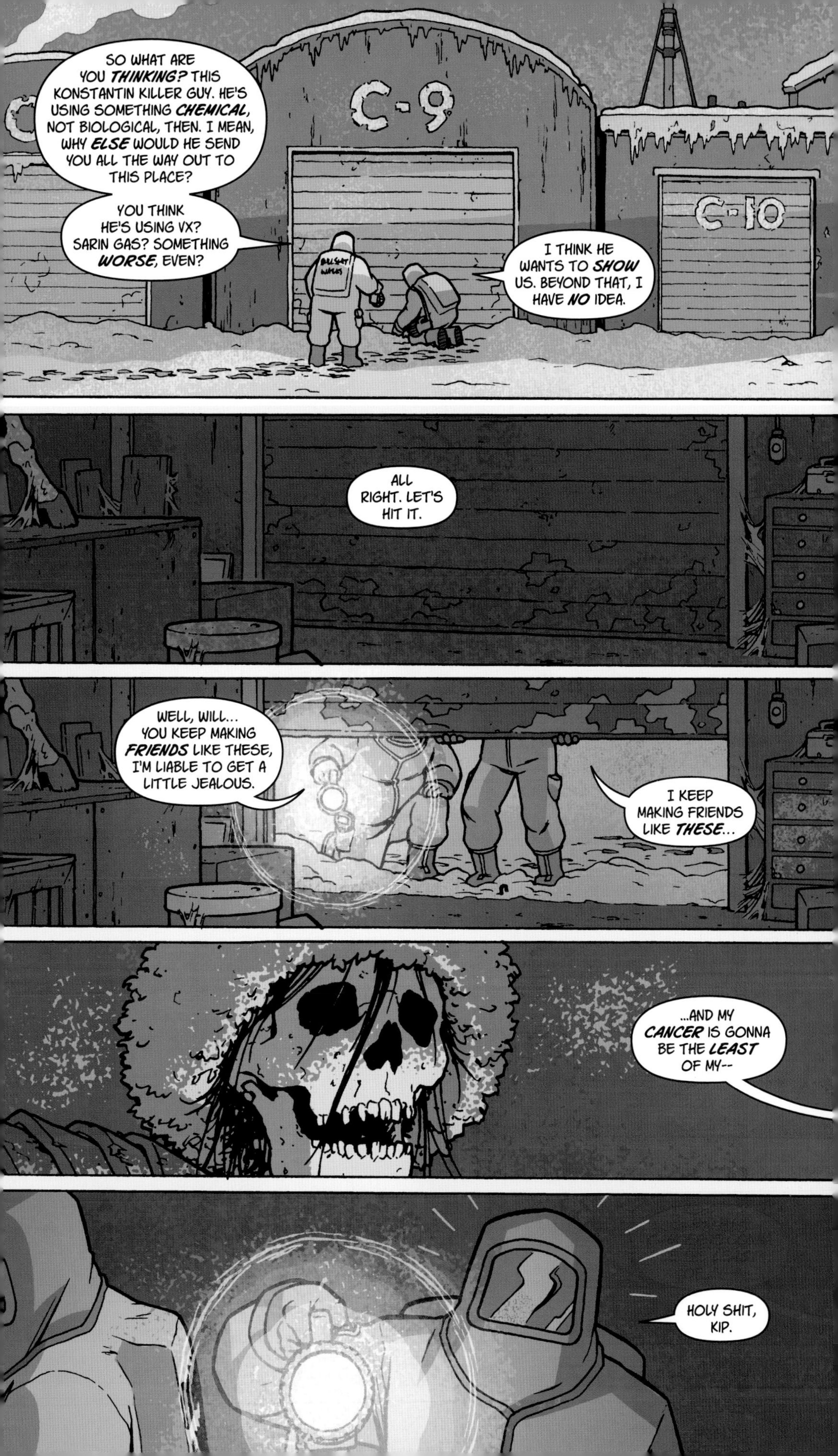
SO WHAT ARE YOU THINKING? THIS KONSTANTIN KILLER GUY. HE'S USING SOMETHING CHEMICAL, NOT BIOLOGICAL, THEN. I MEAN, WHY ELSE WOULD HE SEND YOU ALL THE WAY OUT TO THIS PLACE?
YOU THINK HE'S USING VX? SARIN GAS? SOMETHING WORSE, EVEN?
I THINK HE WANTS TO SHOW US. BEYOND THAT, I HAVE NO IDEA.
C-9
C-10
ALL RIGHT. LET'S HIT IT.
WELL, WILL... YOU KEEP MAKING FRIENDS LIKE THESE, I'M LIABLE TO GET A LITTLE JEALOUS.
I KEEP MAKING FRIENDS LIKE THESE...
...AND MY CANCER IS GONNA BE THE LEAST OF MY--
HOLY SHIT, KIP.

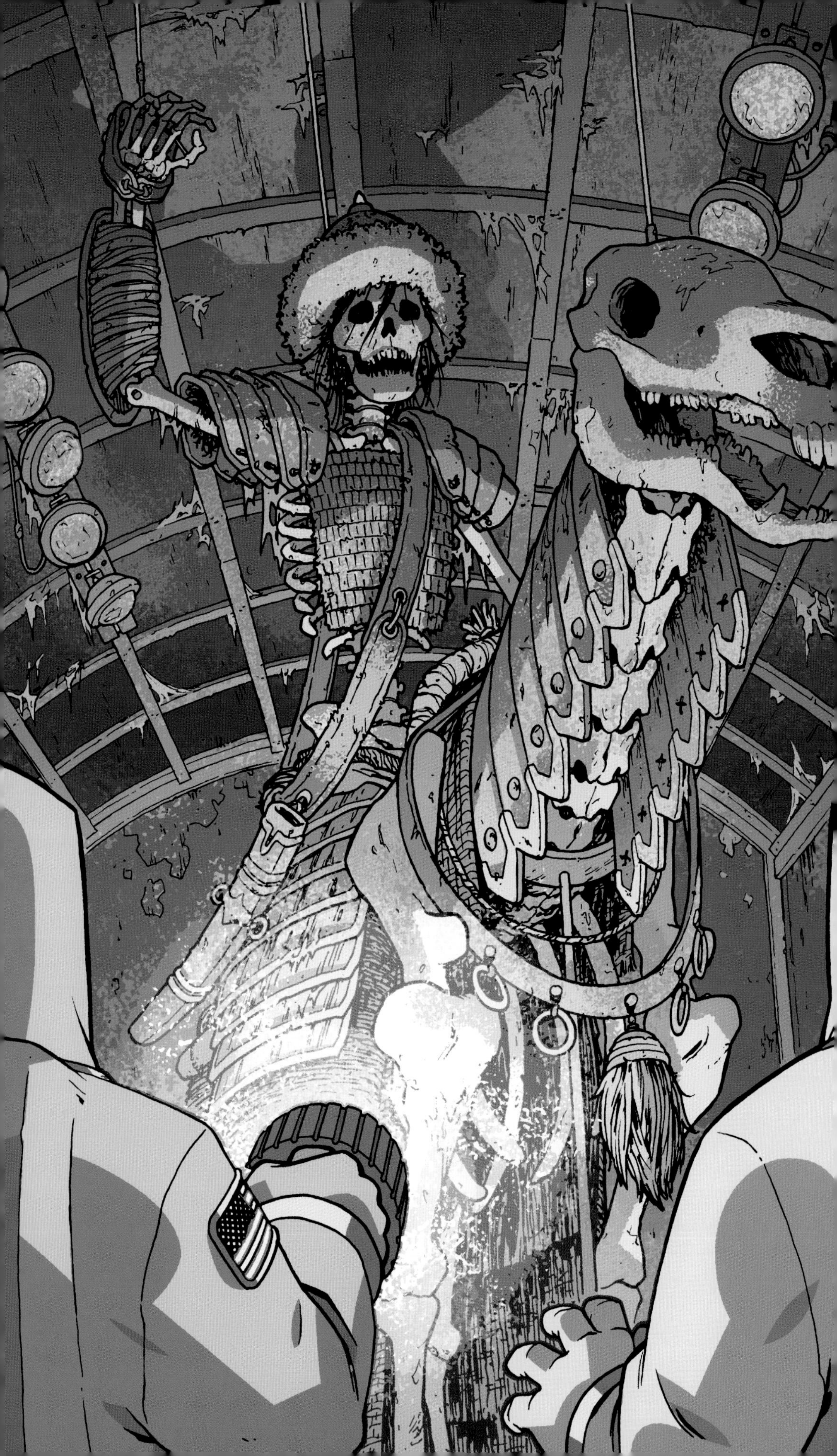

CHAPTER 3:

DARK
RIDERS

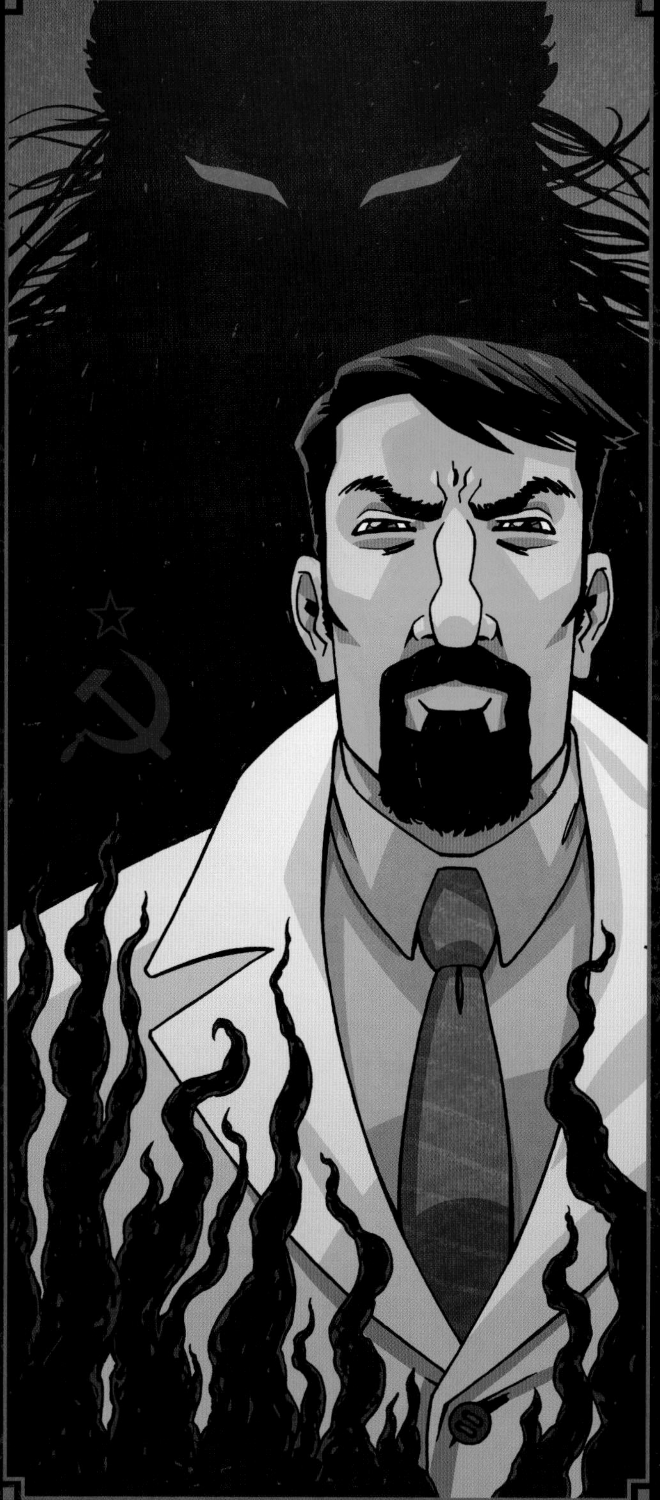

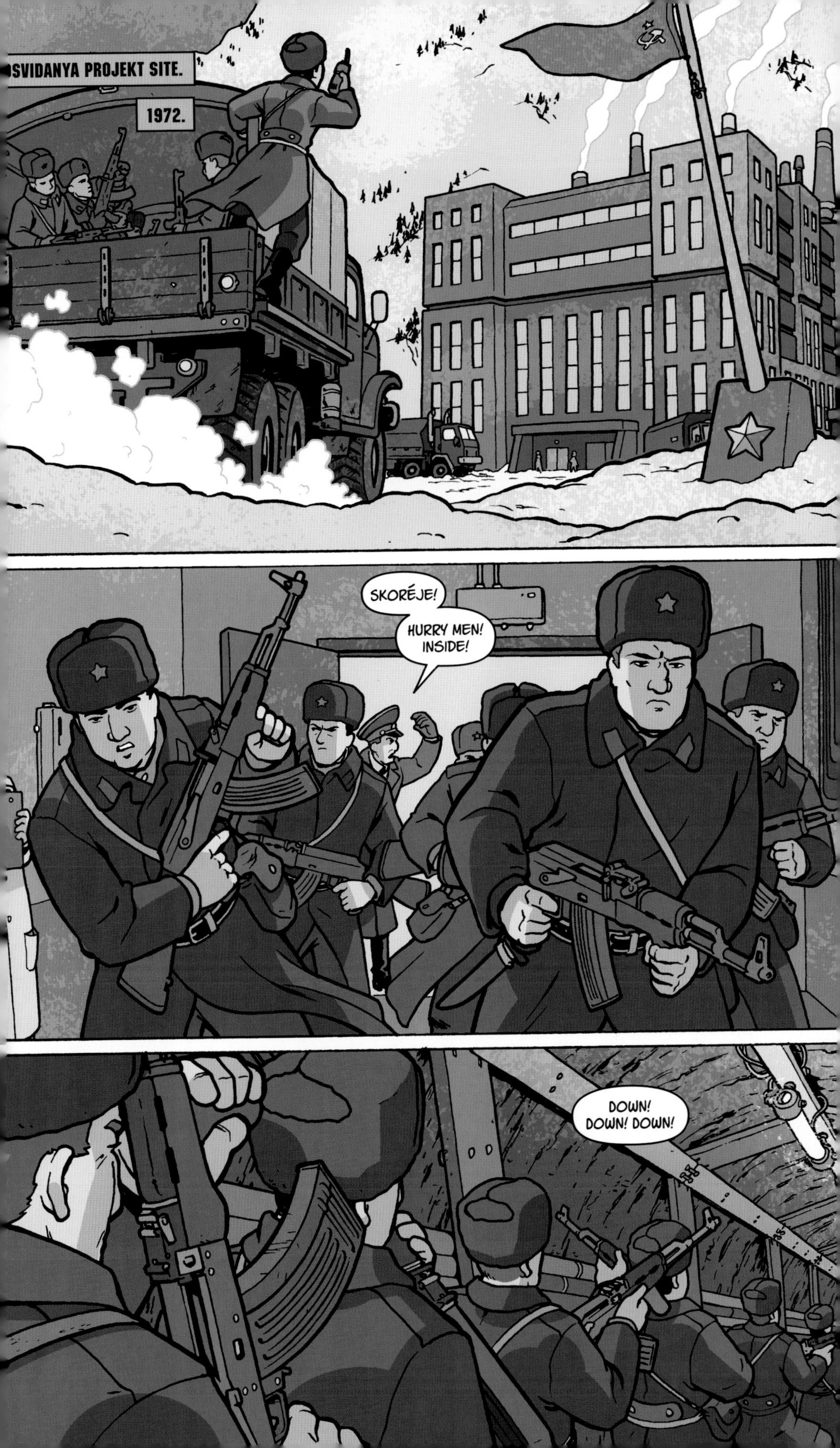

SVIDANYA PROJEKT SITE.
1972.
SKORÉJE!
HURRY MEN! INSIDE!
DOWN! DOWN! DOWN!

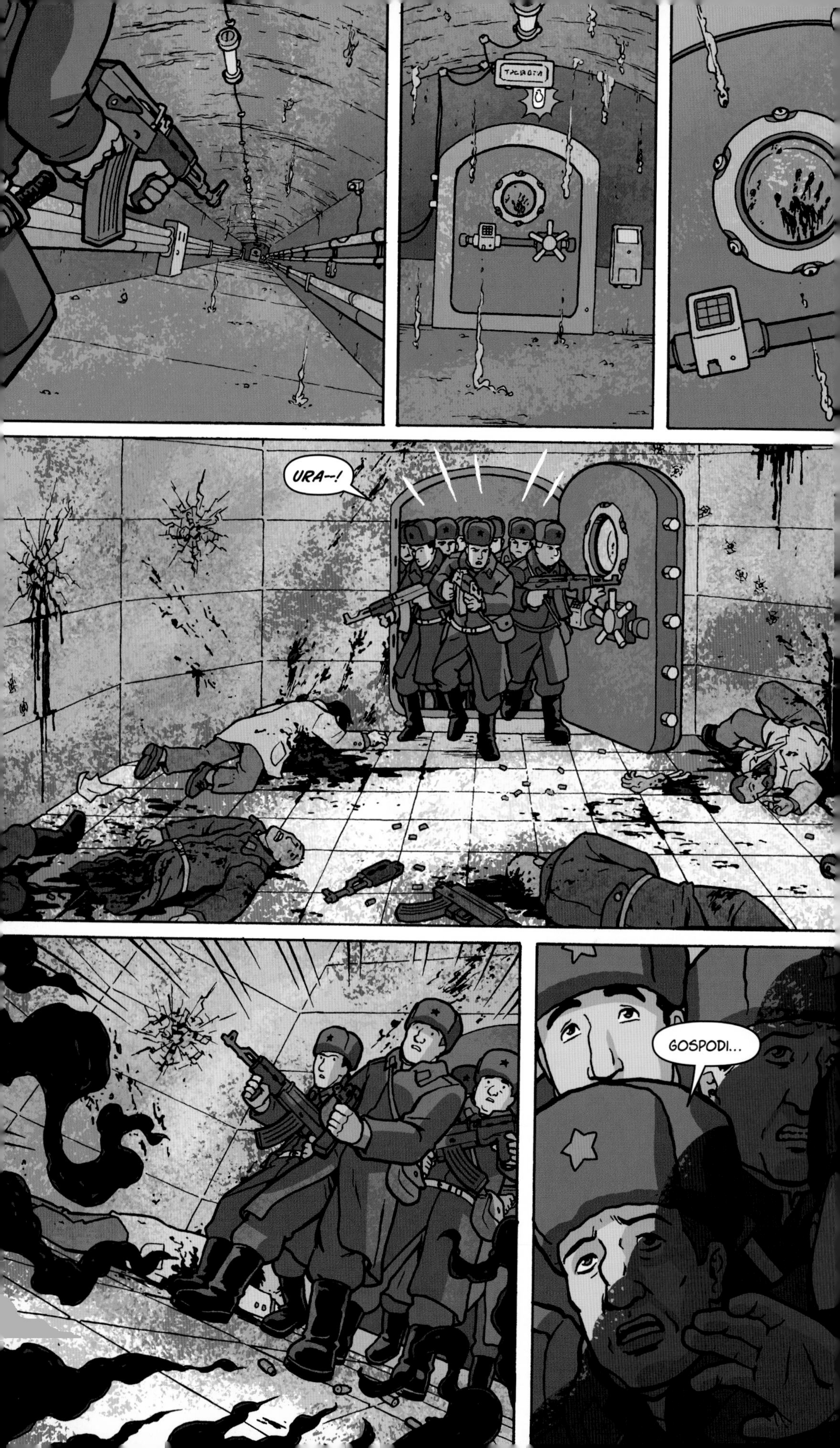
URA--!
GOSPODI...

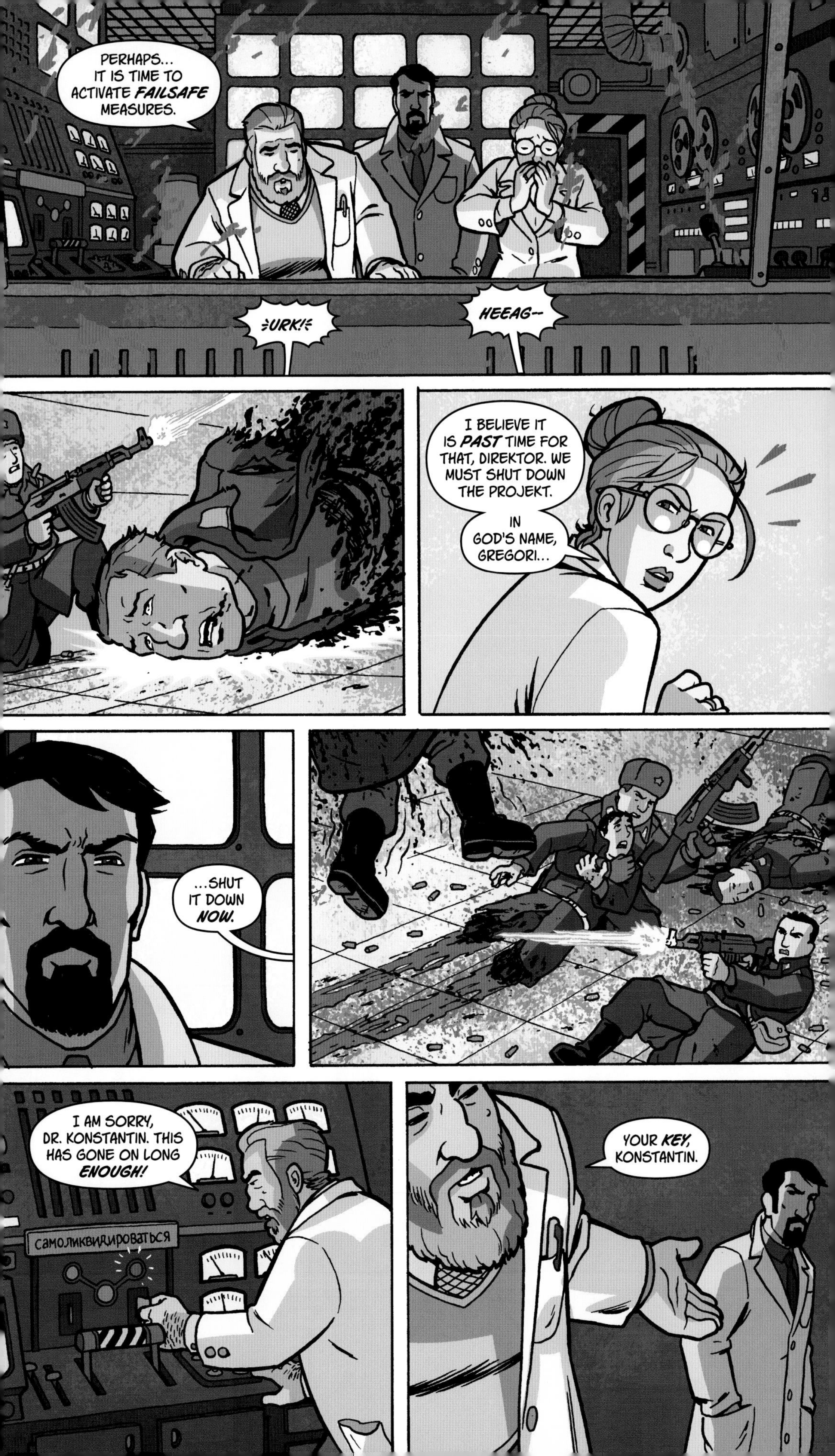
PERHAPS... IT IS TIME TO ACTIVATE FAILSAFE MEASURES.
URK!
HEEAG--
I BELIEVE IT IS PAST TIME FOR THAT, DIREKTOR. WE MUST SHUT DOWN THE PROJEKT.
IN GOD'S NAME, GREGORI...
...SHUT IT DOWN NOW.
I AM SORRY, DR. KONSTANTIN. THIS HAS GONE ON LONG ENOUGH!
самоликвидироваться
YOUR KEY, KONSTANTIN.

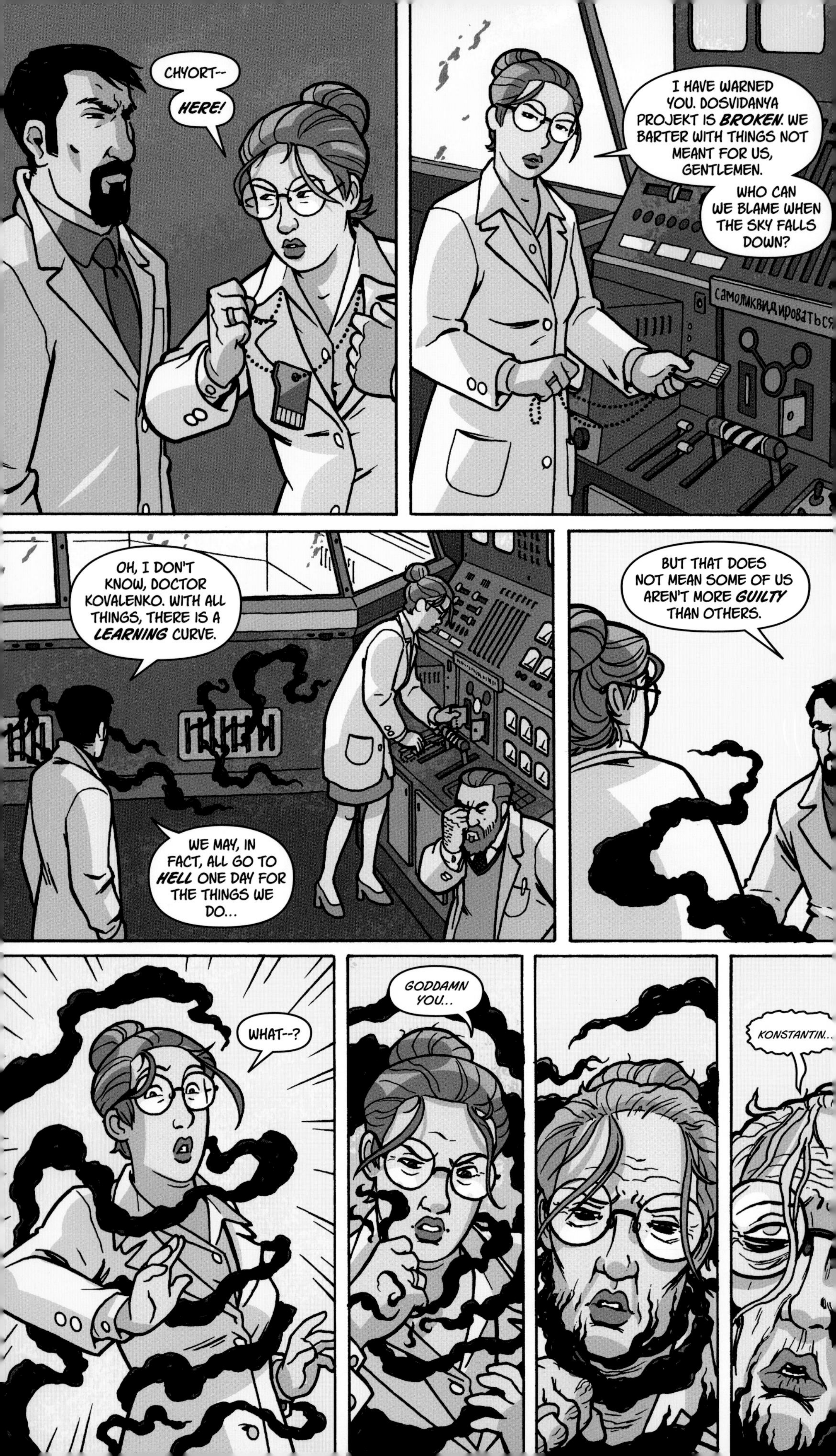
CHYORT--
HERE!
I HAVE WARNED YOU. DOSVIDANYA PROJEKT IS ***BROKEN***. WE BARTER WITH THINGS NOT MEANT FOR US, GENTLEMEN.
WHO CAN WE BLAME WHEN THE SKY FALLS DOWN?
самоликвидироваться
OH, I DON'T KNOW, DOCTOR KOVALENKO. WITH ALL THINGS, THERE IS A ***LEARNING*** CURVE.
WE MAY, IN FACT, ALL GO TO ***HELL*** ONE DAY FOR THE THINGS WE DO...
BUT THAT DOES NOT MEAN SOME OF US AREN'T MORE ***GUILTY*** THAN OTHERS.
WHAT--?
GODDAMN YOU...
KONSTANTIN...

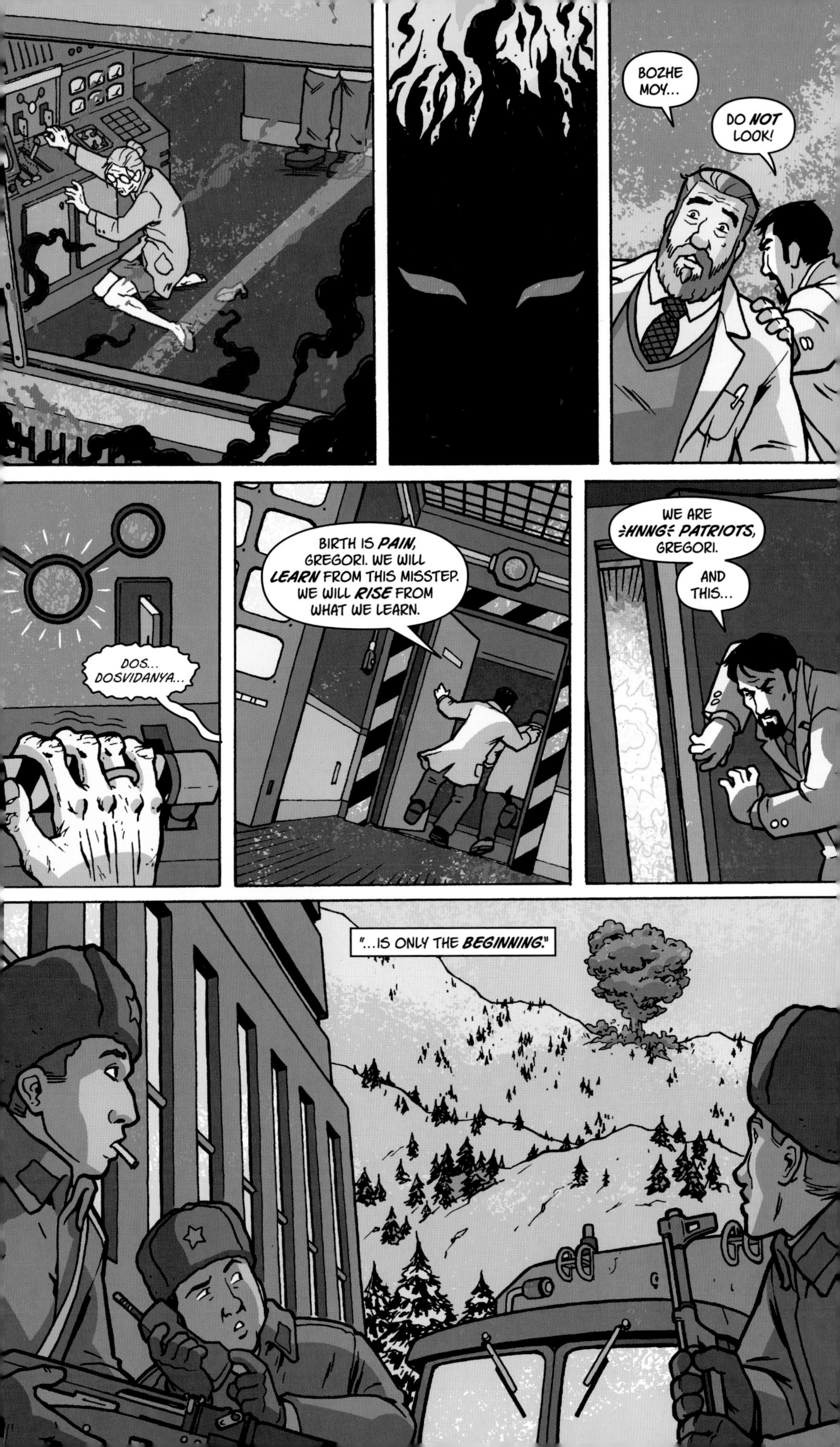
BOZHE MOY...
DO NOT LOOK!
DOS... DOSVIDANYA...
BIRTH IS PAIN, GREGORI. WE WILL LEARN FROM THIS MISSTEP. WE WILL RISE FROM WHAT WE LEARN.
WE ARE HNNG PATRIOTS, GREGORI.
AND THIS...
"...IS ONLY THE BEGINNING."

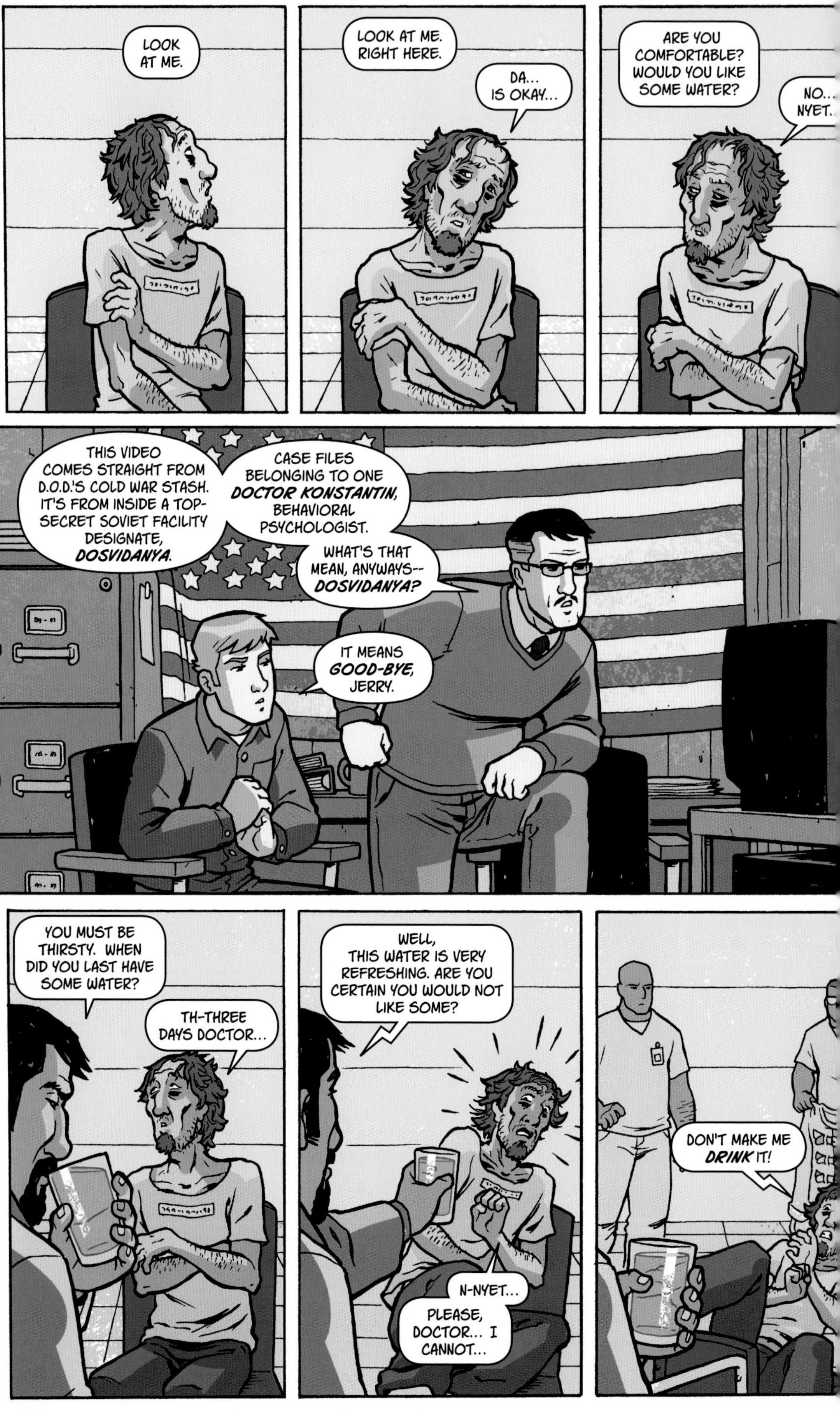

LOOK AT ME.
LOOK AT ME. RIGHT HERE.
DA... IS OKAY...
ARE YOU COMFORTABLE? WOULD YOU LIKE SOME WATER?
NO... NYET.
THIS VIDEO COMES STRAIGHT FROM D.O.D.'S COLD WAR STASH. IT'S FROM INSIDE A TOP-SECRET SOVIET FACILITY DESIGNATE, DOSVIDANYA.
CASE FILES BELONGING TO ONE DOCTOR KONSTANTIN, BEHAVIORAL PSYCHOLOGIST.
WHAT'S THAT MEAN, ANYWAYS-- DOSVIDANYA?
IT MEANS GOOD-BYE, JERRY.
YOU MUST BE THIRSTY. WHEN DID YOU LAST HAVE SOME WATER?
TH-THREE DAYS DOCTOR...
WELL, THIS WATER IS VERY REFRESHING. ARE YOU CERTAIN YOU WOULD NOT LIKE SOME?
N-NYET...
PLEASE, DOCTOR... I CANNOT...
DON'T MAKE ME DRINK IT!

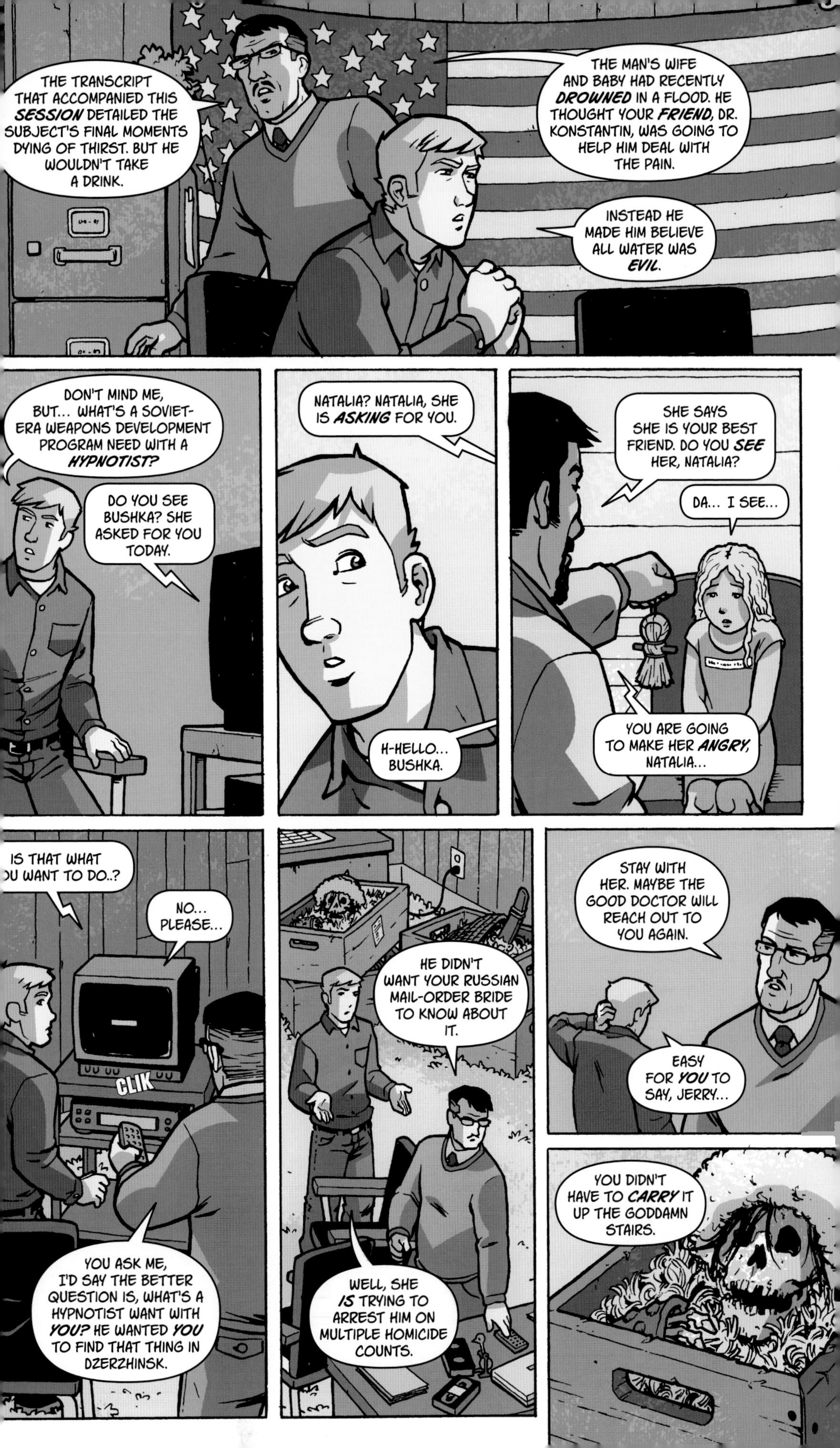
THE TRANSCRIPT THAT ACCOMPANIED THIS *SESSION* DETAILED THE SUBJECT'S FINAL MOMENTS DYING OF THIRST. BUT HE WOULDN'T TAKE A DRINK.
THE MAN'S WIFE AND BABY HAD RECENTLY *DROWNED* IN A FLOOD. HE THOUGHT YOUR *FRIEND*, DR. KONSTANTIN, WAS GOING TO HELP HIM DEAL WITH THE PAIN.
INSTEAD HE MADE HIM BELIEVE ALL WATER WAS *EVIL*.
DON'T MIND ME, BUT... WHAT'S A SOVIET-ERA WEAPONS DEVELOPMENT PROGRAM NEED WITH A *HYPNOTIST?*
DO YOU SEE BUSHKA? SHE ASKED FOR YOU TODAY.
NATALIA? NATALIA, SHE IS *ASKING* FOR YOU.
H-HELLO... BUSHKA.
SHE SAYS SHE IS YOUR BEST FRIEND. DO YOU *SEE* HER, NATALIA?
DA... I SEE...
YOU ARE GOING TO MAKE HER *ANGRY,* NATALIA...
IS THAT WHAT OU WANT TO DO..?
NO... PLEASE...
CLIK
YOU ASK ME, I'D SAY THE BETTER QUESTION IS, WHAT'S A HYPNOTIST WANT WITH *YOU?* HE WANTED *YOU* TO FIND THAT THING IN DZERZHINSK.
HE DIDN'T WANT YOUR RUSSIAN MAIL-ORDER BRIDE TO KNOW ABOUT IT.
WELL, SHE *IS* TRYING TO ARREST HIM ON MULTIPLE HOMICIDE COUNTS.
STAY WITH HER. MAYBE THE GOOD DOCTOR WILL REACH OUT TO YOU AGAIN.
EASY FOR *YOU* TO SAY, JERRY...
YOU DIDN'T HAVE TO *CARRY* IT UP THE GODDAMN STAIRS.

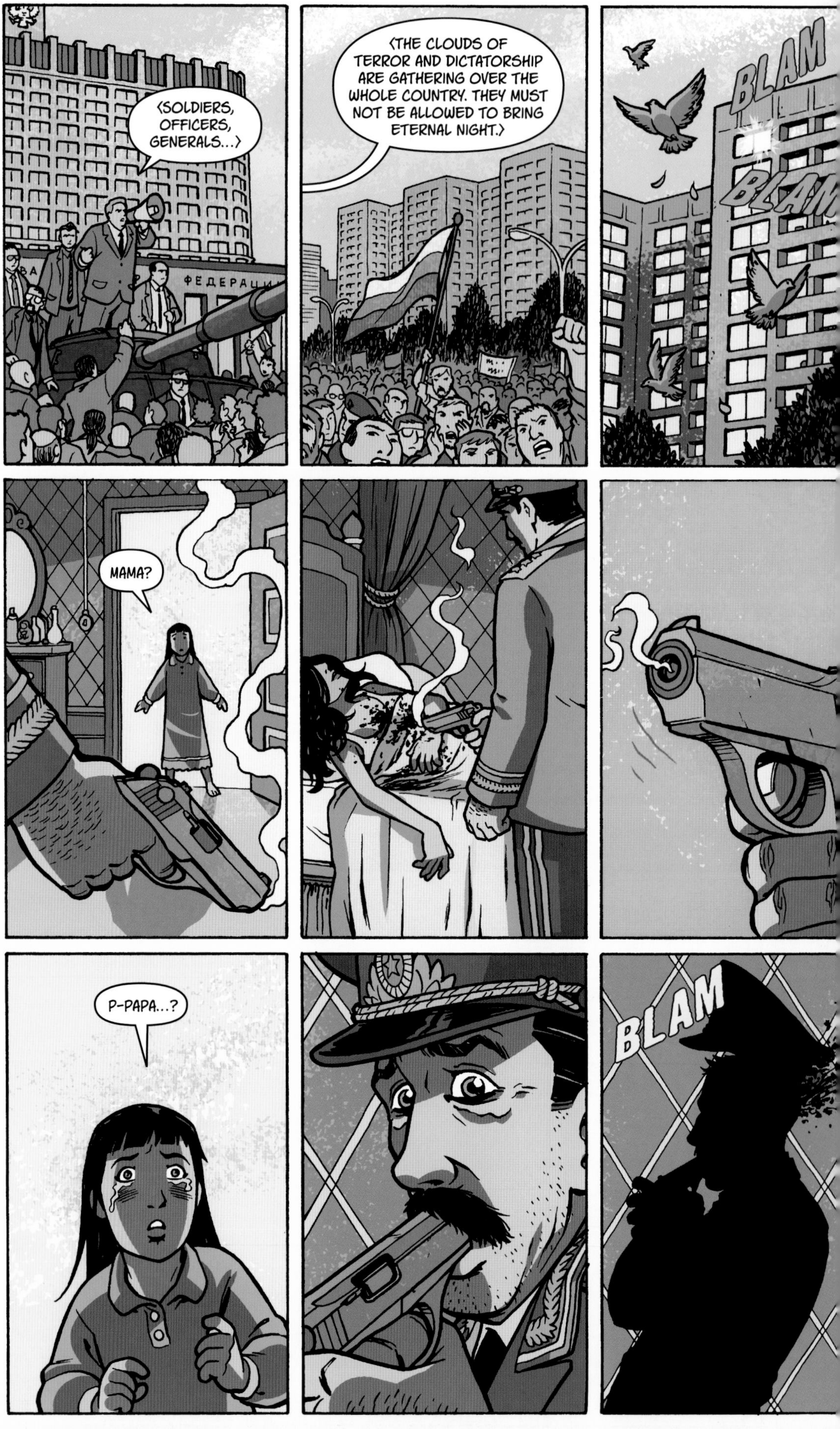
〈SOLDIERS, OFFICERS, GENERALS...〉
ФЕДЕРАЦИ
〈THE CLOUDS OF TERROR AND DICTATORSHIP ARE GATHERING OVER THE WHOLE COUNTRY. THEY MUST NOT BE ALLOWED TO BRING ETERNAL NIGHT.〉
BLAM
BLAM
MAMA?
P-PAPA...?
BLAM

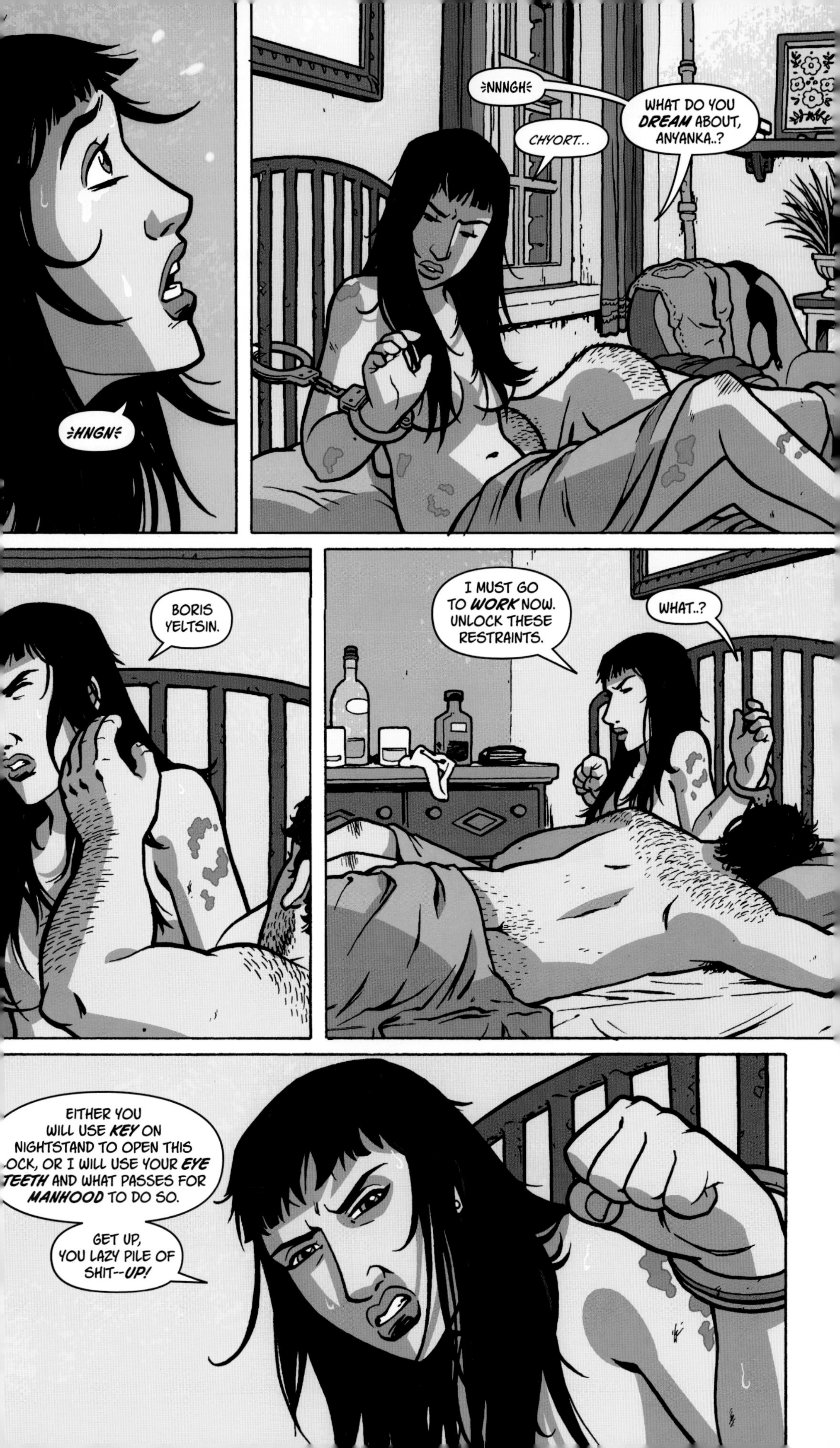

HNGN
NNNGH
CHYORT...
WHAT DO YOU DREAM ABOUT, ANYANKA..?
BORIS YELTSIN.
I MUST GO TO WORK NOW. UNLOCK THESE RESTRAINTS.
WHAT..?
EITHER YOU WILL USE KEY ON NIGHTSTAND TO OPEN THIS LOCK, OR I WILL USE YOUR EYE TEETH AND WHAT PASSES FOR MANHOOD TO DO SO.
GET UP, YOU LAZY PILE OF SHIT--UP!

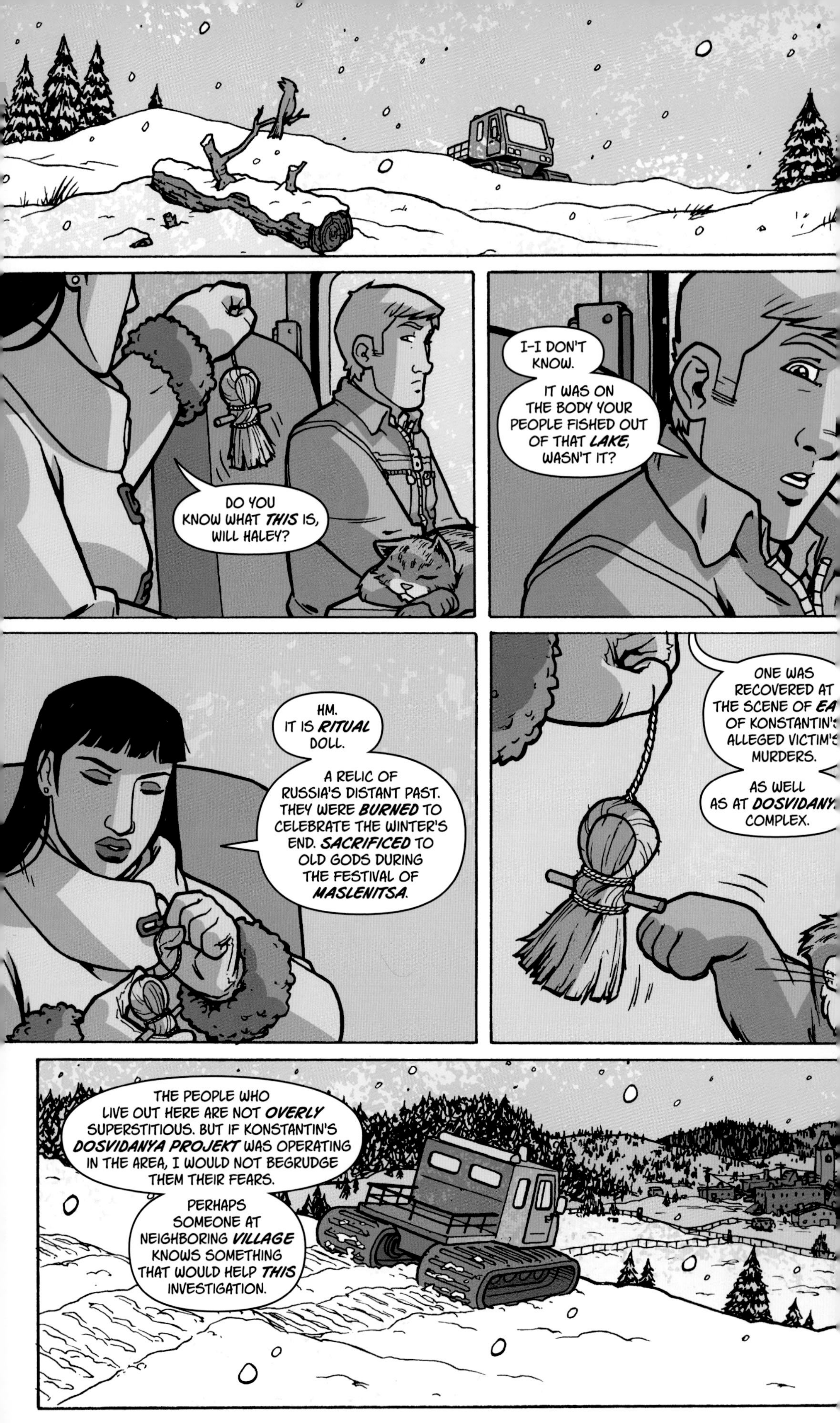
DO YOU KNOW WHAT THIS IS, WILL HALEY?
I-I DON'T KNOW.
IT WAS ON THE BODY YOUR PEOPLE FISHED OUT OF THAT LAKE, WASN'T IT?
HM. IT IS RITUAL DOLL.
A RELIC OF RUSSIA'S DISTANT PAST. THEY WERE BURNED TO CELEBRATE THE WINTER'S END. SACRIFICED TO OLD GODS DURING THE FESTIVAL OF MASLENITSA.
ONE WAS RECOVERED AT THE SCENE OF EA OF KONSTANTIN'S ALLEGED VICTIM'S MURDERS.
AS WELL AS AT DOSVIDANY COMPLEX.
THE PEOPLE WHO LIVE OUT HERE ARE NOT OVERLY SUPERSTITIOUS. BUT IF KONSTANTIN'S DOSVIDANYA PROJEKT WAS OPERATING IN THE AREA, I WOULD NOT BEGRUDGE THEM THEIR FEARS.
PERHAPS SOMEONE AT NEIGHBORING VILLAGE KNOWS SOMETHING THAT WOULD HELP THIS INVESTIGATION.

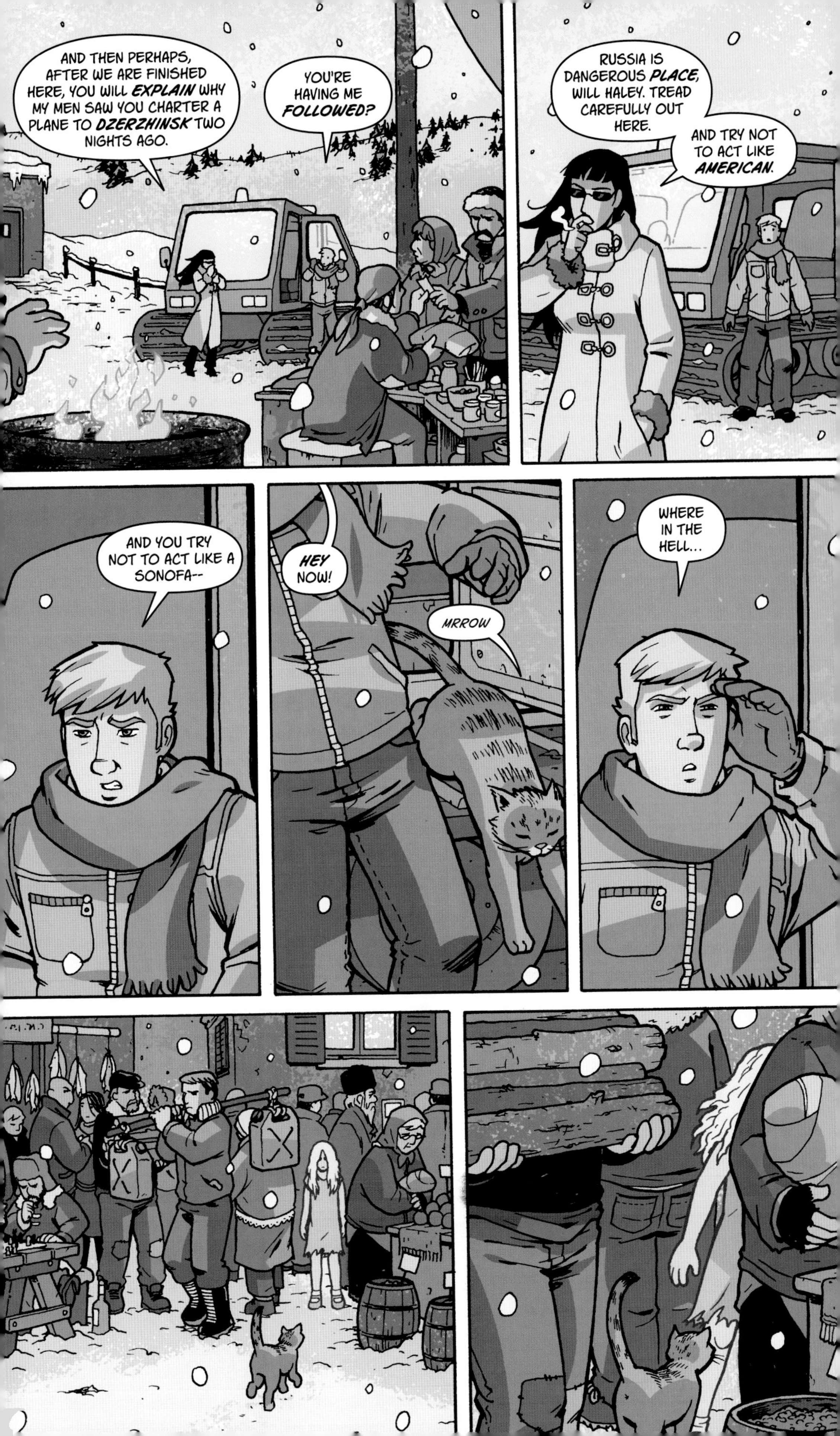
AND THEN PERHAPS, AFTER WE ARE FINISHED HERE, YOU WILL EXPLAIN WHY MY MEN SAW YOU CHARTER A PLANE TO DZERZHINSK TWO NIGHTS AGO.
YOU'RE HAVING ME FOLLOWED?
RUSSIA IS DANGEROUS PLACE, WILL HALEY. TREAD CAREFULLY OUT HERE.
AND TRY NOT TO ACT LIKE AMERICAN.
AND YOU TRY NOT TO ACT LIKE A SONOFA--
HEY NOW!
MRROW
WHERE IN THE HELL...

AW HELL.

≋COUGH≋

WHERE YOU OFF TO ≋KEFF≋... FRANKENCAT?

LET ME-- LET ME JUST--

≋HK≋ ≋HNGH≋ ≋KOFF≋

NIIILLLLLLLLLLHALLLLLLLLEY

HELLO?

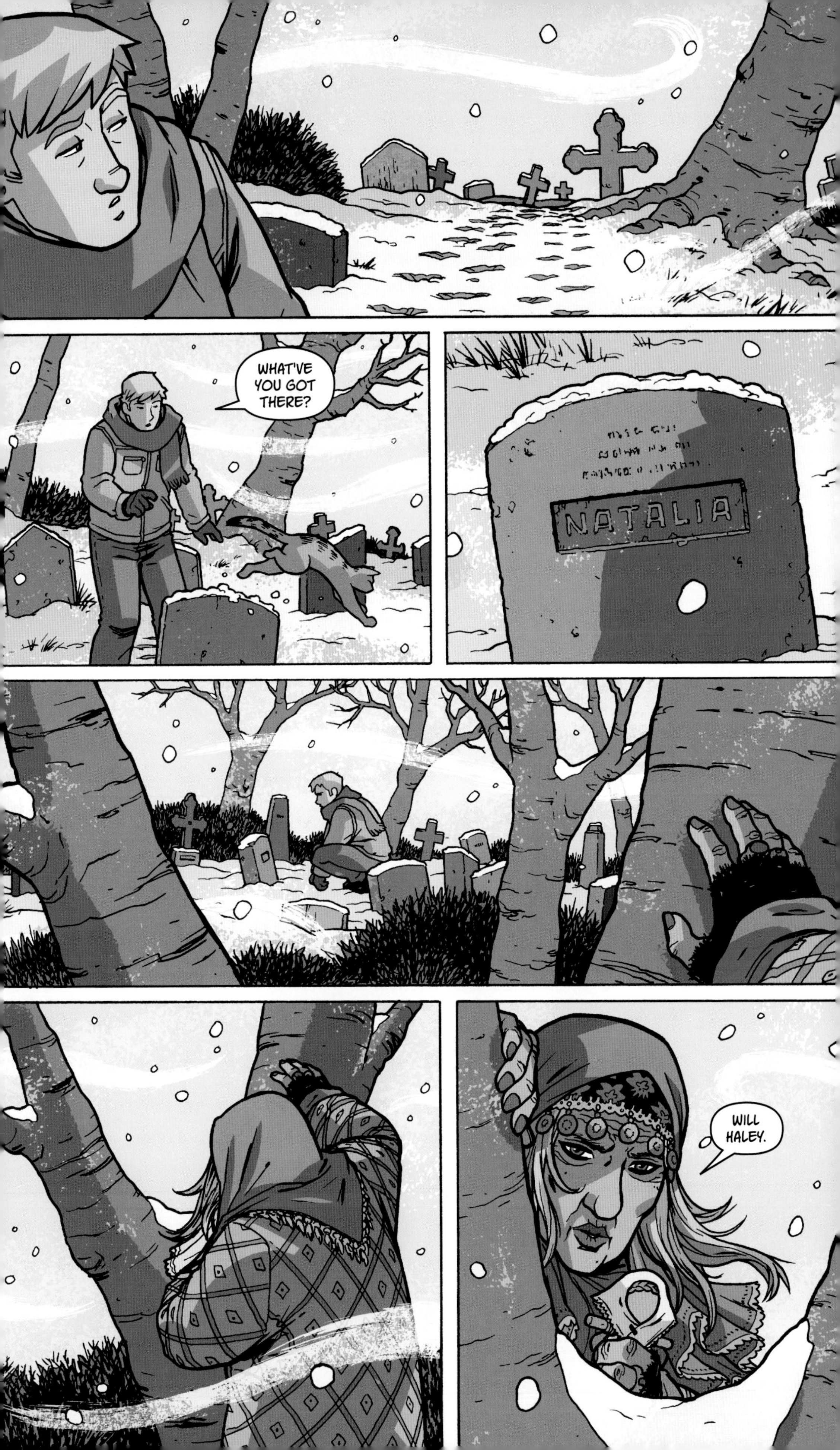
WHAT'VE YOU GOT THERE?
NATALIA
WILL HALEY.

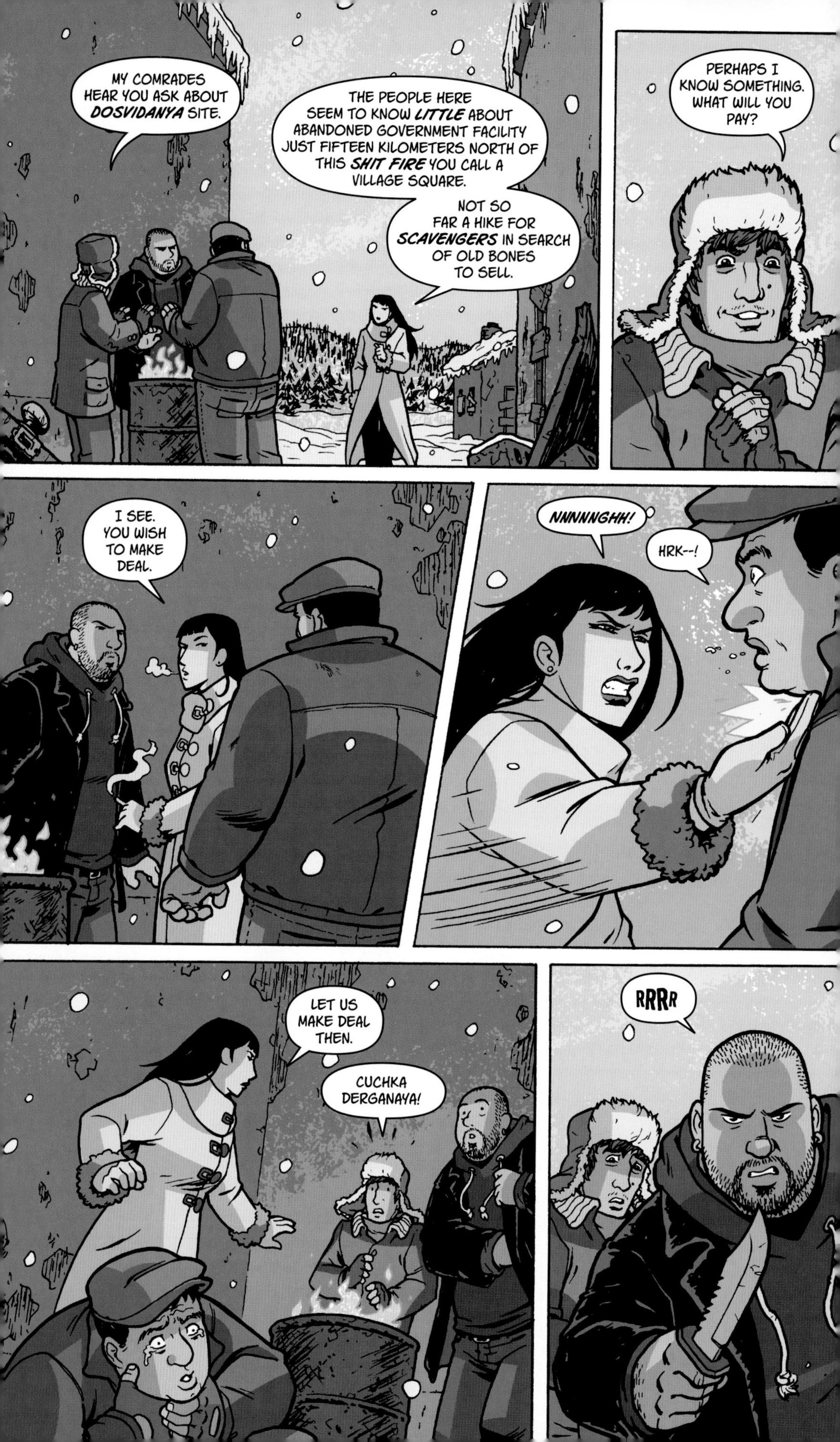

MY COMRADES HEAR YOU ASK ABOUT DOSVIDANYA SITE.
THE PEOPLE HERE SEEM TO KNOW LITTLE ABOUT ABANDONED GOVERNMENT FACILITY JUST FIFTEEN KILOMETERS NORTH OF THIS SHIT FIRE YOU CALL A VILLAGE SQUARE.
NOT SO FAR A HIKE FOR SCAVENGERS IN SEARCH OF OLD BONES TO SELL.
PERHAPS I KNOW SOMETHING. WHAT WILL YOU PAY?
I SEE. YOU WISH TO MAKE DEAL.
NNNNNGHH!
HRK--!
LET US MAKE DEAL THEN.
CUCHKA DERGANAYA!
RRRR

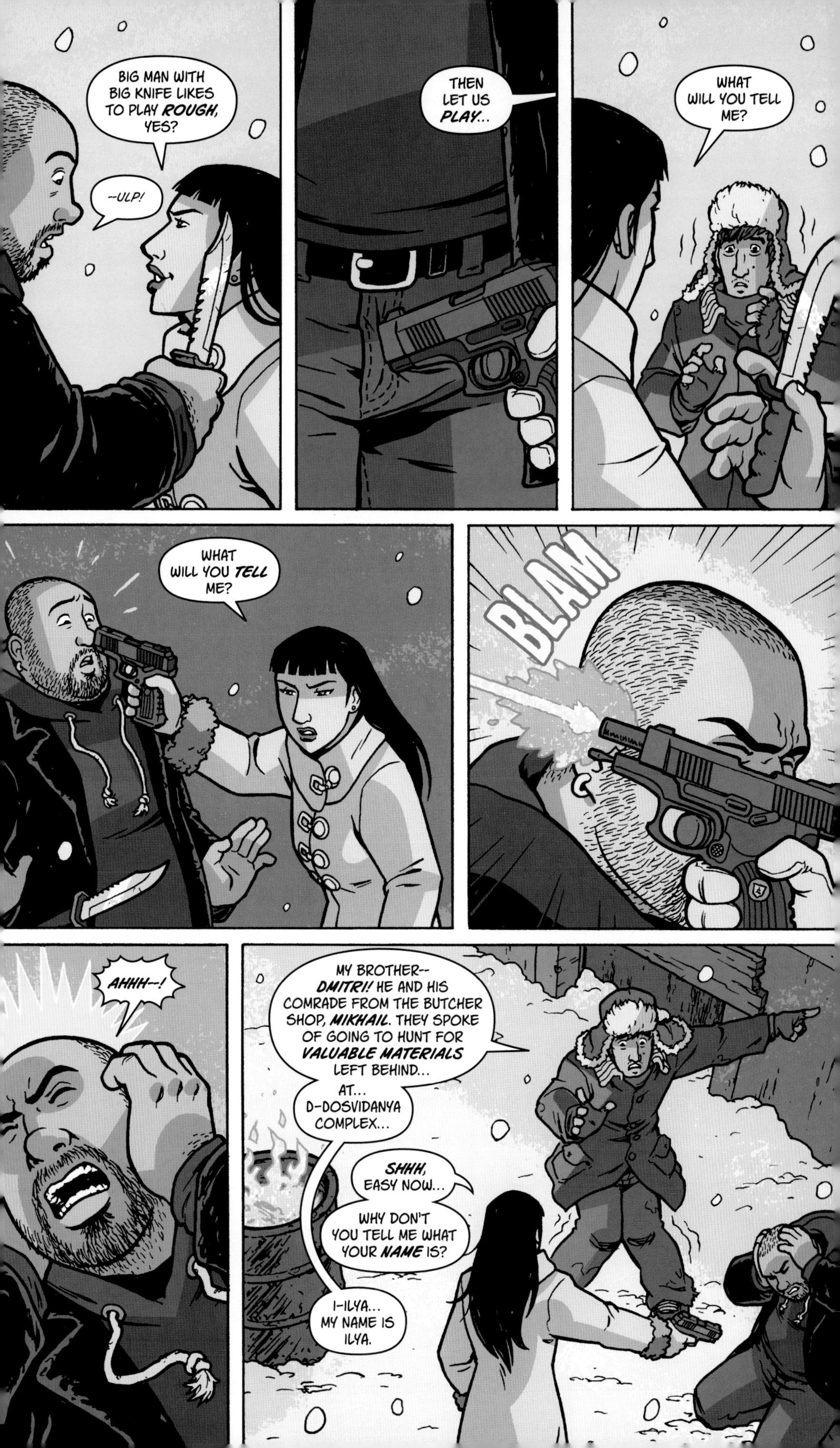
BIG MAN WITH BIG KNIFE LIKES TO PLAY ROUGH, YES?
--ULP!
THEN LET US PLAY...
WHAT WILL YOU TELL ME?
WHAT WILL YOU TELL ME?
BLAM
AHHH--!
MY BROTHER-- DMITRI! HE AND HIS COMRADE FROM THE BUTCHER SHOP, MIKHAIL. THEY SPOKE OF GOING TO HUNT FOR VALUABLE MATERIALS LEFT BEHIND...
AT... D-DOSVIDANYA COMPLEX...
SHHH, EASY NOW...
WHY DON'T YOU TELL ME WHAT YOUR NAME IS?
I-ILYA... MY NAME IS ILYA.

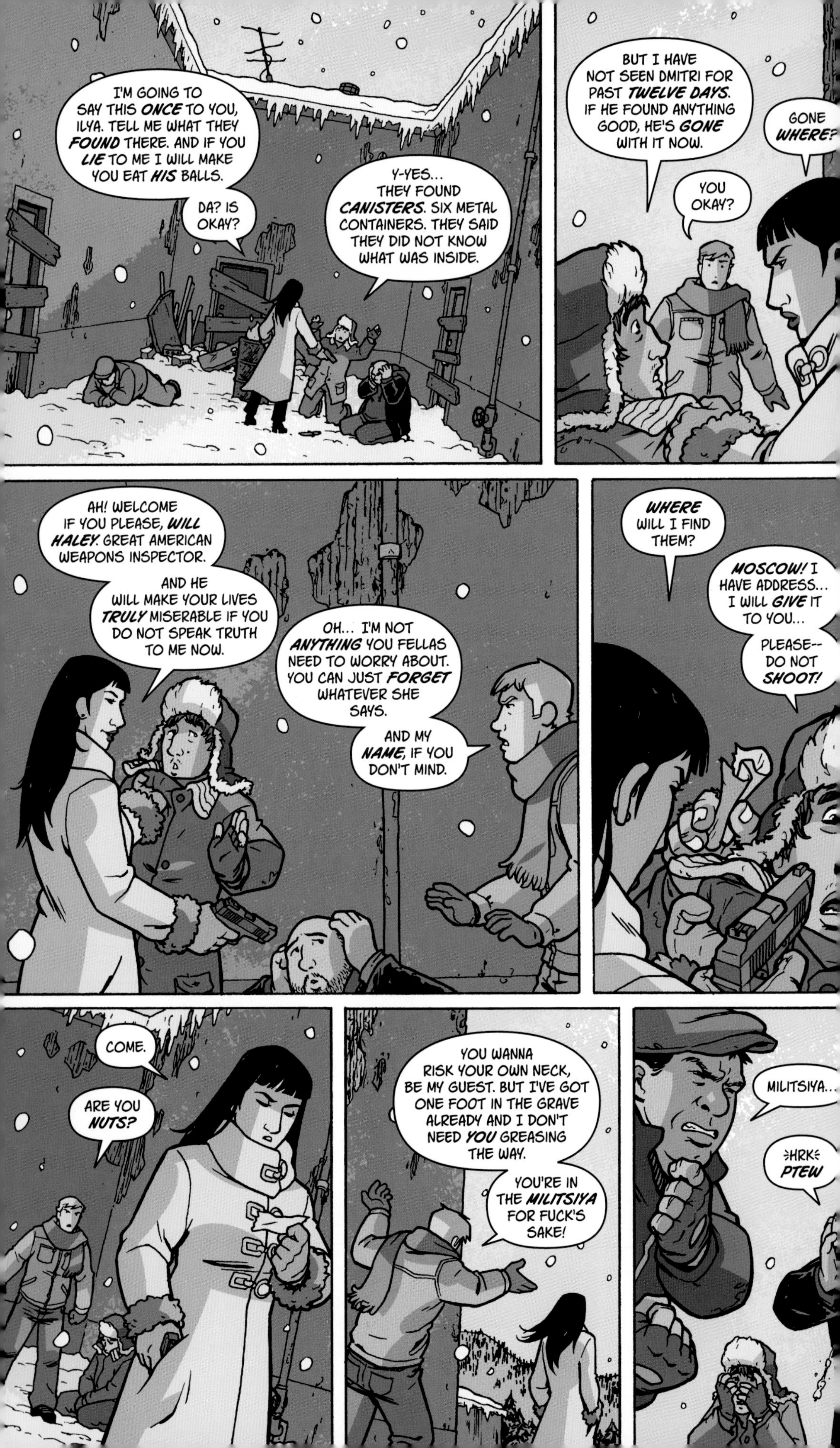
I'M GOING TO SAY THIS ONCE TO YOU, ILYA. TELL ME WHAT THEY FOUND THERE. AND IF YOU LIE TO ME I WILL MAKE YOU EAT HIS BALLS.
DA? IS OKAY?
Y-YES... THEY FOUND CANISTERS. SIX METAL CONTAINERS. THEY SAID THEY DID NOT KNOW WHAT WAS INSIDE.
BUT I HAVE NOT SEEN DMITRI FOR PAST TWELVE DAYS. IF HE FOUND ANYTHING GOOD, HE'S GONE WITH IT NOW.
GONE WHERE?
YOU OKAY?
AH! WELCOME IF YOU PLEASE, WILL HALEY. GREAT AMERICAN WEAPONS INSPECTOR.
AND HE WILL MAKE YOUR LIVES TRULY MISERABLE IF YOU DO NOT SPEAK TRUTH TO ME NOW.
OH... I'M NOT ANYTHING YOU FELLAS NEED TO WORRY ABOUT. YOU CAN JUST FORGET WHATEVER SHE SAYS.
AND MY NAME, IF YOU DON'T MIND.
WHERE WILL I FIND THEM?
MOSCOW! I HAVE ADDRESS... I WILL GIVE IT TO YOU...
PLEASE-- DO NOT SHOOT!
COME.
ARE YOU NUTS?
YOU WANNA RISK YOUR OWN NECK, BE MY GUEST. BUT I'VE GOT ONE FOOT IN THE GRAVE ALREADY AND I DON'T NEED YOU GREASING THE WAY.
YOU'RE IN THE MILITSIYA FOR FUCK'S SAKE!
MILITSIYA...
HRK PTEW

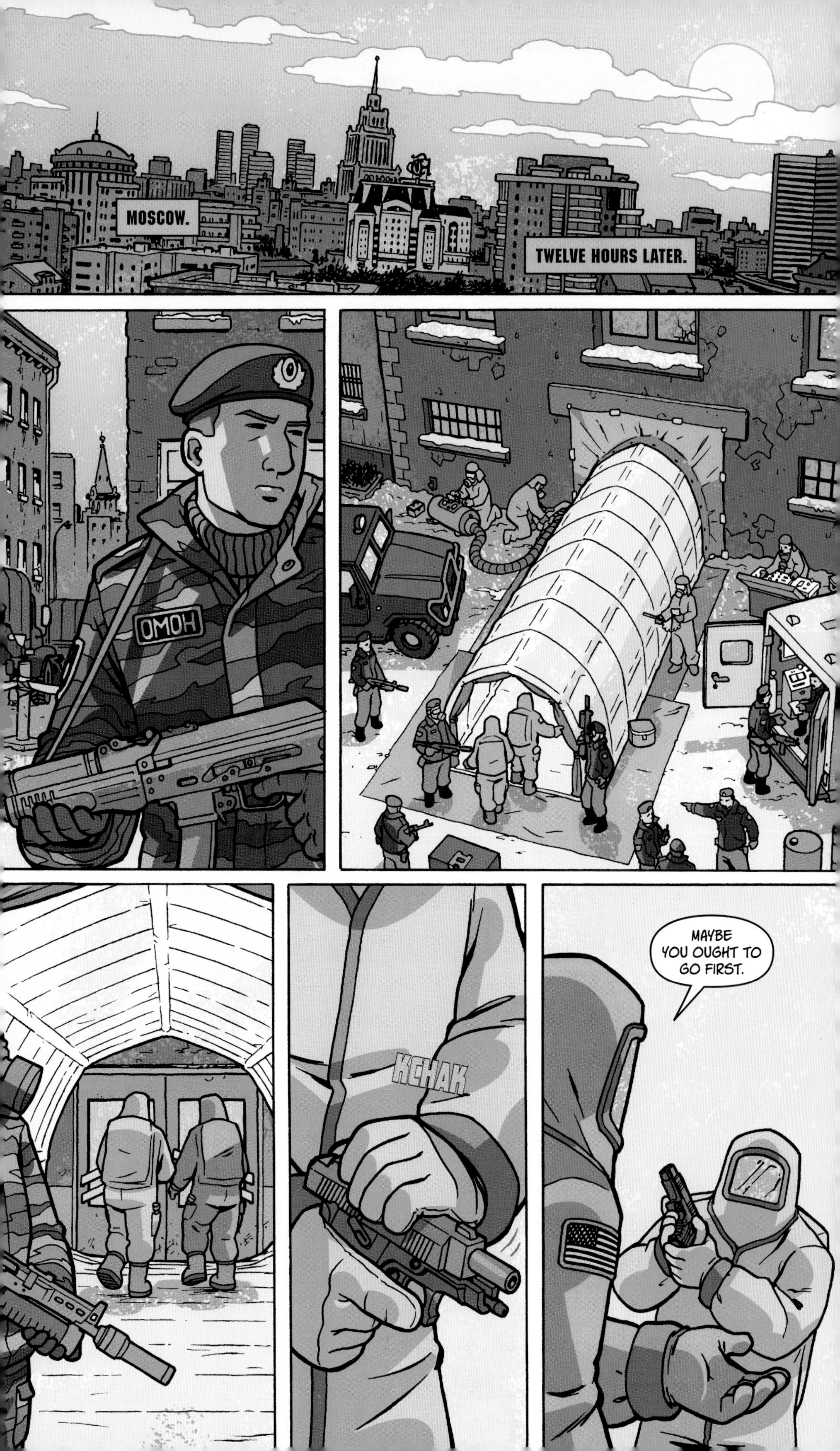
MOSCOW.
TWELVE HOURS LATER.
ОМОН
KCHAK
MAYBE YOU OUGHT TO GO FIRST.

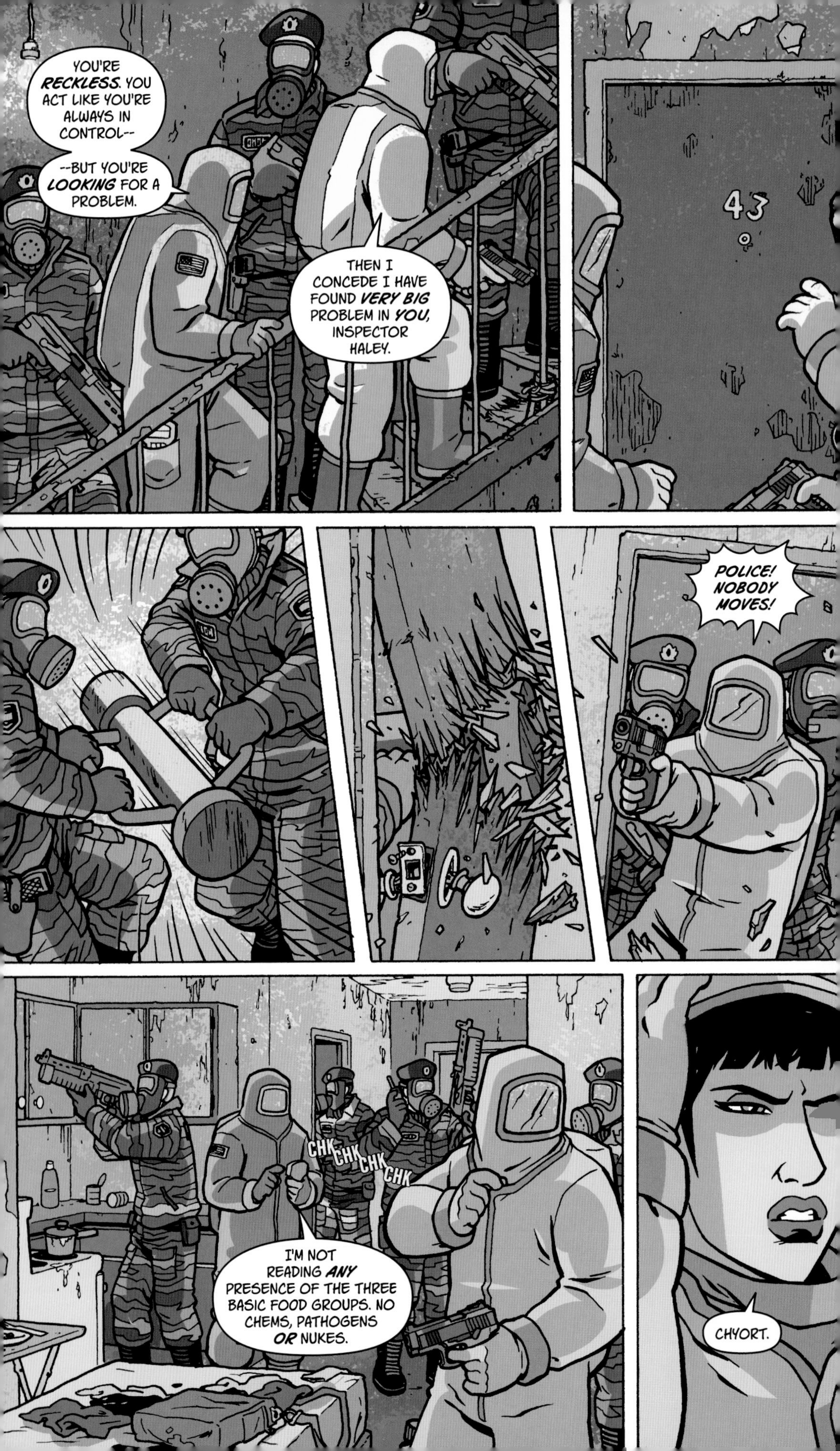
YOU'RE RECKLESS. YOU ACT LIKE YOU'RE ALWAYS IN CONTROL--
--BUT YOU'RE LOOKING FOR A PROBLEM.
THEN I CONCEDE I HAVE FOUND VERY BIG PROBLEM IN YOU, INSPECTOR HALEY.
43
POLICE! NOBODY MOVES!
CHK CHK CHK CHK
I'M NOT READING ANY PRESENCE OF THE THREE BASIC FOOD GROUPS. NO CHEMS, PATHOGENS OR NUKES.
CHYORT.

DA. I AM IN *MOSCOW*.

DA. DA, I UNDERSTAND. I WILL COME TO *YOU* THEN. GIVE ME THE *ADDRESS* AND I COME RIGHT AWAY.

YES. I WILL NOT BE LATE.

3:00
NW c near K-G
Красная

HM.

3:00
NW c near K-G
Красная
Площадо

IT APPEARS OUR QUARRY HAS ESCAPED. BUT NOT WITHOUT LEAVING *CLUES* TO HIS WHEREABOUTS.

OH, HE LEFT *SOMETHING* ALL RIGHT.

YOU'RE GONNA WANT TO TAKE A *LOOK* AT THIS...

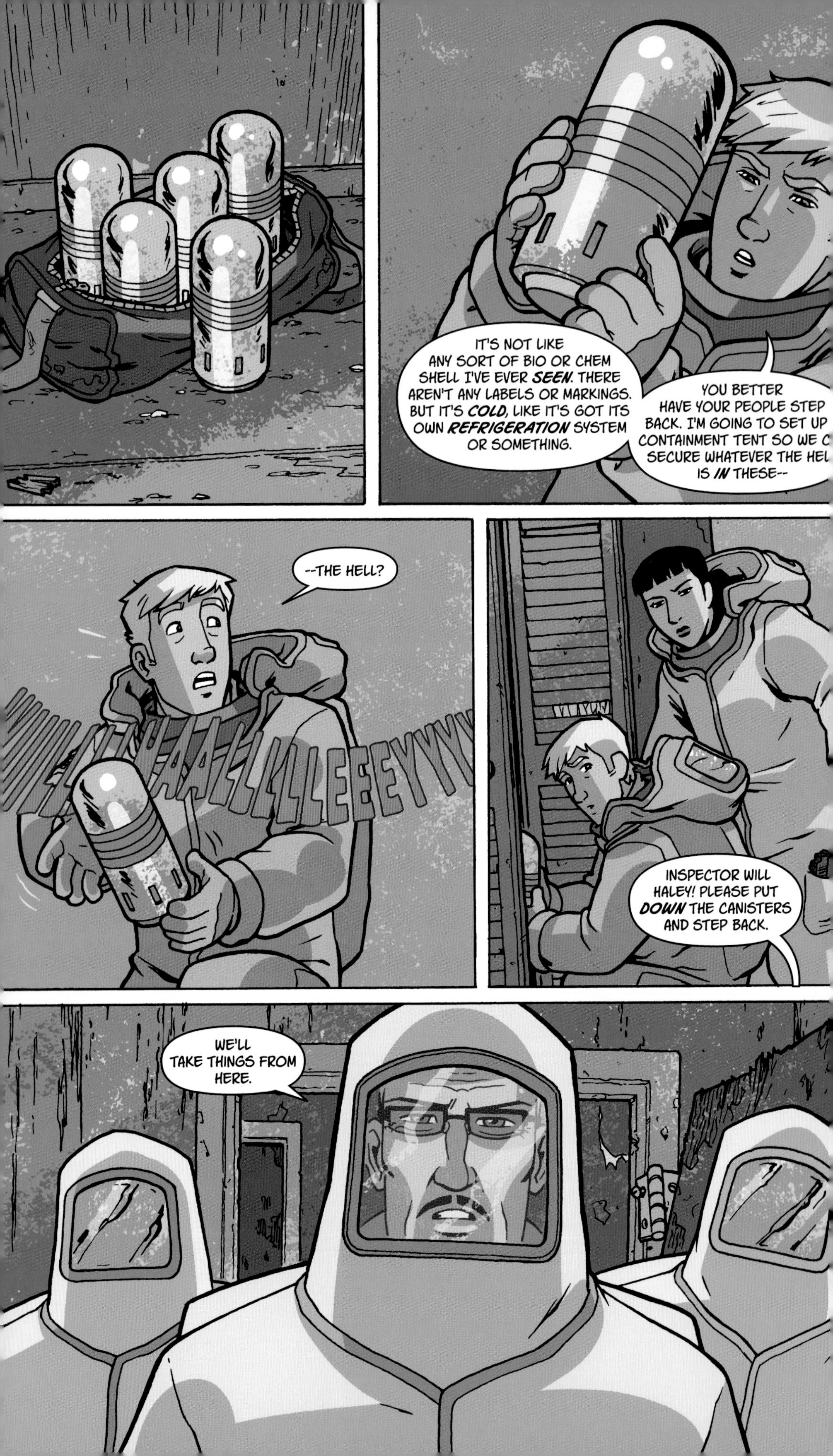

IT'S NOT LIKE ANY SORT OF BIO OR CHEM SHELL I'VE EVER SEEN. THERE AREN'T ANY LABELS OR MARKINGS. BUT IT'S COLD, LIKE IT'S GOT ITS OWN REFRIGERATION SYSTEM OR SOMETHING.
YOU BETTER HAVE YOUR PEOPLE STEP BACK. I'M GOING TO SET UP CONTAINMENT TENT SO WE C SECURE WHATEVER THE HEL IS IN THESE--
--THE HELL?
WHHUUUAALLLLLEEEEYYYY
INSPECTOR WILL HALEY! PLEASE PUT DOWN THE CANISTERS AND STEP BACK.
WE'LL TAKE THINGS FROM HERE.

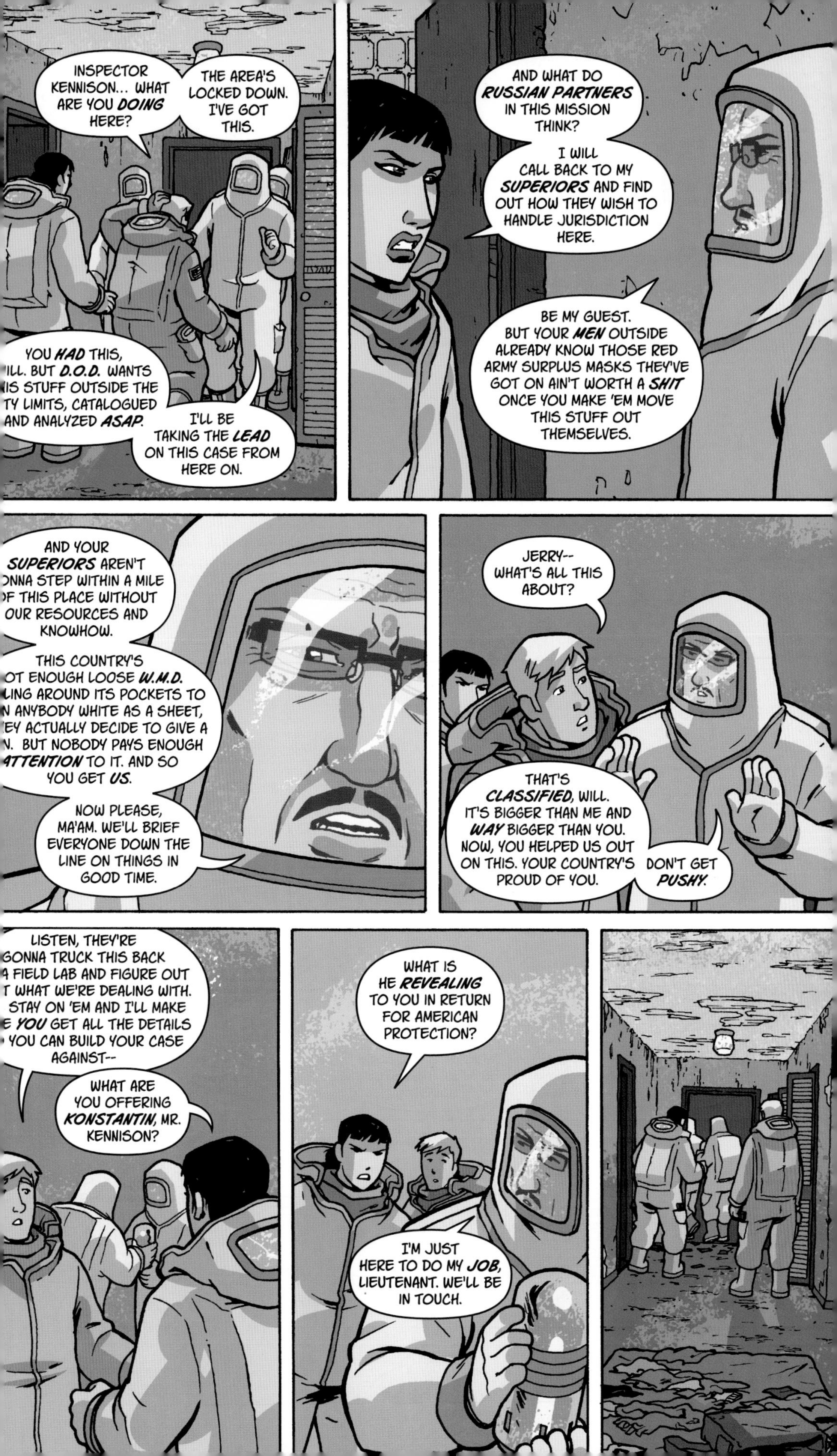
INSPECTOR KENNISON... WHAT ARE YOU DOING HERE?
THE AREA'S LOCKED DOWN. I'VE GOT THIS.
YOU HAD THIS, ILL. BUT D.O.D. WANTS IS STUFF OUTSIDE THE TY LIMITS, CATALOGUED AND ANALYZED ASAP.
I'LL BE TAKING THE LEAD ON THIS CASE FROM HERE ON.
AND WHAT DO RUSSIAN PARTNERS IN THIS MISSION THINK?
I WILL CALL BACK TO MY SUPERIORS AND FIND OUT HOW THEY WISH TO HANDLE JURISDICTION HERE.
BE MY GUEST. BUT YOUR MEN OUTSIDE ALREADY KNOW THOSE RED ARMY SURPLUS MASKS THEY'VE GOT ON AIN'T WORTH A SHIT ONCE YOU MAKE 'EM MOVE THIS STUFF OUT THEMSELVES.
AND YOUR SUPERIORS AREN'T ONNA STEP WITHIN A MILE OF THIS PLACE WITHOUT OUR RESOURCES AND KNOWHOW.
THIS COUNTRY'S OT ENOUGH LOOSE W.M.D. LING AROUND ITS POCKETS TO N ANYBODY WHITE AS A SHEET, EY ACTUALLY DECIDE TO GIVE A N. BUT NOBODY PAYS ENOUGH ATTENTION TO IT. AND SO YOU GET US.
NOW PLEASE, MA'AM. WE'LL BRIEF EVERYONE DOWN THE LINE ON THINGS IN GOOD TIME.
JERRY-- WHAT'S ALL THIS ABOUT?
THAT'S CLASSIFIED, WILL. IT'S BIGGER THAN ME AND WAY BIGGER THAN YOU. NOW, YOU HELPED US OUT ON THIS. YOUR COUNTRY'S PROUD OF YOU.
DON'T GET PUSHY.
LISTEN, THEY'RE GONNA TRUCK THIS BACK A FIELD LAB AND FIGURE OUT T WHAT WE'RE DEALING WITH. STAY ON 'EM AND I'LL MAKE E YOU GET ALL THE DETAILS YOU CAN BUILD YOUR CASE AGAINST--
WHAT ARE YOU OFFERING KONSTANTIN, MR. KENNISON?
WHAT IS HE REVEALING TO YOU IN RETURN FOR AMERICAN PROTECTION?
I'M JUST HERE TO DO MY JOB, LIEUTENANT. WE'LL BE IN TOUCH.

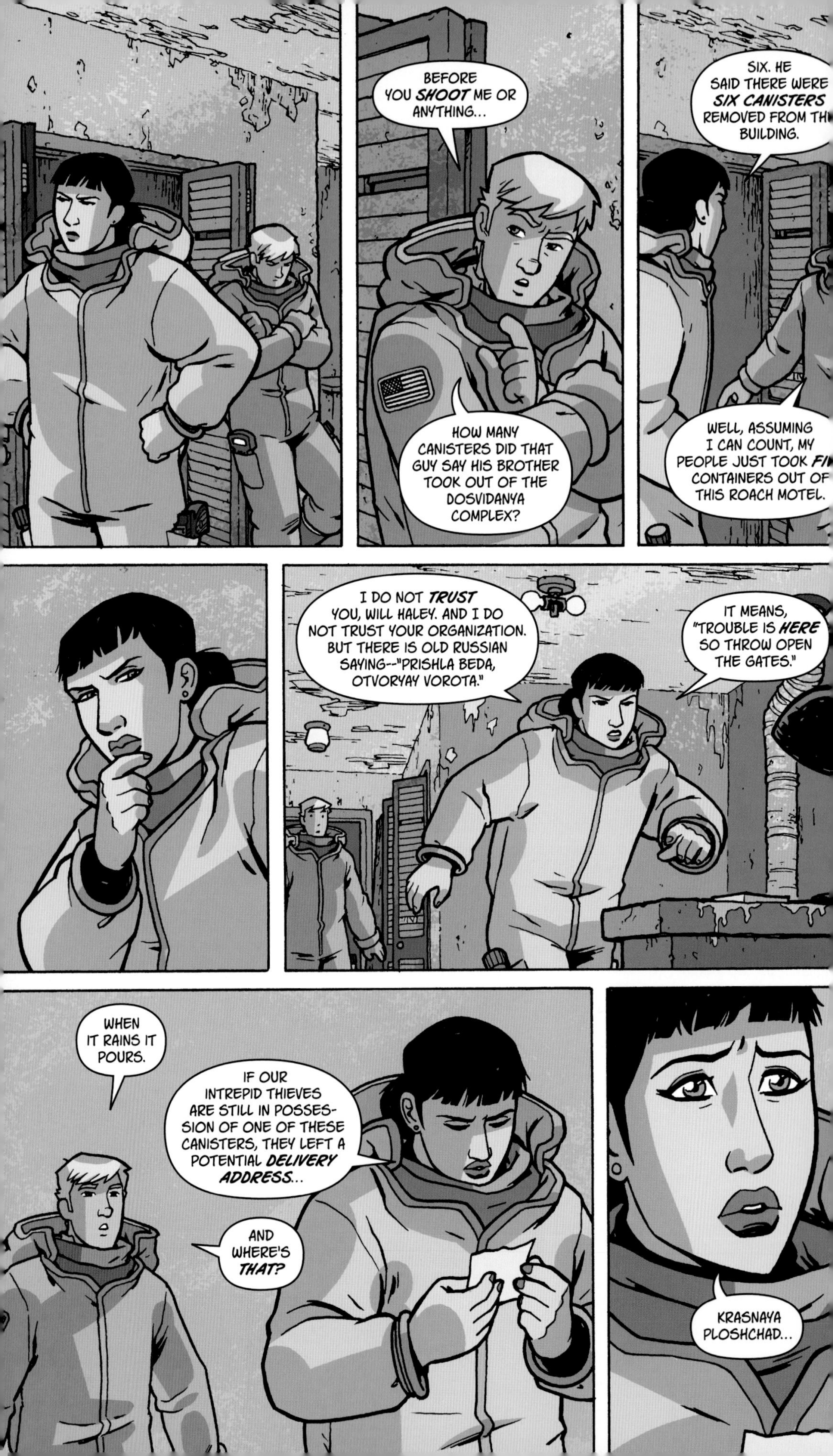
BEFORE YOU SHOOT ME OR ANYTHING...
HOW MANY CANISTERS DID THAT GUY SAY HIS BROTHER TOOK OUT OF THE DOSVIDANYA COMPLEX?
SIX. HE SAID THERE WERE SIX CANISTERS REMOVED FROM TH BUILDING.
WELL, ASSUMING I CAN COUNT, MY PEOPLE JUST TOOK FI CONTAINERS OUT OF THIS ROACH MOTEL.
I DO NOT TRUST YOU, WILL HALEY. AND I DO NOT TRUST YOUR ORGANIZATION. BUT THERE IS OLD RUSSIAN SAYING--"PRISHLA BEDA, OTVORYAY VOROTA."
IT MEANS, "TROUBLE IS HERE SO THROW OPEN THE GATES."
WHEN IT RAINS IT POURS.
IF OUR INTREPID THIEVES ARE STILL IN POSSES- SION OF ONE OF THESE CANISTERS, THEY LEFT A POTENTIAL DELIVERY ADDRESS...
AND WHERE'S THAT?
KRASNAYA PLOSHCHAD...

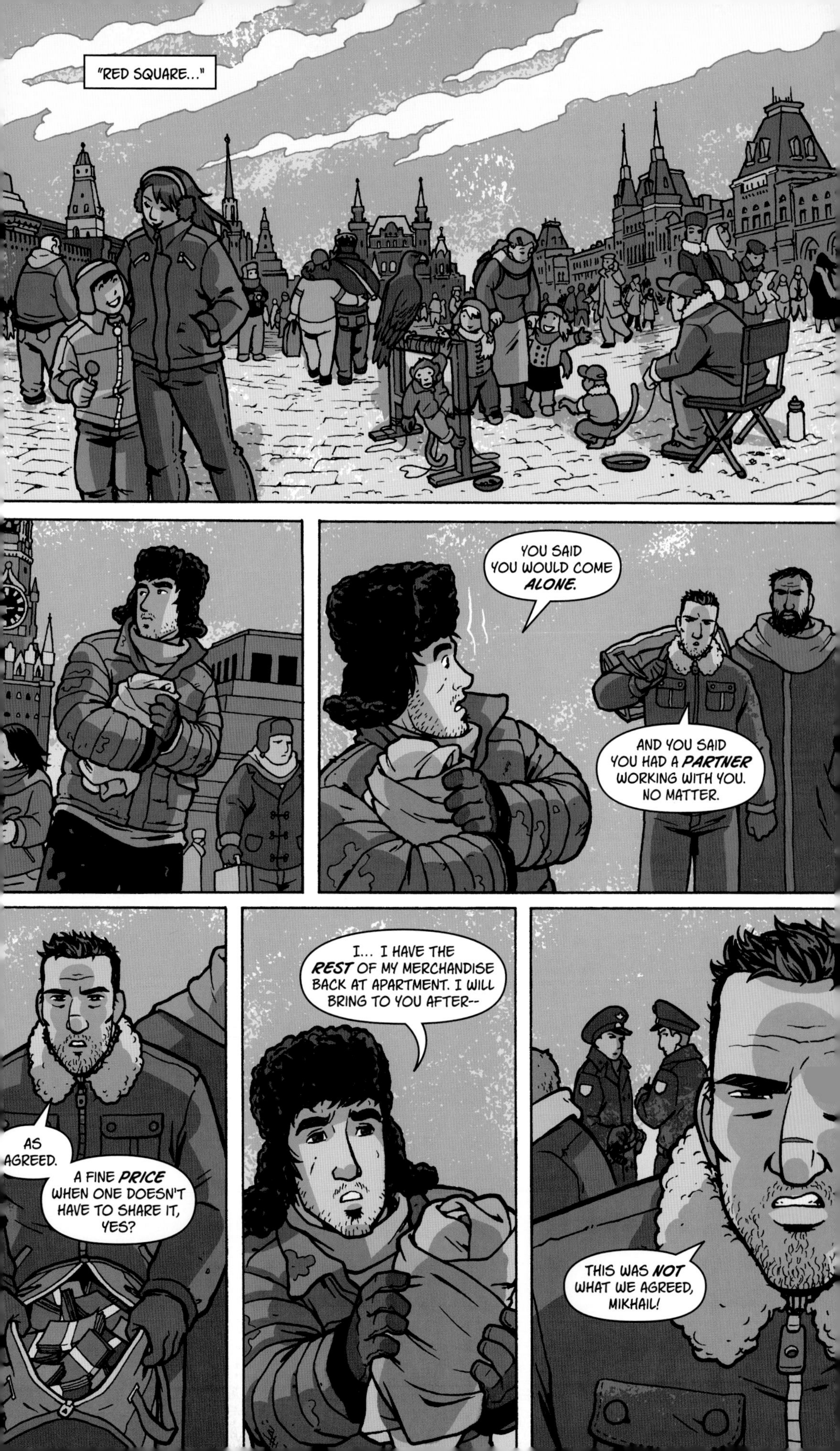
"RED SQUARE..."
YOU SAID YOU WOULD COME ALONE.
AND YOU SAID YOU HAD A PARTNER WORKING WITH YOU. NO MATTER.
AS AGREED.
A FINE PRICE WHEN ONE DOESN'T HAVE TO SHARE IT, YES?
I... I HAVE THE REST OF MY MERCHANDISE BACK AT APARTMENT. I WILL BRING TO YOU AFTER--
THIS WAS NOT WHAT WE AGREED, MIKHAIL!

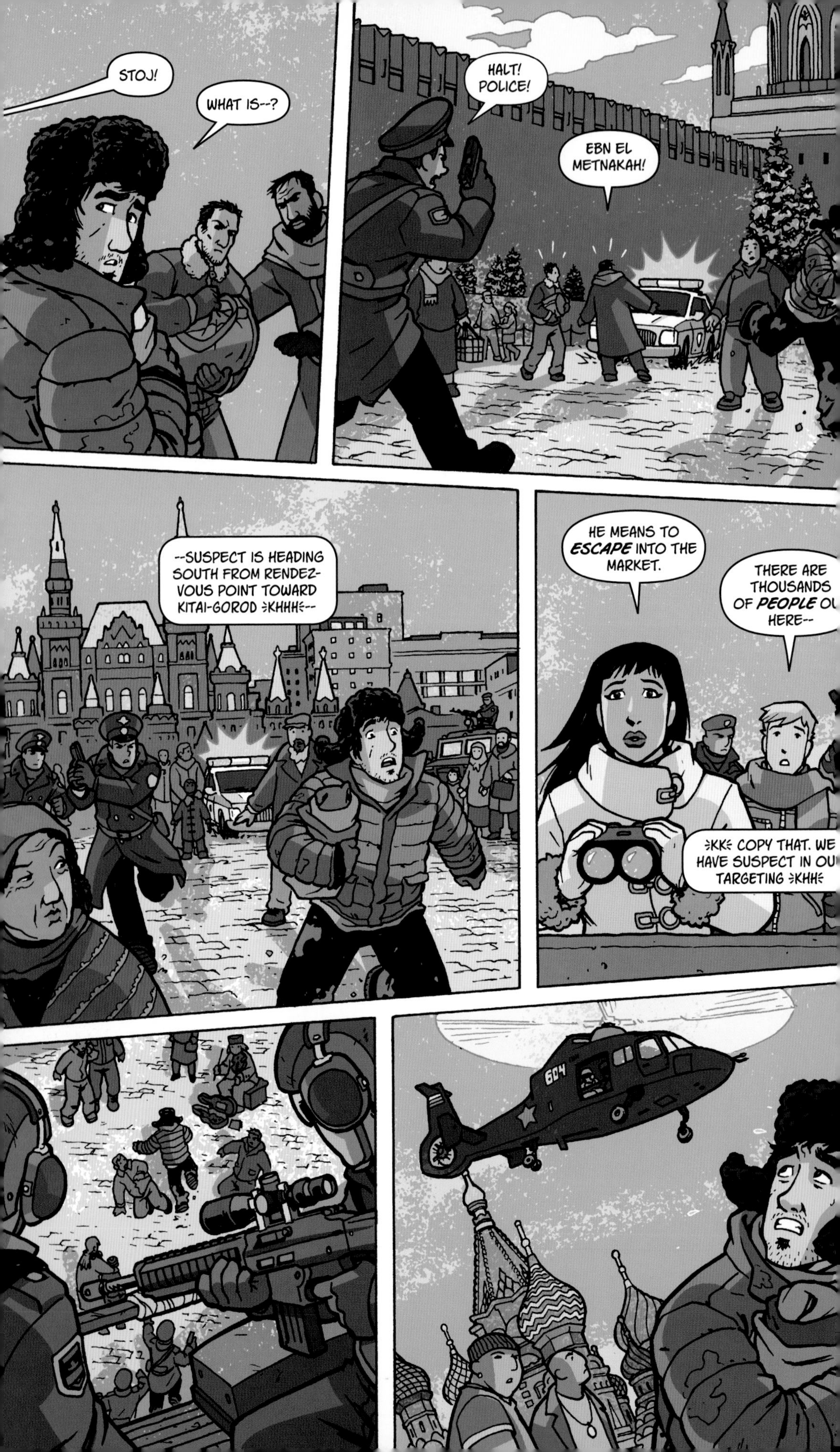
STOJ!
WHAT IS--?
HALT! POLICE!
EBN EL METNAKAH!
--SUSPECT IS HEADING SOUTH FROM RENDEZ-VOUS POINT TOWARD KITAI-GOROD ⋛KHHH⋚--
HE MEANS TO *ESCAPE* INTO THE MARKET.
THERE ARE THOUSANDS OF *PEOPLE* OU HERE--
⋛KK⋚ COPY THAT. WE HAVE SUSPECT IN OU TARGETING ⋛KHH⋚
604

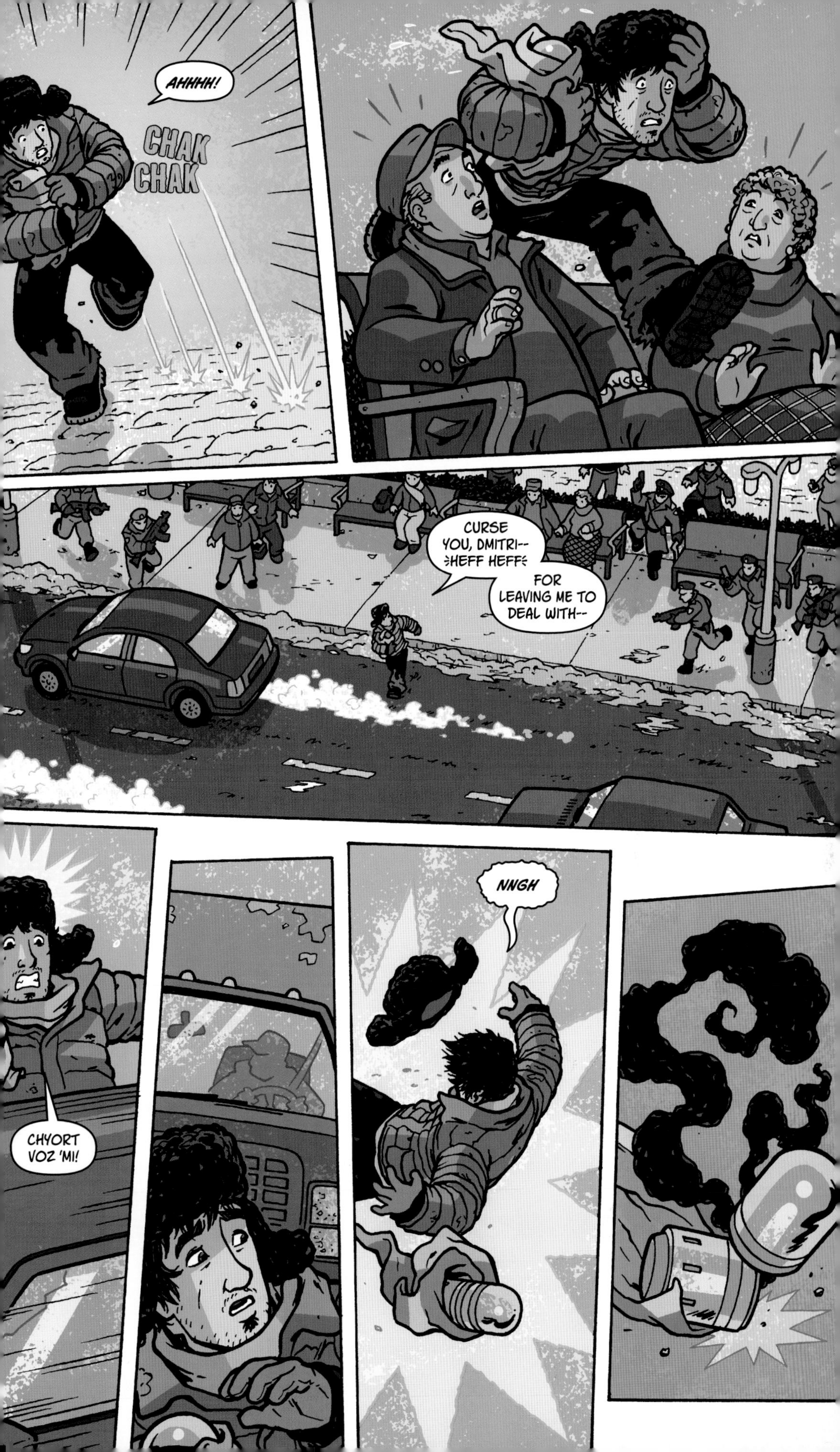
AHHHH!
CHAK CHAK
CURSE YOU, DMITRI-- ≷HEFF HEFF≷
FOR LEAVING ME TO DEAL WITH--
CHYORT VOZ 'MI!
NNGH

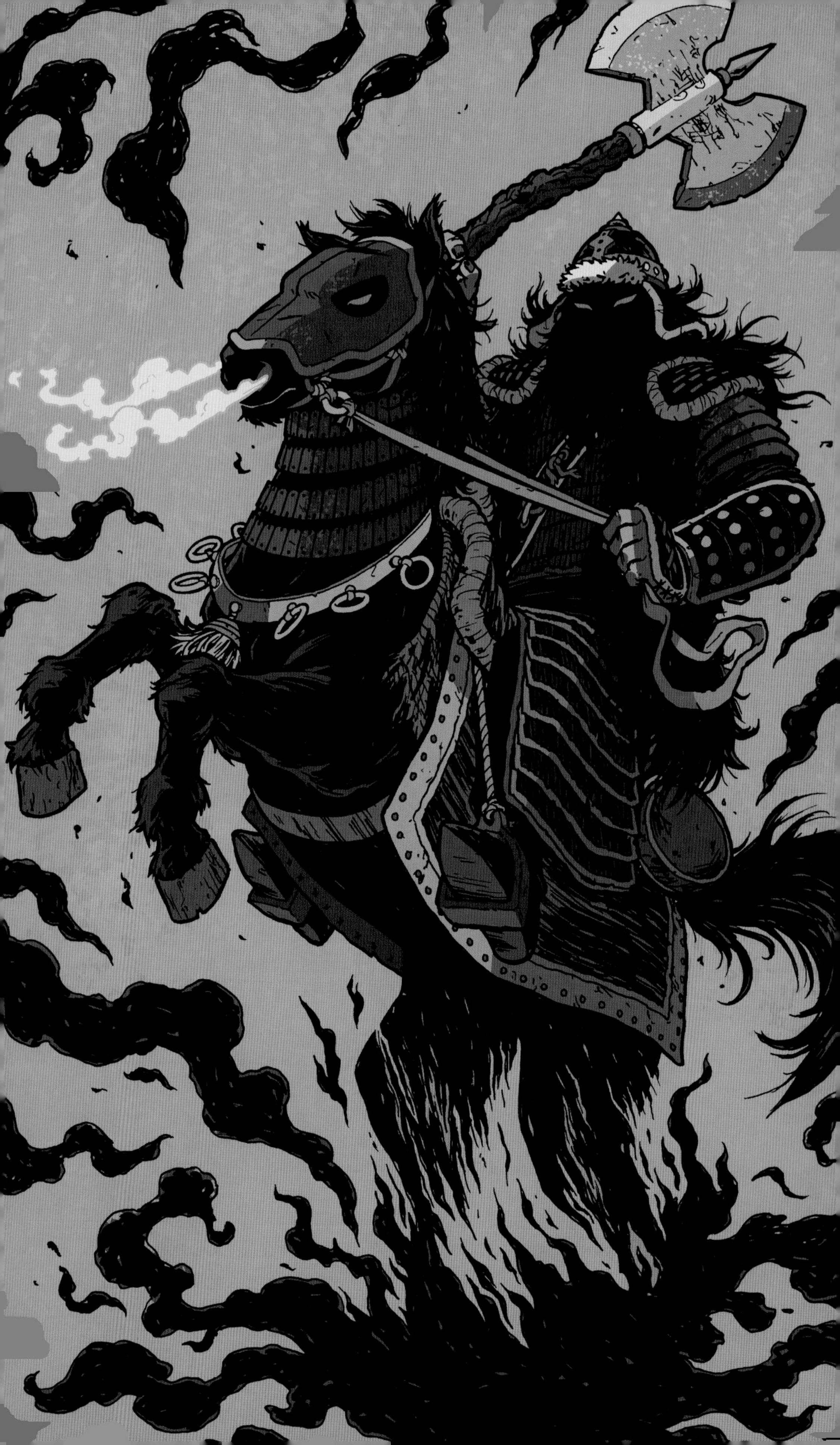

CHAPTER 4:

RED
SNOW

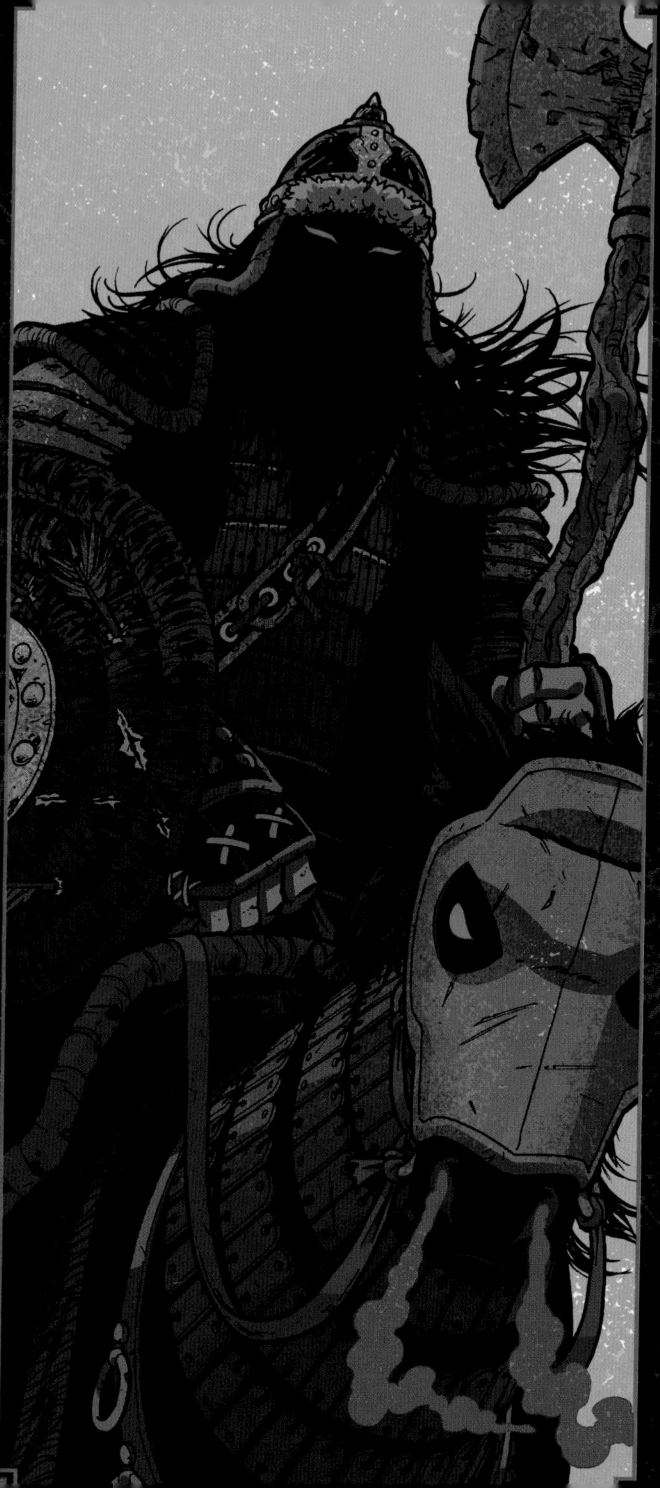

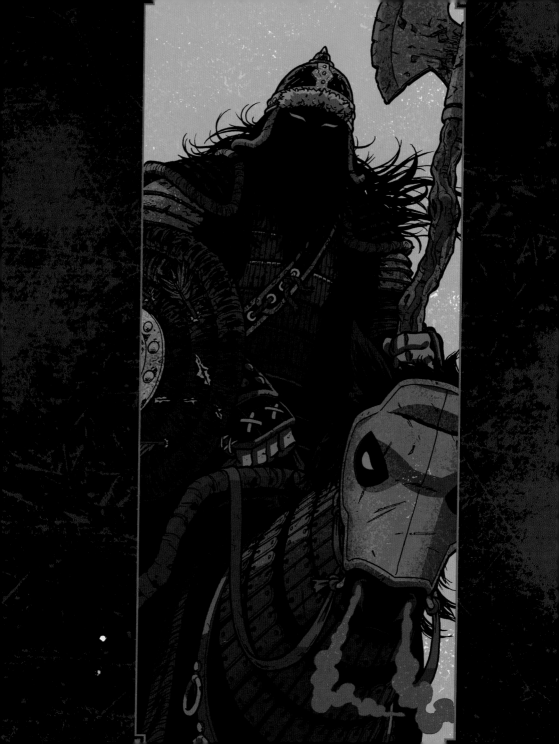

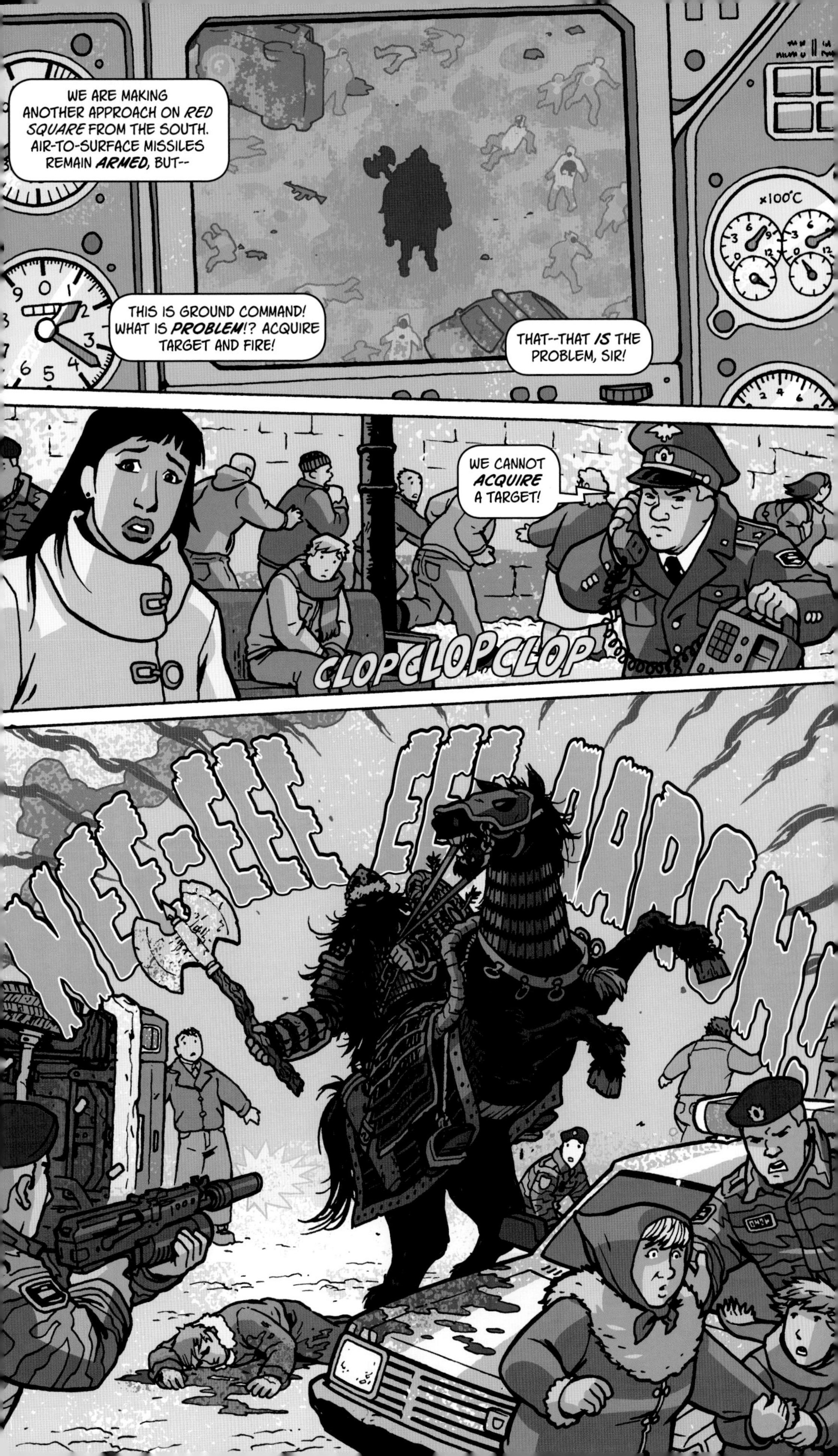
WE ARE MAKING ANOTHER APPROACH ON RED SQUARE FROM THE SOUTH. AIR-TO-SURFACE MISSILES REMAIN ARMED, BUT--
THIS IS GROUND COMMAND! WHAT IS PROBLEM!? ACQUIRE TARGET AND FIRE!
THAT--THAT IS THE PROBLEM, SIR!
WE CANNOT ACQUIRE A TARGET!
CLOPCLOPCLOP

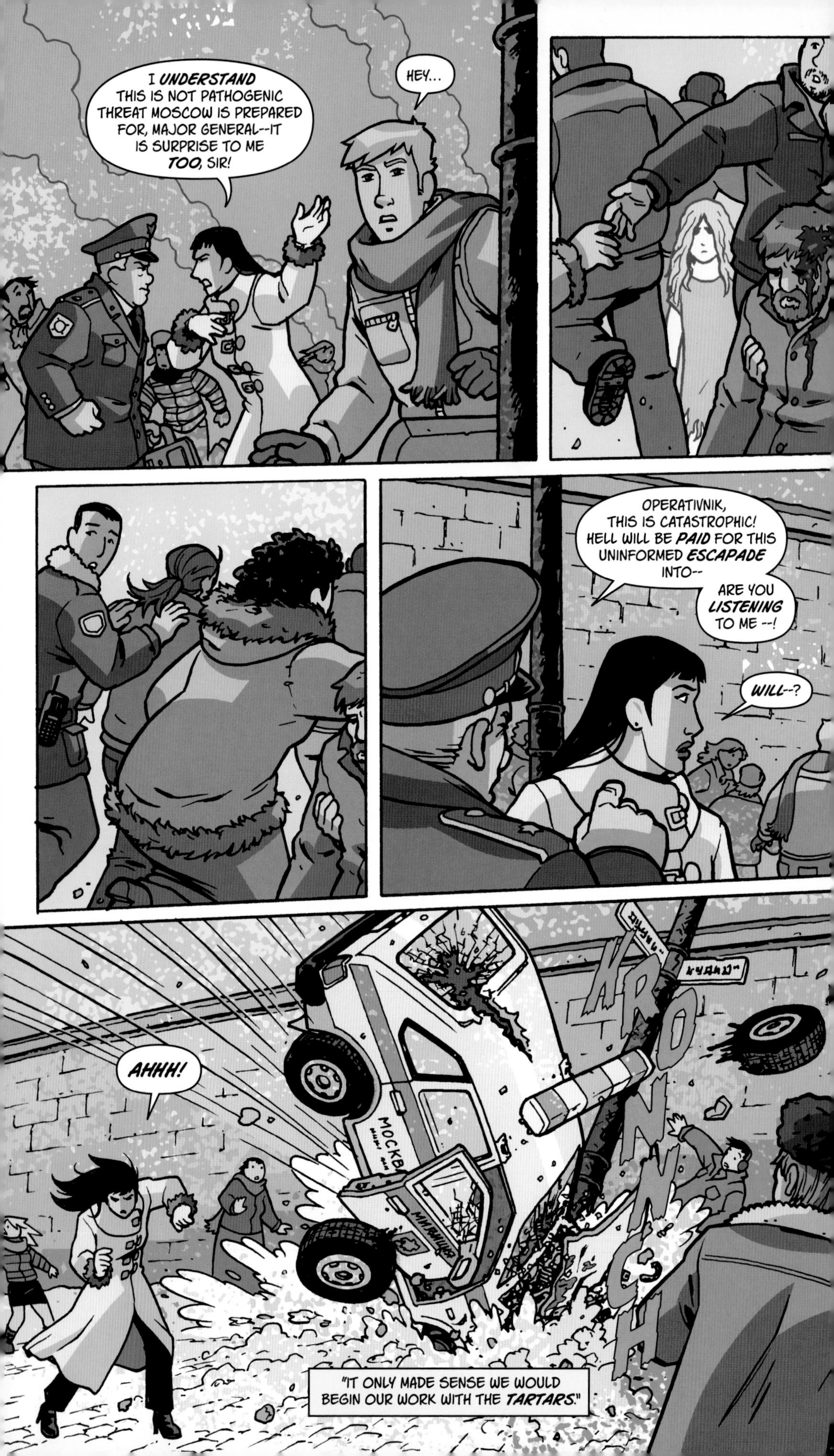
I UNDERSTAND THIS IS NOT PATHOGENIC THREAT MOSCOW IS PREPARED FOR, MAJOR GENERAL--IT IS SURPRISE TO ME TOO, SIR!
HEY...
OPERATIVNIK, THIS IS CATASTROPHIC! HELL WILL BE PAID FOR THIS UNINFORMED ESCAPADE INTO--
ARE YOU LISTENING TO ME --!
WILL--?
AHHH!
KRONNCH
"IT ONLY MADE SENSE WE WOULD BEGIN OUR WORK WITH THE TARTARS."

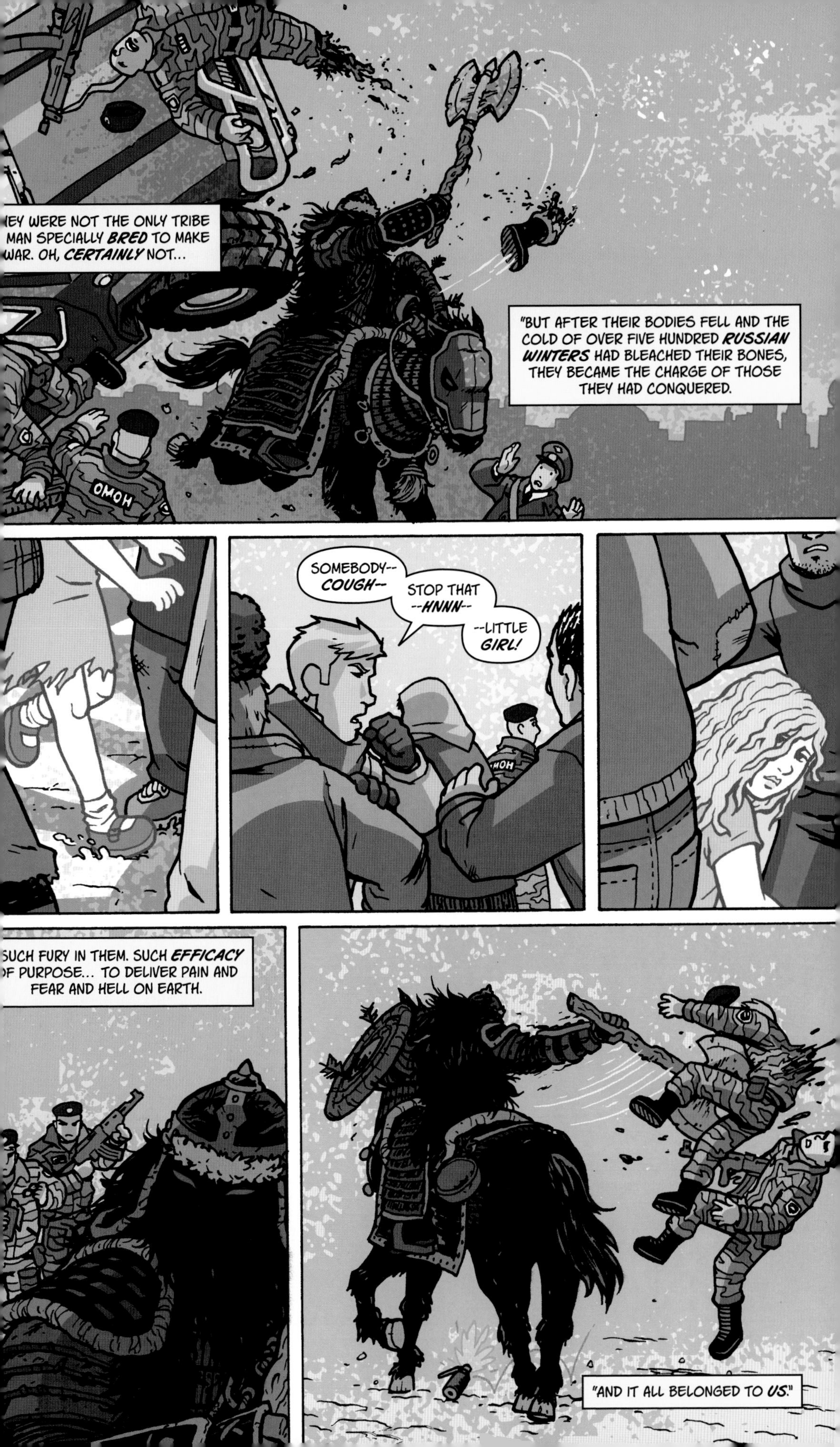

HEY WERE NOT THE ONLY TRIBE
MAN SPECIALLY BRED TO MAKE
WAR. OH, CERTAINLY NOT...
"BUT AFTER THEIR BODIES FELL AND THE COLD OF OVER FIVE HUNDRED RUSSIAN WINTERS HAD BLEACHED THEIR BONES, THEY BECAME THE CHARGE OF THOSE THEY HAD CONQUERED.
ОМОН
SOMEBODY-- COUGH--
STOP THAT --HNNN--
--LITTLE GIRL!
ОМОН
SUCH FURY IN THEM. SUCH EFFICACY
OF PURPOSE... TO DELIVER PAIN AND FEAR AND HELL ON EARTH.
"AND IT ALL BELONGED TO US."

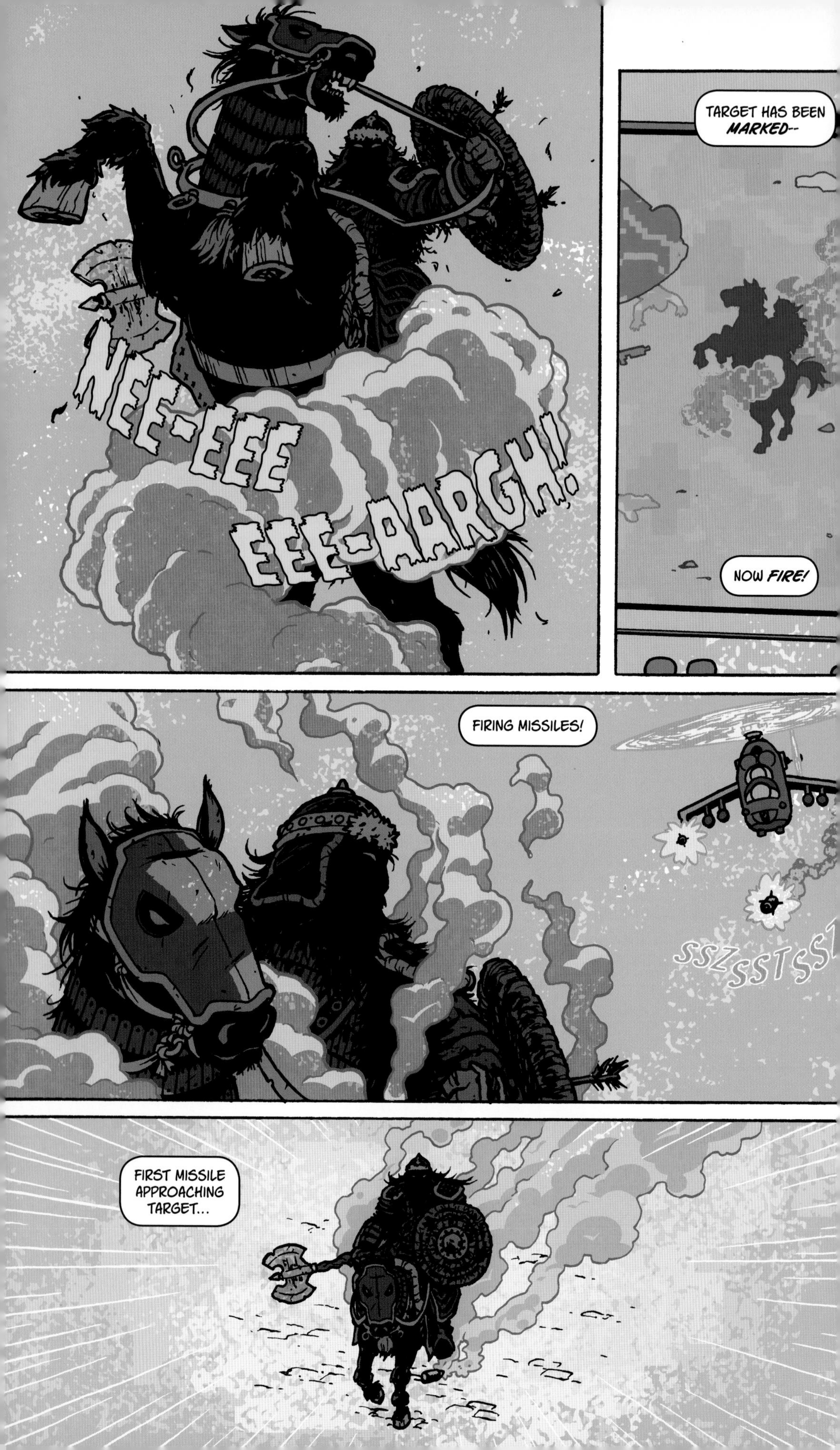
NEE-EEE EEE-AARGH!
TARGET HAS BEEN MARKED--
NOW FIRE!
FIRING MISSILES!
SSZSSTSSZ
FIRST MISSILE APPROACHING TARGET...

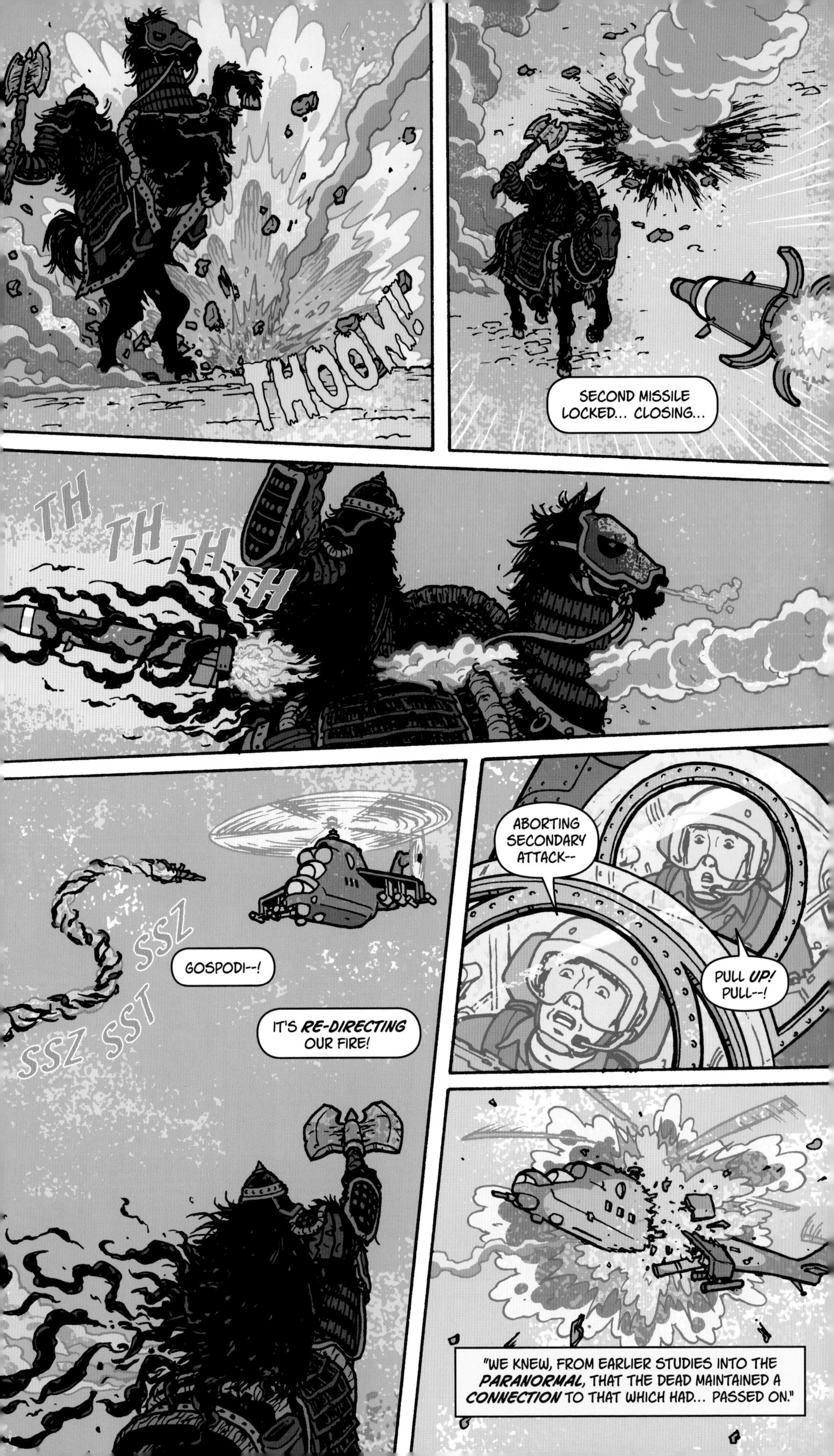
THOOM!!
SECOND MISSILE LOCKED... CLOSING...
TH TH TH TH
GOSPODI--!
SSZ SSZ SST
IT'S *RE-DIRECTING* OUR FIRE!
ABORTING SECONDARY ATTACK--
PULL *UP!* PULL--!
"WE KNEW, FROM EARLIER STUDIES INTO THE *PARANORMAL*, THAT THE DEAD MAINTAINED A *CONNECTION* TO THAT WHICH HAD... PASSED ON."

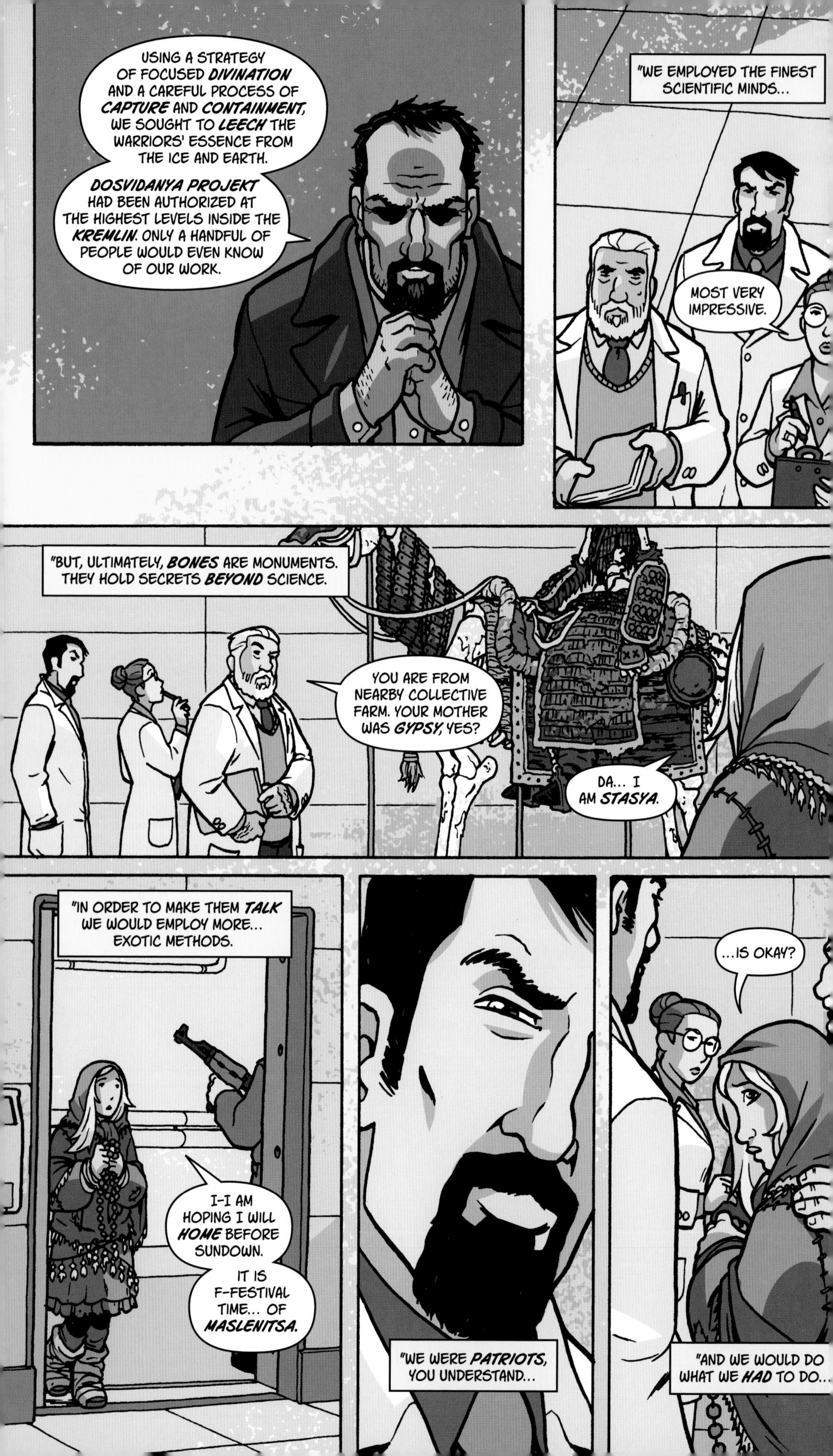
USING A STRATEGY OF FOCUSED DIVINATION AND A CAREFUL PROCESS OF CAPTURE AND CONTAINMENT, WE SOUGHT TO LEECH THE WARRIORS' ESSENCE FROM THE ICE AND EARTH.
DOSVIDANYA PROJEKT HAD BEEN AUTHORIZED AT THE HIGHEST LEVELS INSIDE THE KREMLIN. ONLY A HANDFUL OF PEOPLE WOULD EVEN KNOW OF OUR WORK.
"WE EMPLOYED THE FINEST SCIENTIFIC MINDS...
MOST VERY IMPRESSIVE.
"BUT, ULTIMATELY, BONES ARE MONUMENTS. THEY HOLD SECRETS BEYOND SCIENCE.
YOU ARE FROM NEARBY COLLECTIVE FARM. YOUR MOTHER WAS GYPSY, YES?
DA... I AM STASYA.
"IN ORDER TO MAKE THEM TALK WE WOULD EMPLOY MORE... EXOTIC METHODS.
I-I AM HOPING I WILL HOME BEFORE SUNDOWN.
IT IS F-FESTIVAL TIME... OF MASLENITSA.
"WE WERE PATRIOTS, YOU UNDERSTAND...
...IS OKAY?
"AND WE WOULD DO WHAT WE HAD TO DO...

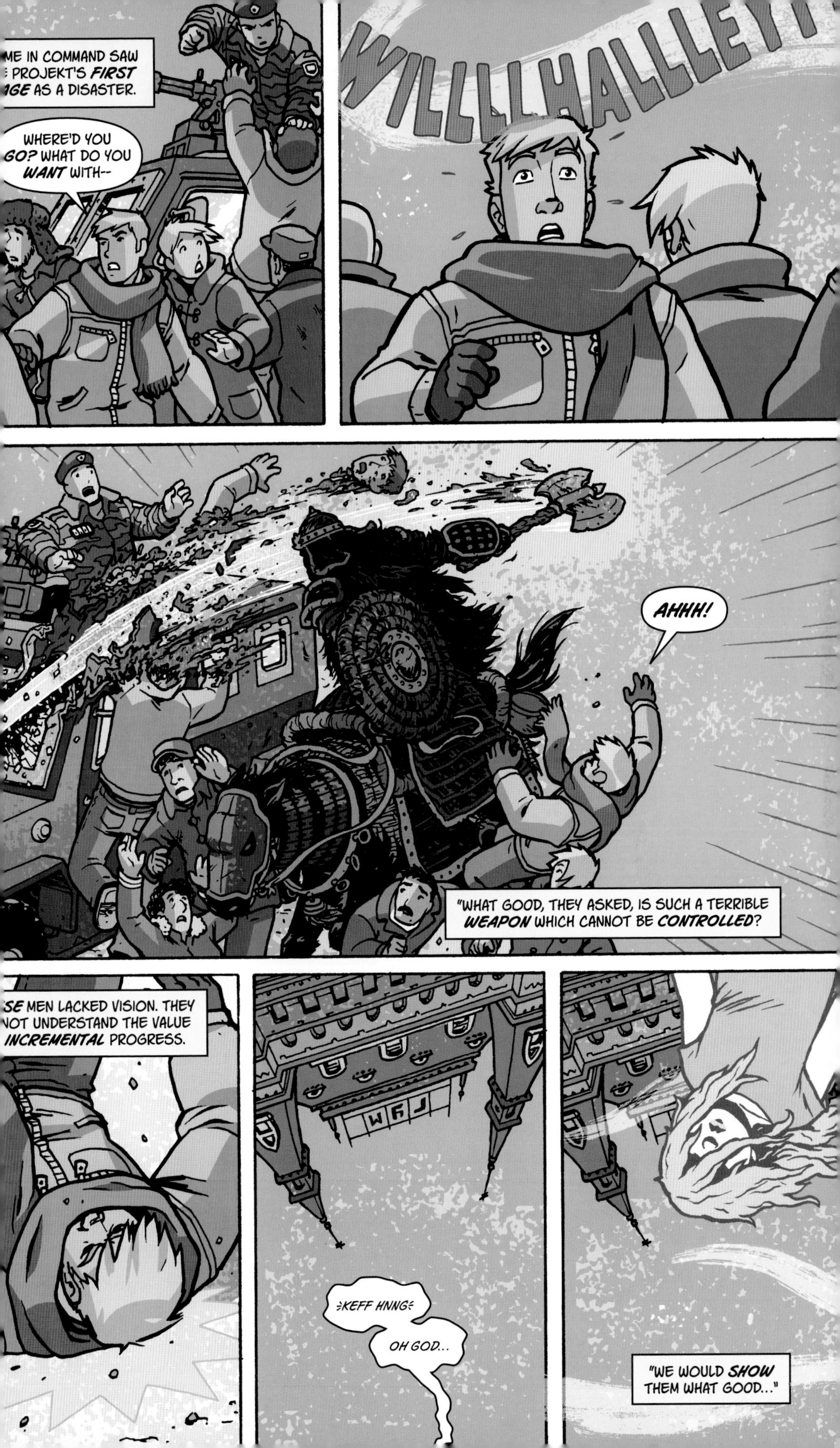
ME IN COMMAND SAW
PROJEKT'S FIRST
GE AS A DISASTER.
WHERE'D YOU GO? WHAT DO YOU WANT WITH--
WILLLHALLLEY!!
AHHH!
"WHAT GOOD, THEY ASKED, IS SUCH A TERRIBLE WEAPON WHICH CANNOT BE CONTROLLED?
SE MEN LACKED VISION. THEY
NOT UNDERSTAND THE VALUE
INCREMENTAL PROGRESS.
WFJ
KEFF HNNG
OH GOD...
"WE WOULD SHOW THEM WHAT GOOD..."

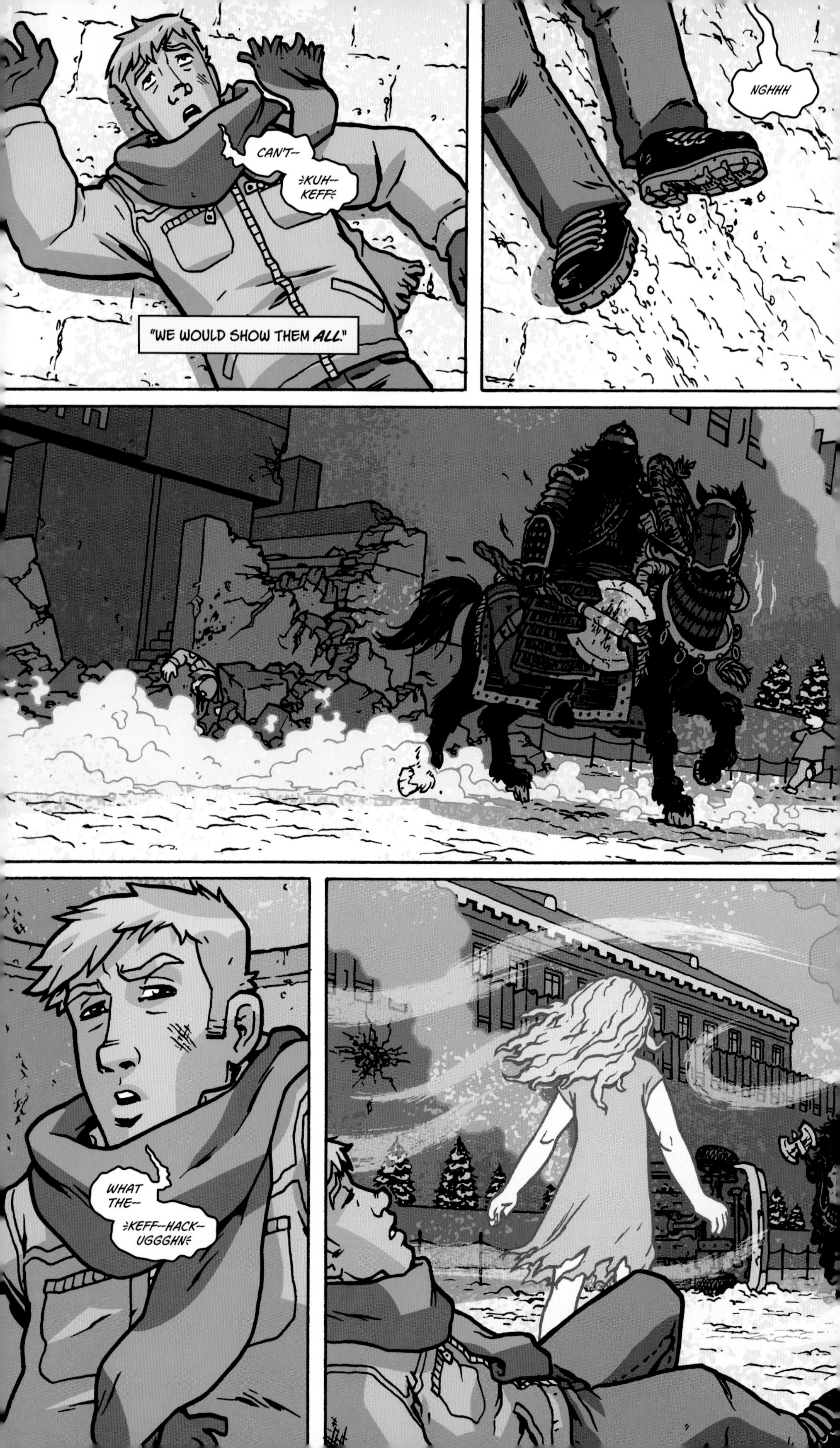

CAN'T--
KUH--KEFF
"WE WOULD SHOW THEM ALL."
NGHHH
WHAT THE--
KEFF--HACK--UGGGHN

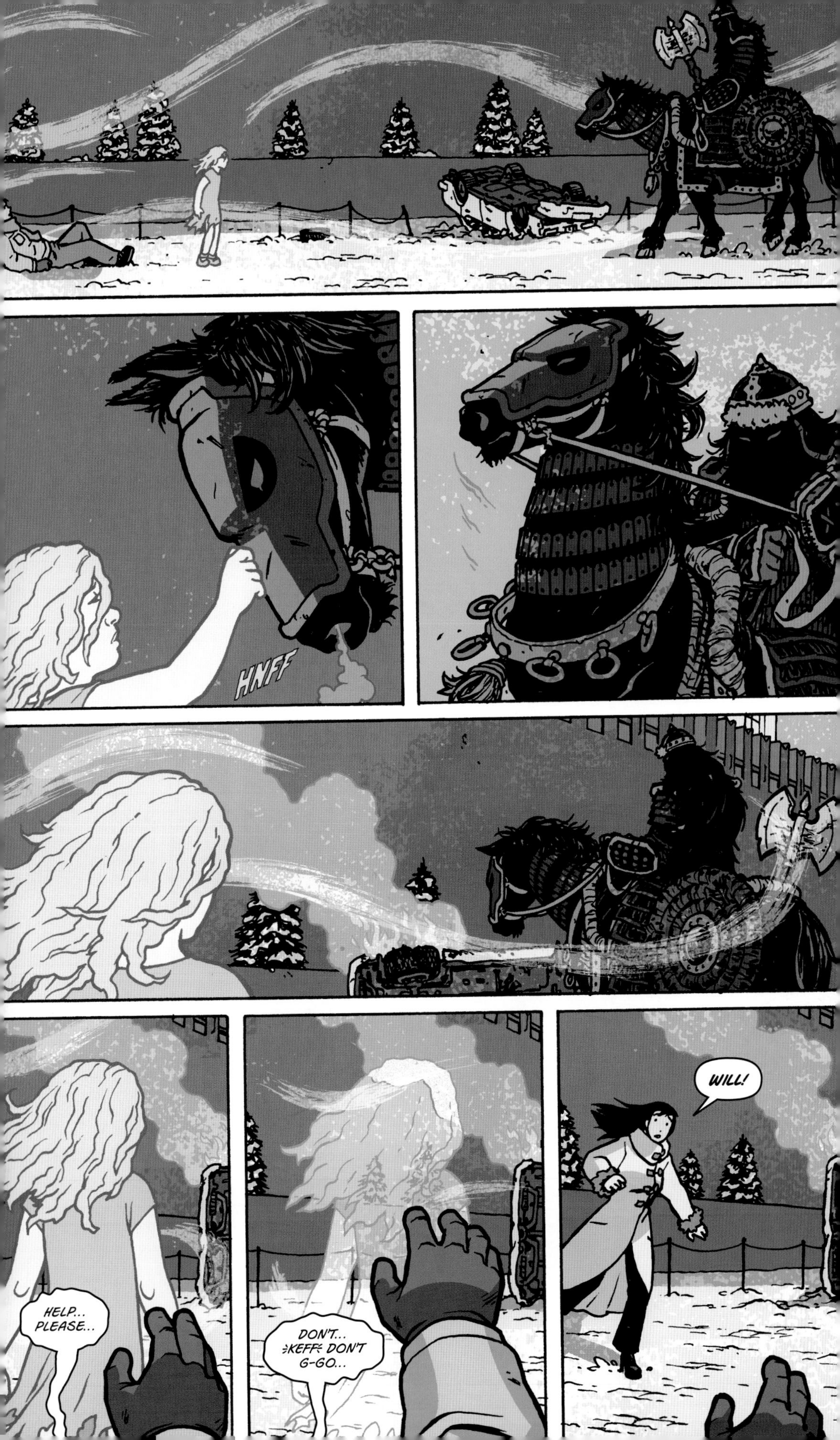
HNFF
HELP... PLEASE...
DON'T... *KEFF* DON'T G-GO...
WILL!

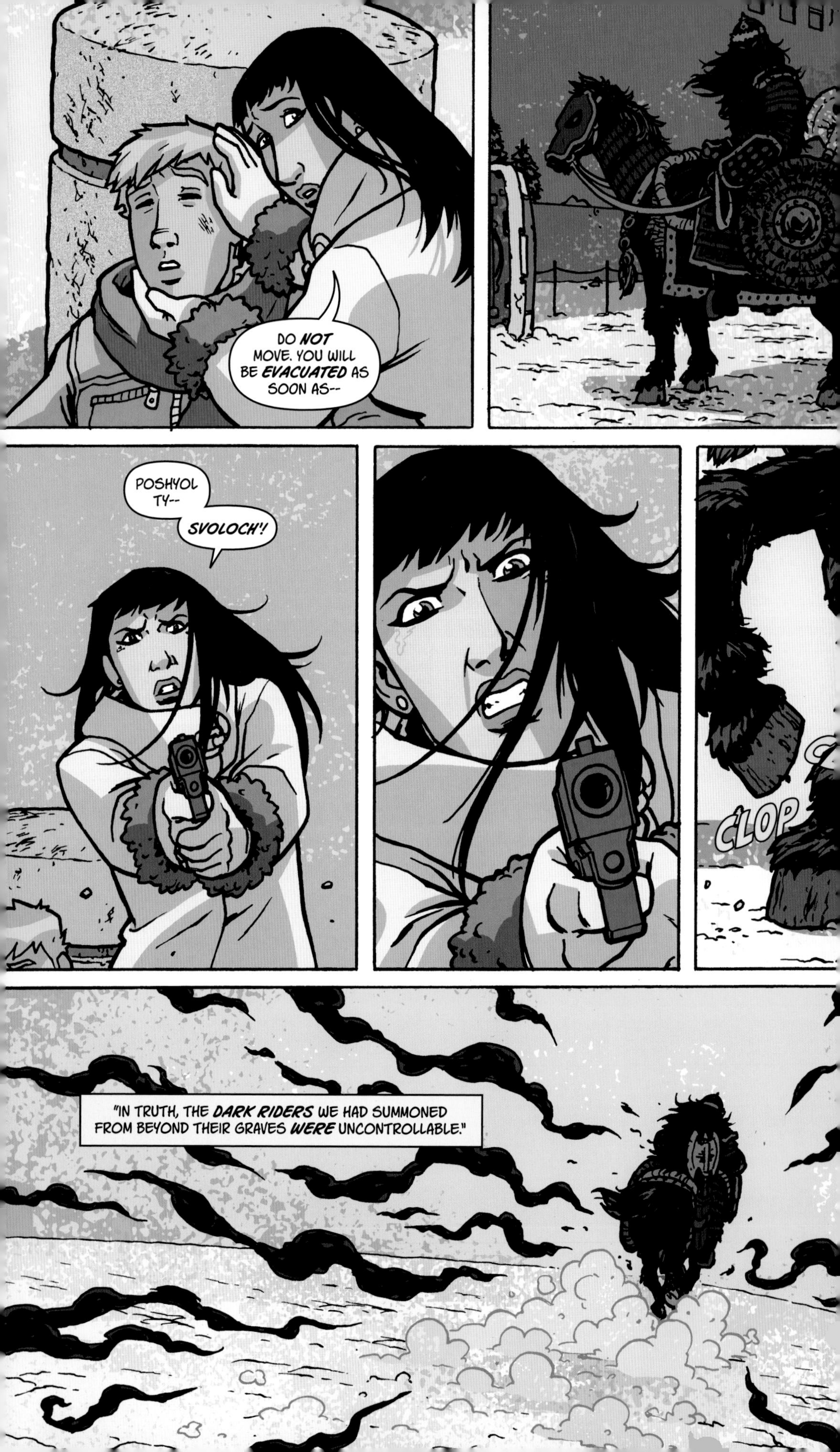

DO NOT MOVE. YOU WILL BE EVACUATED AS SOON AS--
POSHYOL TY--
SVOLOCH'!
CLOP
"IN TRUTH, THE DARK RIDERS WE HAD SUMMONED FROM BEYOND THEIR GRAVES WERE UNCONTROLLABLE."

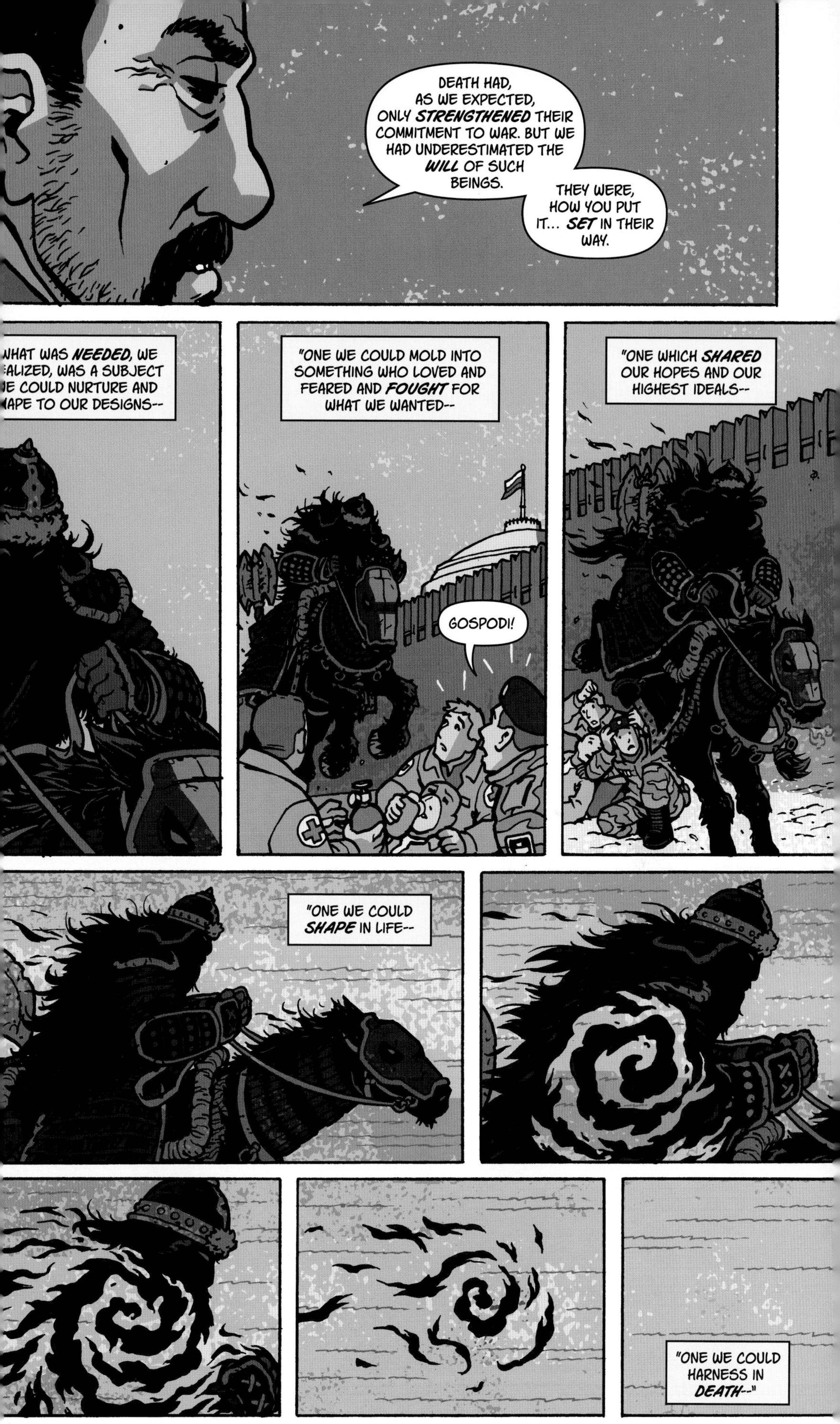
DEATH HAD, AS WE EXPECTED, ONLY STRENGTHENED THEIR COMMITMENT TO WAR. BUT WE HAD UNDERESTIMATED THE WILL OF SUCH BEINGS.
THEY WERE, HOW YOU PUT IT... SET IN THEIR WAY.
WHAT WAS NEEDED, WE EALIZED, WAS A SUBJECT E COULD NURTURE AND APE TO OUR DESIGNS--
"ONE WE COULD MOLD INTO SOMETHING WHO LOVED AND FEARED AND FOUGHT FOR WHAT WE WANTED--
GOSPODI!
"ONE WHICH SHARED OUR HOPES AND OUR HIGHEST IDEALS--
"ONE WE COULD SHAPE IN LIFE--
"ONE WE COULD HARNESS IN DEATH--"

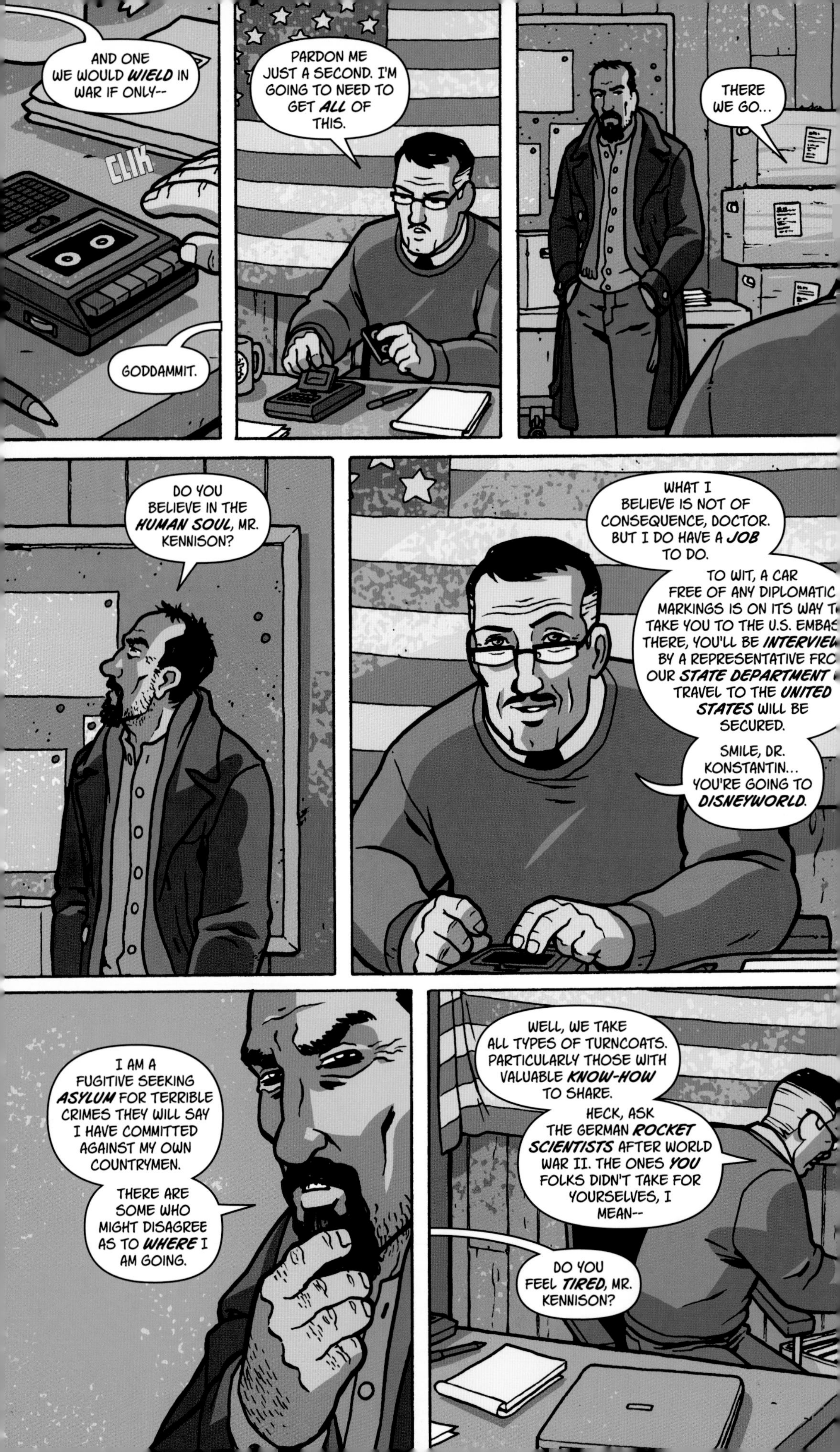
AND ONE WE WOULD WIELD IN WAR IF ONLY--
CLIK
GODDAMMIT.
PARDON ME JUST A SECOND. I'M GOING TO NEED TO GET ALL OF THIS.
THERE WE GO...
DO YOU BELIEVE IN THE HUMAN SOUL, MR. KENNISON?
WHAT I BELIEVE IS NOT OF CONSEQUENCE, DOCTOR. BUT I DO HAVE A JOB TO DO.
TO WIT, A CAR FREE OF ANY DIPLOMATIC MARKINGS IS ON ITS WAY T TAKE YOU TO THE U.S. EMBAS THERE, YOU'LL BE INTERVIEW BY A REPRESENTATIVE FRO OUR STATE DEPARTMENT TRAVEL TO THE UNITED STATES WILL BE SECURED.
SMILE, DR. KONSTANTIN... YOU'RE GOING TO DISNEYWORLD.
I AM A FUGITIVE SEEKING ASYLUM FOR TERRIBLE CRIMES THEY WILL SAY I HAVE COMMITTED AGAINST MY OWN COUNTRYMEN.
THERE ARE SOME WHO MIGHT DISAGREE AS TO WHERE I AM GOING.
WELL, WE TAKE ALL TYPES OF TURNCOATS. PARTICULARLY THOSE WITH VALUABLE KNOW-HOW TO SHARE.
HECK, ASK THE GERMAN ROCKET SCIENTISTS AFTER WORLD WAR II. THE ONES YOU FOLKS DIDN'T TAKE FOR YOURSELVES, I MEAN--
DO YOU FEEL TIRED, MR. KENNISON?

WHAT DO YOU MEAN, DO I FEEL--

YOU ARE *VERY* TIRED, MR. KENNISON...

YOU *ARE* GROWING TIRED... I CAN TELL. LISTENING LONG TO MY *VOICE* AS YOU HAVE N, HOW COULD THAT NOT BE? MY CE IS ALL YOU HAVE HEARD THESE PAST FEW HOURS WE HAVE SPENT TOGETHER.

ALL THAT YOU HEAR *NOW* IS MY VOICE...

I... I AM...

...TIRED...

OF COURSE YOU ARE...

SINCE YOU ARE O TIRED, I WILL LET SLEEP, BUT BEFORE CAN ALLOW THAT, I NEED YOU TO DO *TWO THINGS* FOR ME.

IS THAT ALL RIGHT...?

WHATEVER... YOU WANT... DOCTOR...

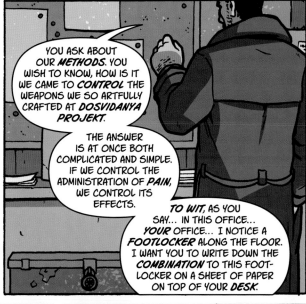

YOU ASK ABOUT OUR *METHODS*. YOU WISH TO KNOW, HOW IS IT WE CAME TO *CONTROL* THE WEAPONS WE SO ARTFULLY CRAFTED AT *DOSVIDANYA PROJEKT*.

THE ANSWER IS AT ONCE BOTH COMPLICATED AND SIMPLE. IF WE CONTROL THE ADMINISTRATION OF *PAIN*, WE CONTROL ITS EFFECTS.

TO WIT, AS YOU SAY... IN THIS OFFICE... *YOUR* OFFICE... I NOTICE A *FOOTLOCKER* ALONG THE FLOOR. I WANT YOU TO WRITE DOWN THE *COMBINATION* TO THIS FOOT-LOCKER ON A SHEET OF PAPER ON TOP OF YOUR *DESK*.

NEXT, I WANT YOU TO *SLAM YOUR FACE* INTO THE DESK-TOP WITH ALL OF YOUR STRENGTH...

THEN, I WANT FOR YOU TO DO IT *AGAIN*...

AND STILL *AGAIN* AFTER THAT...

EACH TIME, I WANT YOU TO REDOUBLE YOUR EFFORT. I WANT YOU TO SUMMON *EACH DROP* OF STRENGTH UNTIL THE LAST. AND I WANT YOU TO KEEP DOING THIS UNTIL YOU'VE GIVEN *ALL* THAT YOU CAN.

SPASIBA. YOU MUST BE *TERRIBLY* TIRED BY NOW, MR. KENNISON...

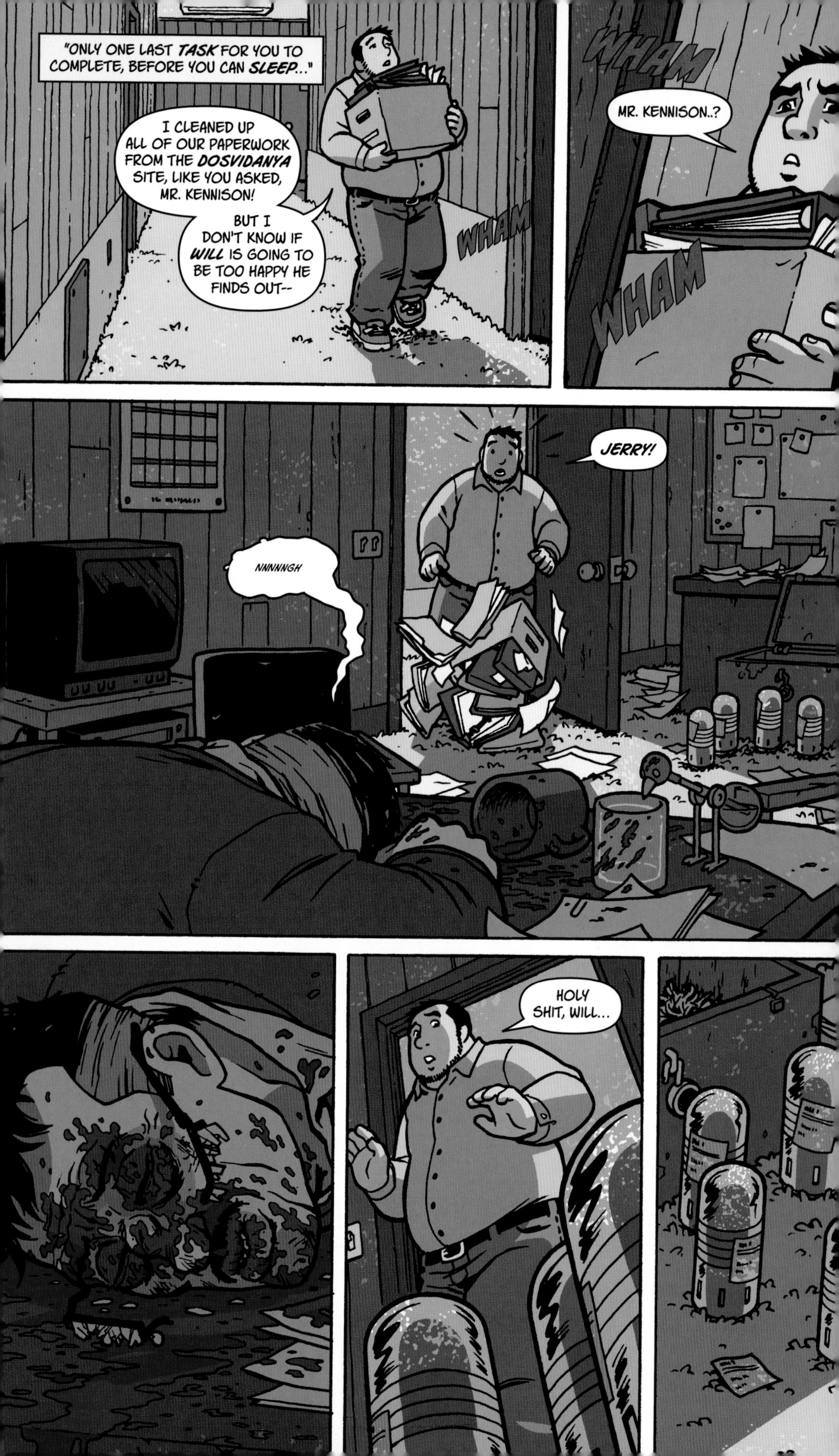
"ONLY ONE LAST TASK FOR YOU TO COMPLETE, BEFORE YOU CAN SLEEP..."
I CLEANED UP ALL OF OUR PAPERWORK FROM THE DOSVIDANYA SITE, LIKE YOU ASKED, MR. KENNISON!
BUT I DON'T KNOW IF WILL IS GOING TO BE TOO HAPPY HE FINDS OUT--
WHAM
WHAM
MR. KENNISON..?
WHAM
JERRY!
NNNNNGH
HOLY SHIT, WILL...

"WHAT SORT OF *WEAPONS PROJECT* DID WE UNCOVER...?"

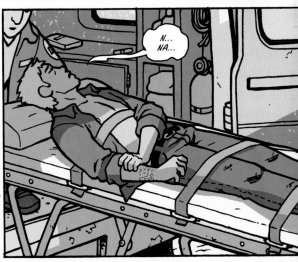

N...
NA...

NAT...

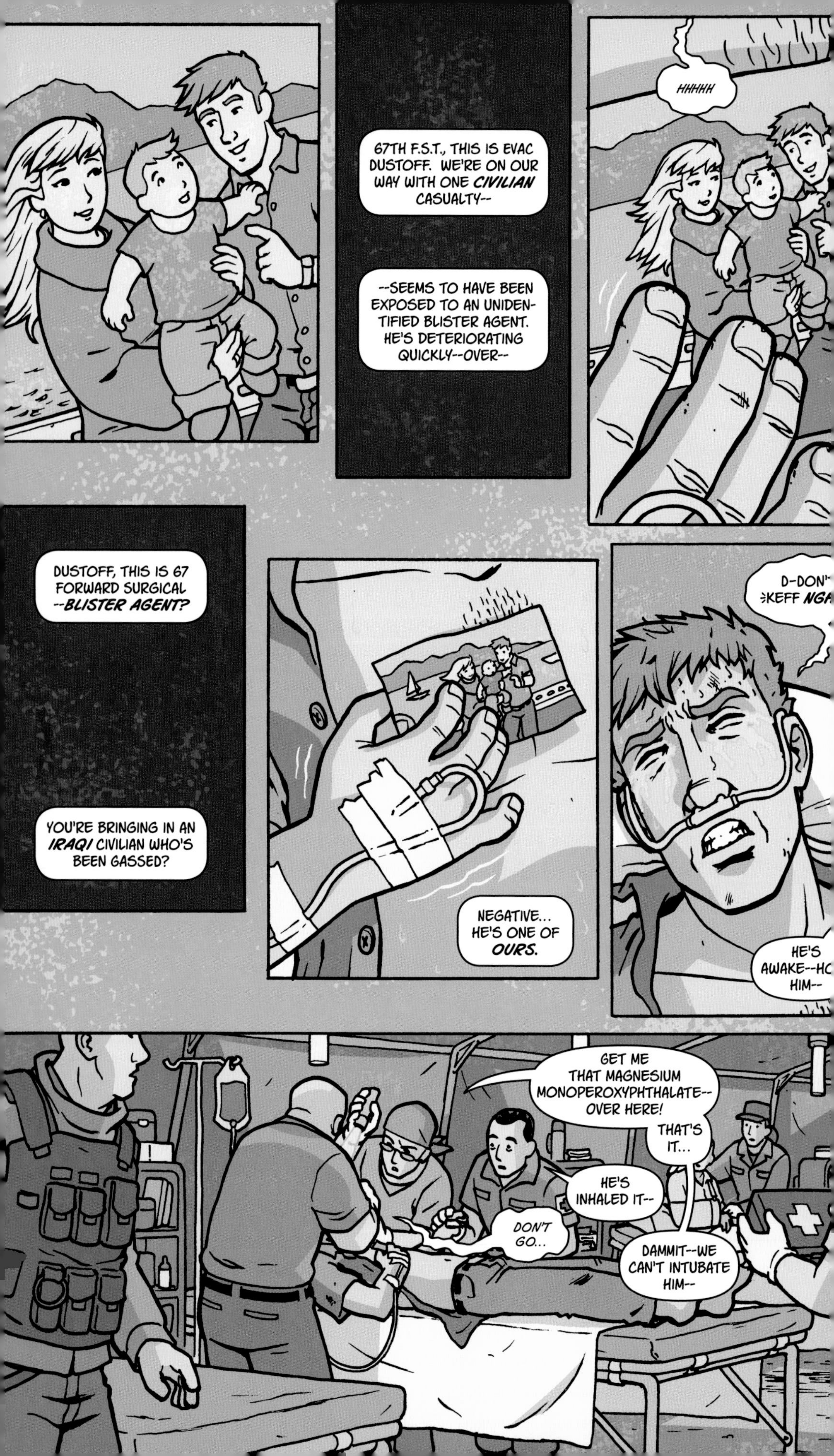
67TH F.S.T., THIS IS EVAC DUSTOFF. WE'RE ON OUR WAY WITH ONE *CIVILIAN* CASUALTY--
--SEEMS TO HAVE BEEN EXPOSED TO AN UNIDENTIFIED BLISTER AGENT. HE'S DETERIORATING QUICKLY--OVER--
HHHHH
DUSTOFF, THIS IS 67 FORWARD SURGICAL --***BLISTER AGENT?***
YOU'RE BRINGING IN AN ***IRAQI*** CIVILIAN WHO'S BEEN GASSED?
NEGATIVE... HE'S ONE OF ***OURS.***
D-DON'T KEFF NGA
HE'S AWAKE--HO HIM--
GET ME THAT MAGNESIUM MONOPEROXYPHTHALATE--OVER HERE!
THAT'S IT...
HE'S INHALED IT--
DON'T GO...
DAMMIT--WE CAN'T INTUBATE HIM--

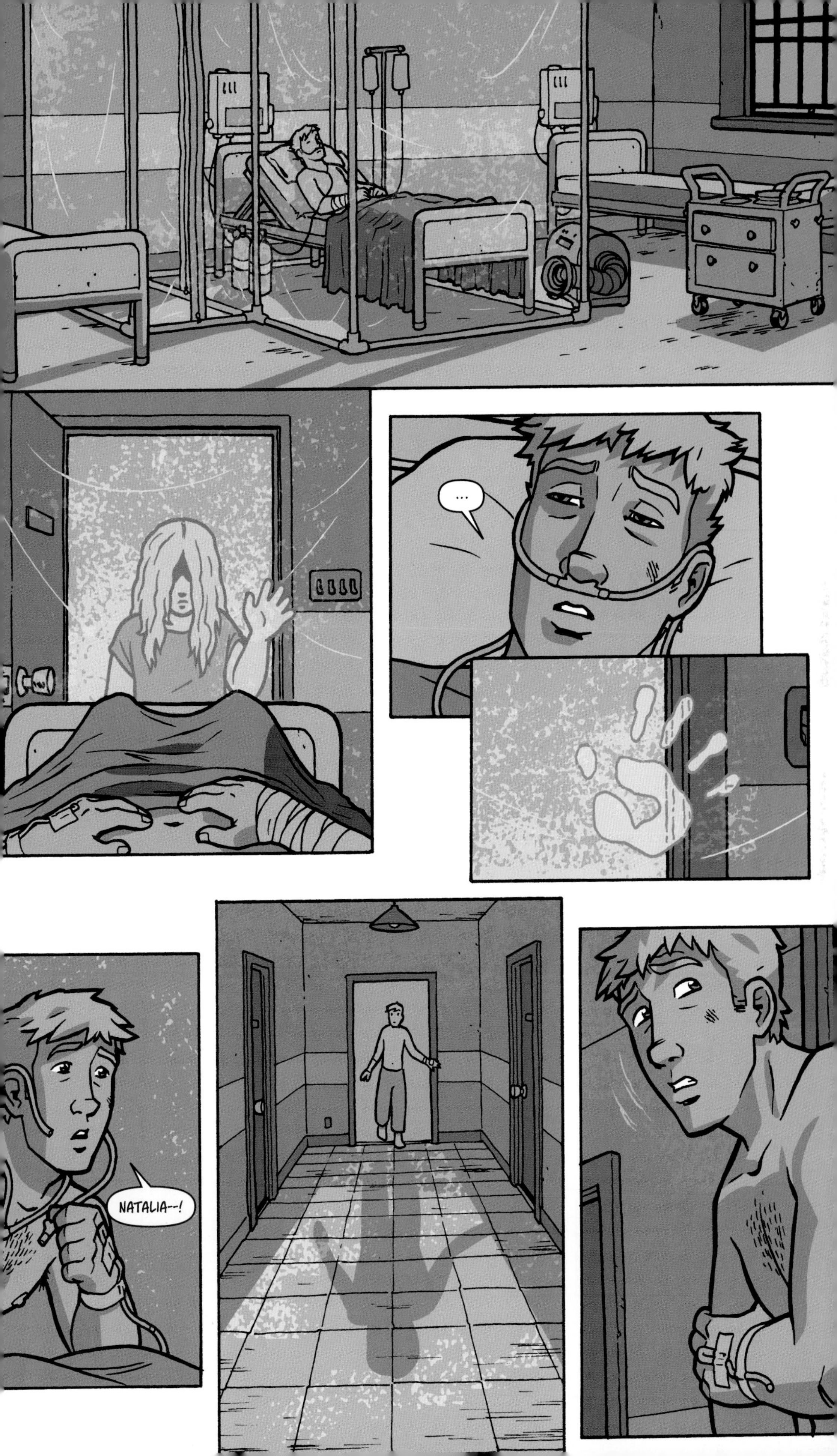

...
NATALIA--!

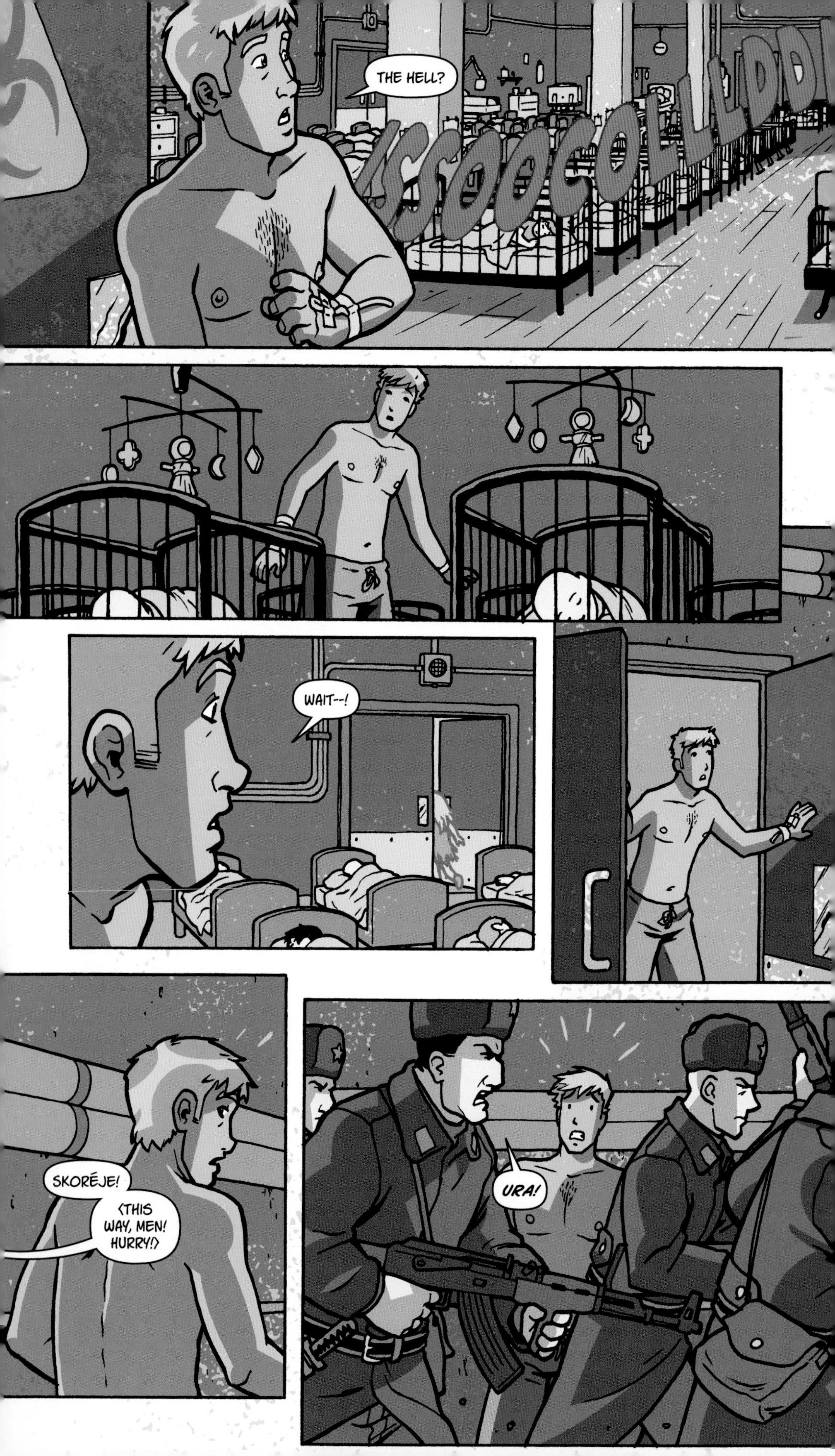
THE HELL?
SSOOCOLLLDD
WAIT--!
SKORÉJE!
<THIS WAY, MEN! HURRY!>
URA!

WHAT ARE YOU?

PLEASE--

I NEED TO--

HNN

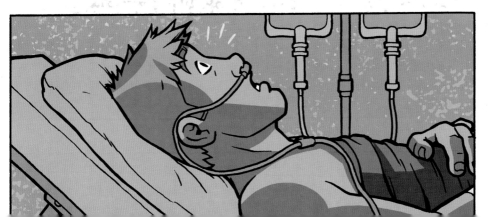

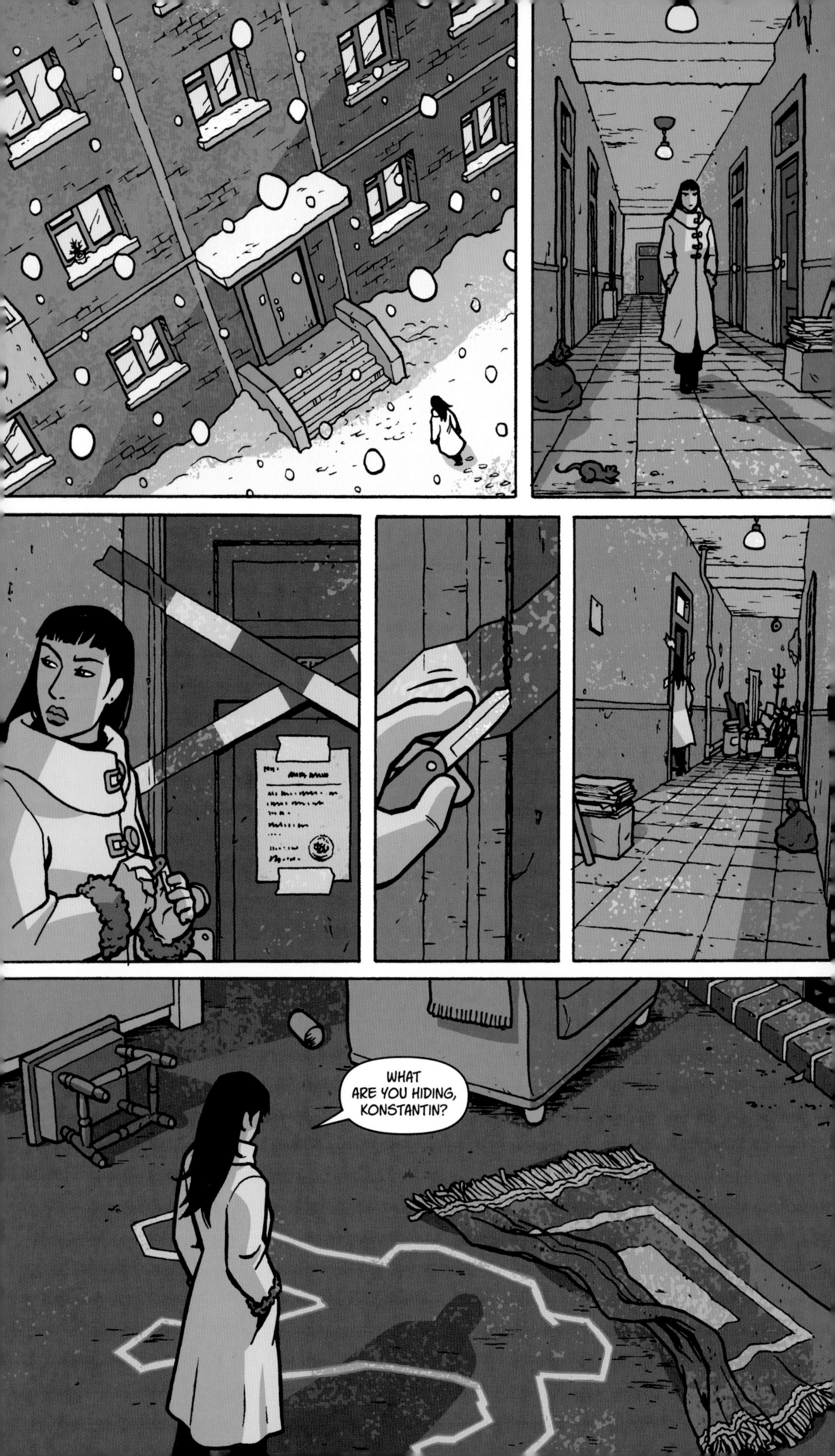
WHAT ARE YOU HIDING, KONSTANTIN?

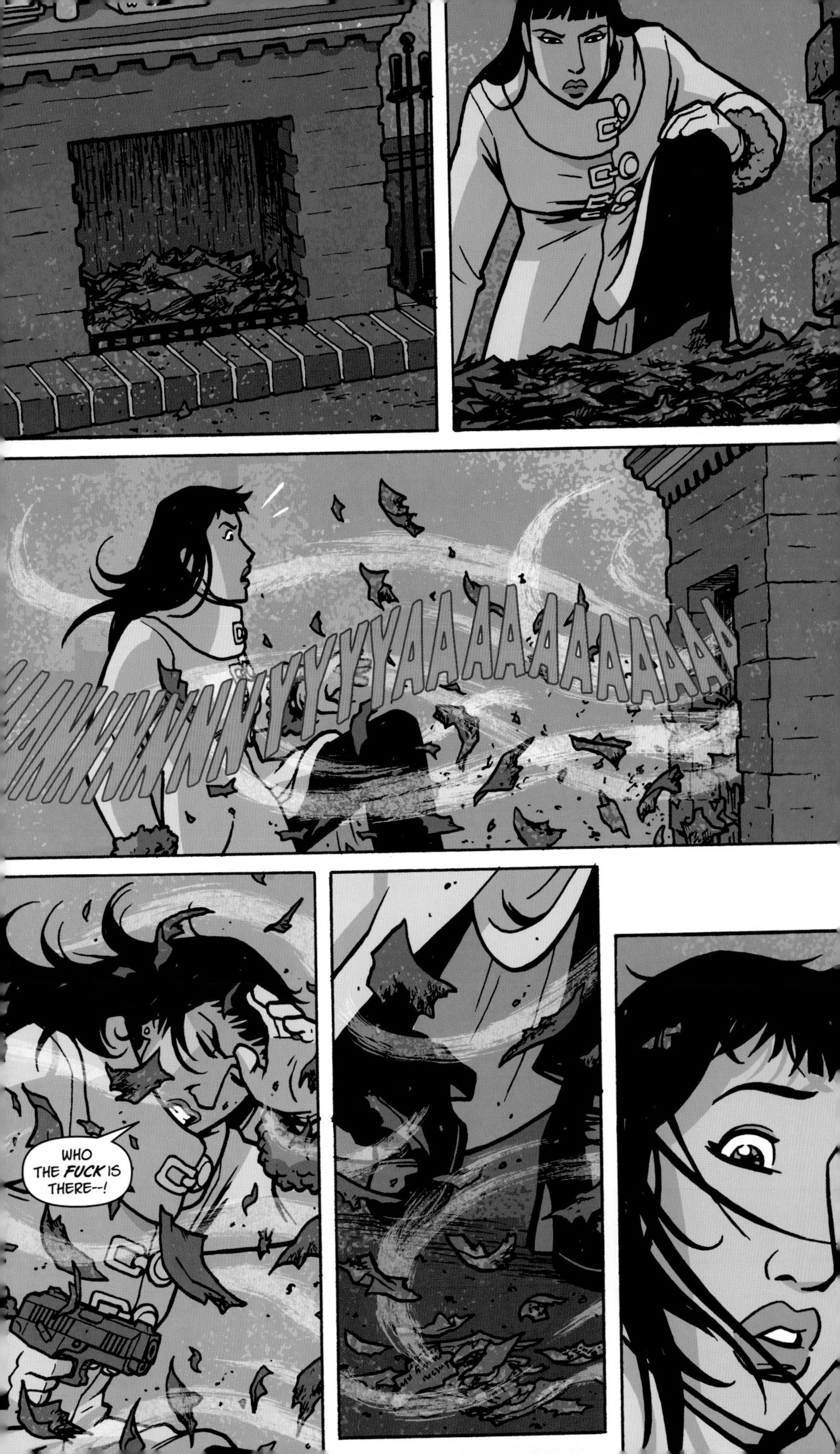

WHO THE *FUCK* IS THERE--!

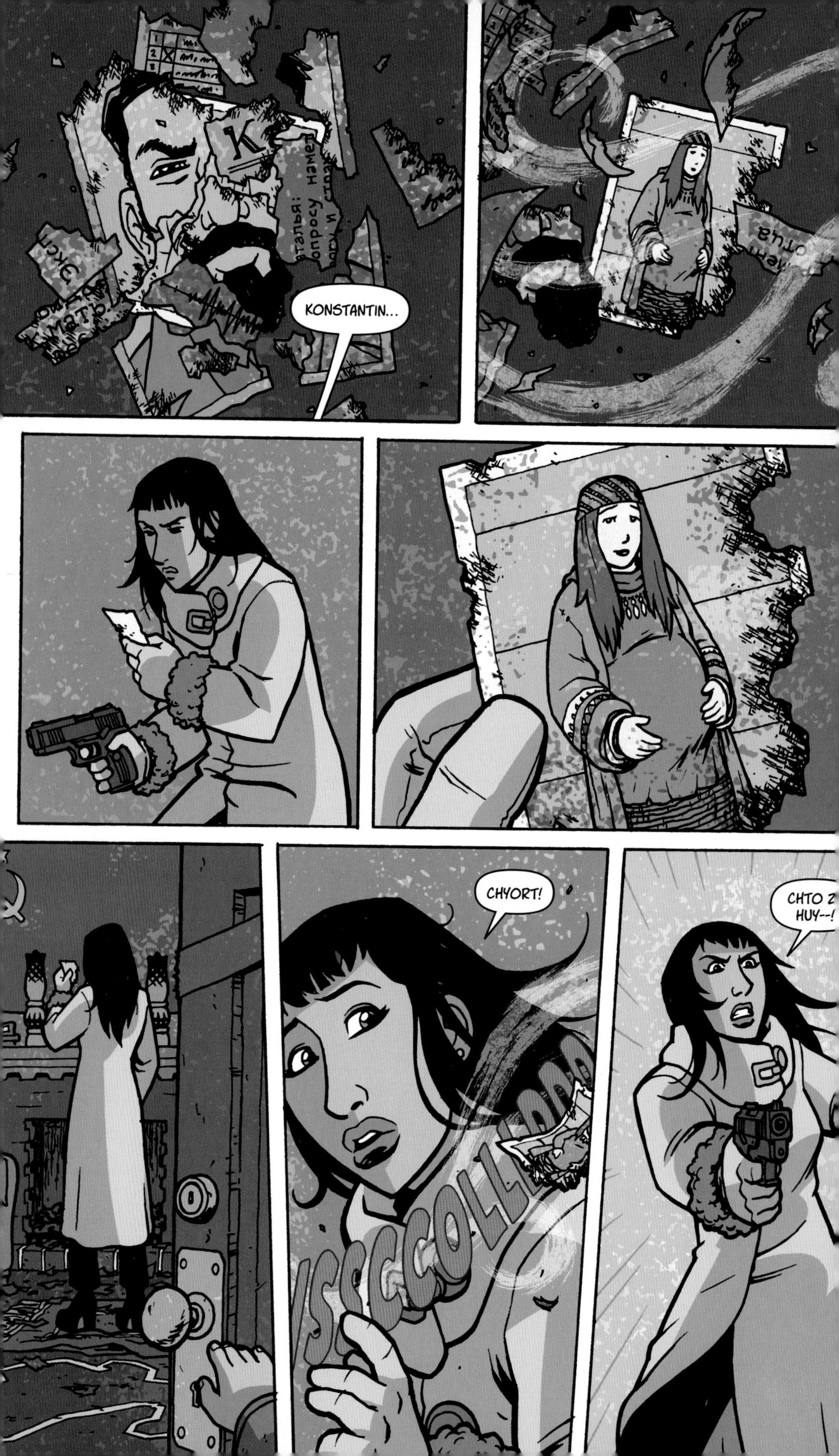
KONSTANTIN...
CHYORT!
VSSCCCOLLDDD
CHTO Z
HUY--!

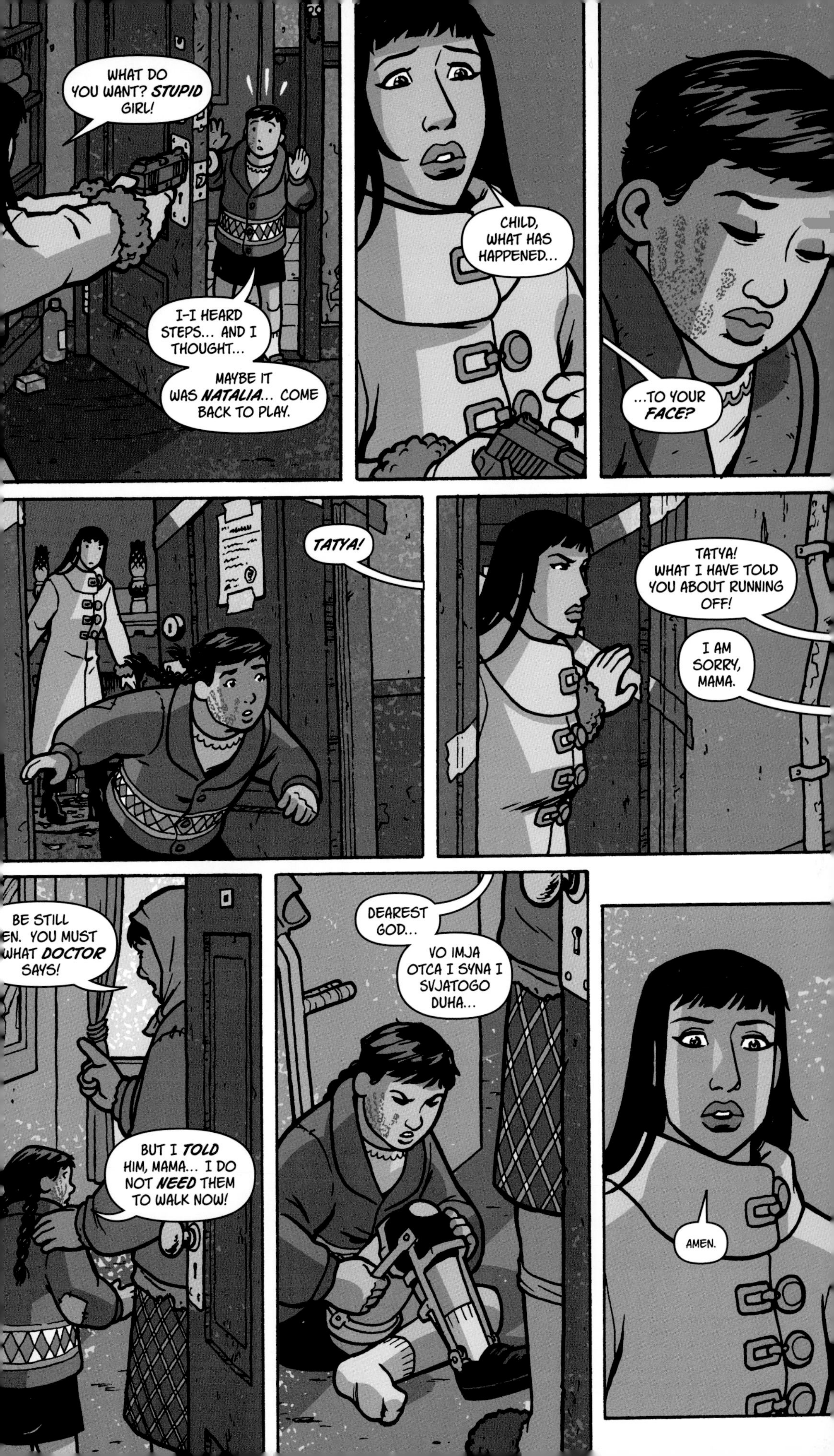
WHAT DO YOU WANT? STUPID GIRL!
I-I HEARD STEPS... AND I THOUGHT...
MAYBE IT WAS NATALIA... COME BACK TO PLAY.
CHILD, WHAT HAS HAPPENED...
...TO YOUR FACE?
TATYA!
TATYA! WHAT I HAVE TOLD YOU ABOUT RUNNING OFF!
I AM SORRY, MAMA.
BE STILL
EN. YOU MUST
WHAT DOCTOR SAYS!
BUT I TOLD HIM, MAMA... I DO NOT NEED THEM TO WALK NOW!
DEAREST GOD...
VO IMJA OTCA I SYNA I SVJATOGO DUHA...
AMEN.

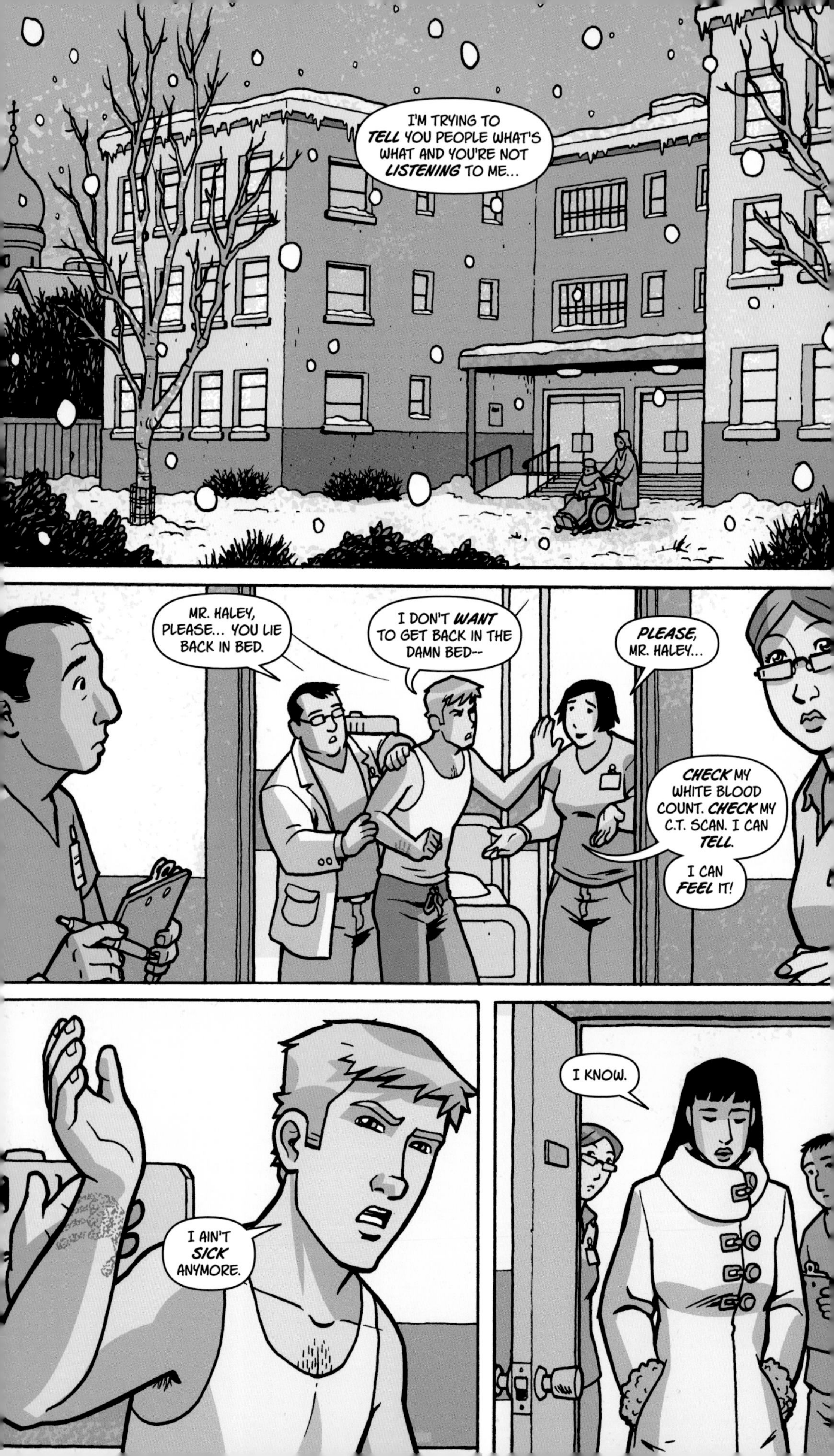

I'M TRYING TO **TELL** YOU PEOPLE WHAT'S WHAT AND YOU'RE NOT **LISTENING** TO ME...
MR. HALEY, PLEASE... YOU LIE BACK IN BED.
I DON'T **WANT** TO GET BACK IN THE DAMN BED--
PLEASE, MR. HALEY...
CHECK MY WHITE BLOOD COUNT. **CHECK** MY C.T. SCAN. I CAN **TELL**.
I CAN **FEEL** IT!
I AIN'T **SICK** ANYMORE.
I KNOW.

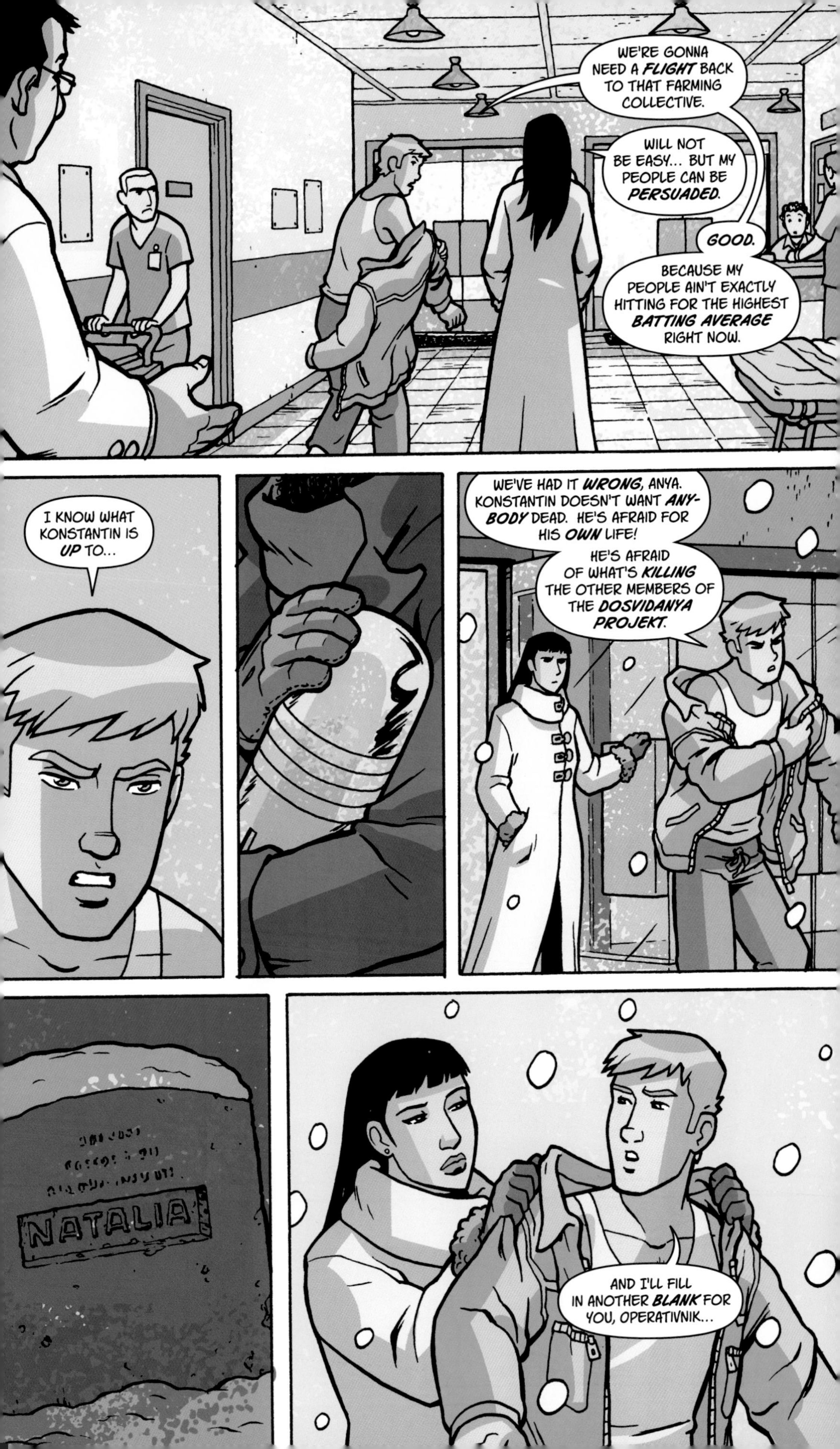
WE'RE GONNA NEED A FLIGHT BACK TO THAT FARMING COLLECTIVE.
WILL NOT BE EASY... BUT MY PEOPLE CAN BE PERSUADED.
GOOD.
BECAUSE MY PEOPLE AIN'T EXACTLY HITTING FOR THE HIGHEST BATTING AVERAGE RIGHT NOW.
I KNOW WHAT KONSTANTIN IS UP TO...
WE'VE HAD IT WRONG, ANYA. KONSTANTIN DOESN'T WANT ANYBODY DEAD. HE'S AFRAID FOR HIS OWN LIFE!
HE'S AFRAID OF WHAT'S KILLING THE OTHER MEMBERS OF THE DOSVIDANYA PROJEKT.
NATALIA
AND I'LL FILL IN ANOTHER BLANK FOR YOU, OPERATIVNIK...

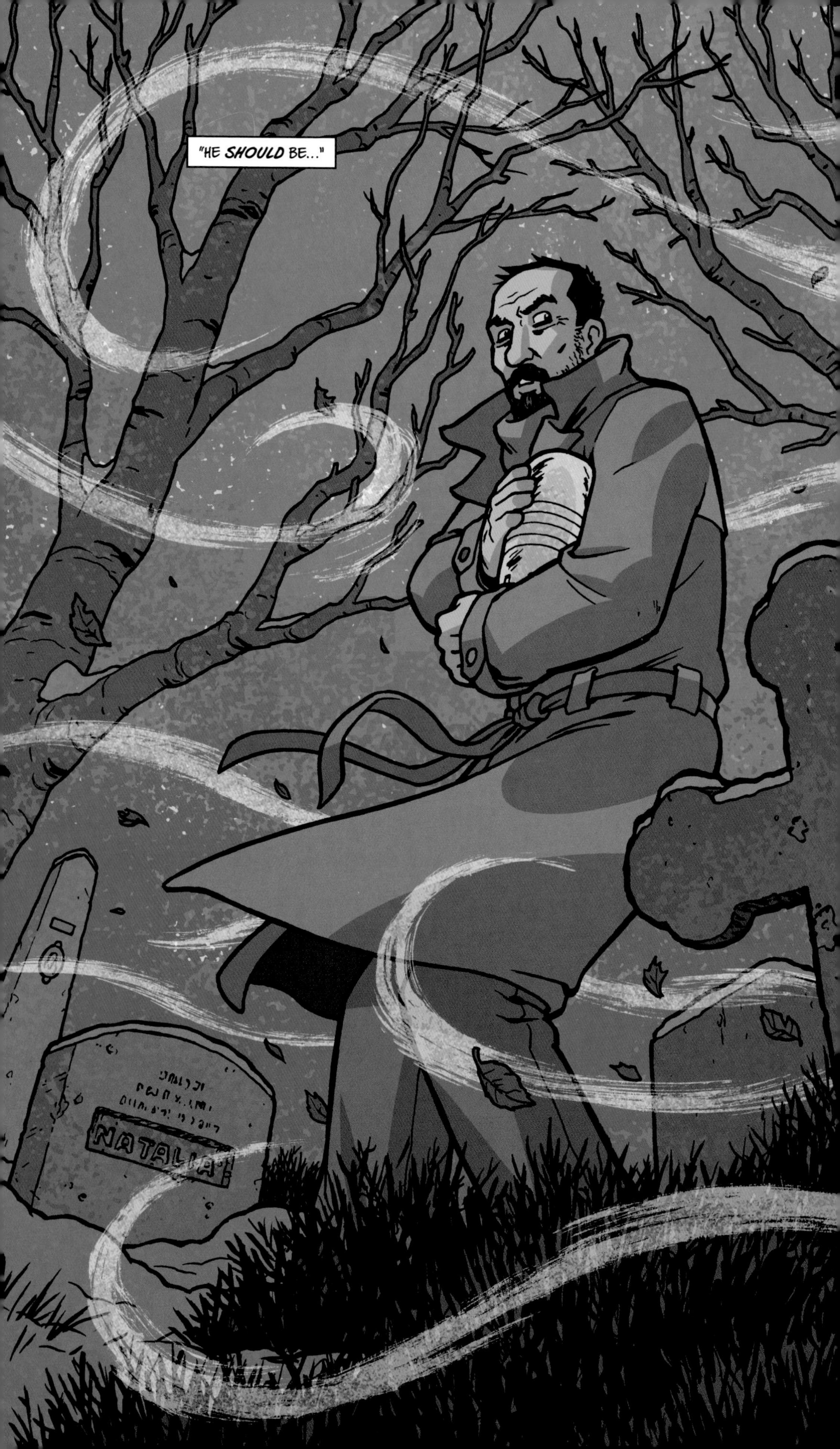
"HE SHOULD BE..."
NATALIA

CHAPTER 5:

REQUIEM

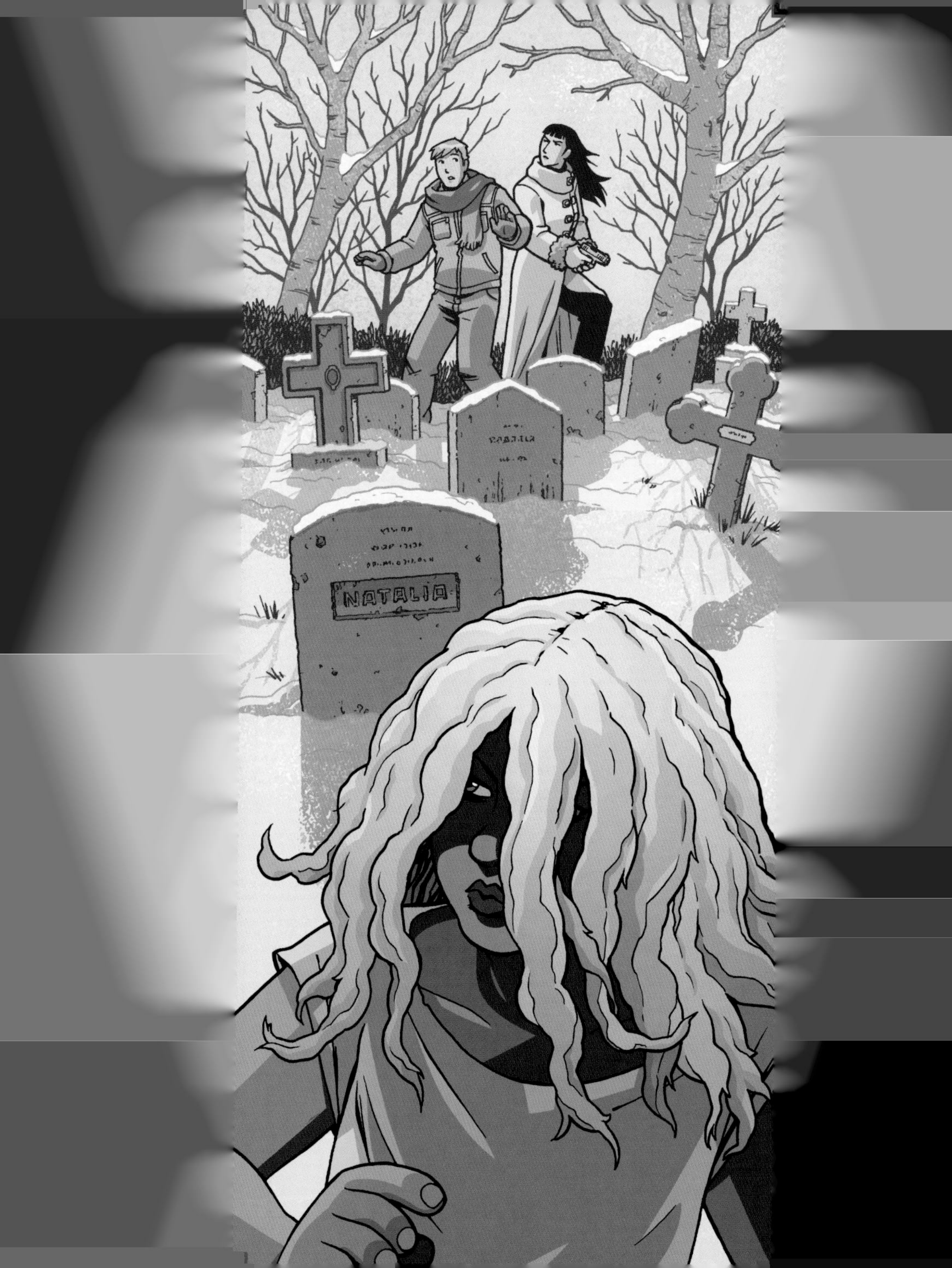
NATALIA

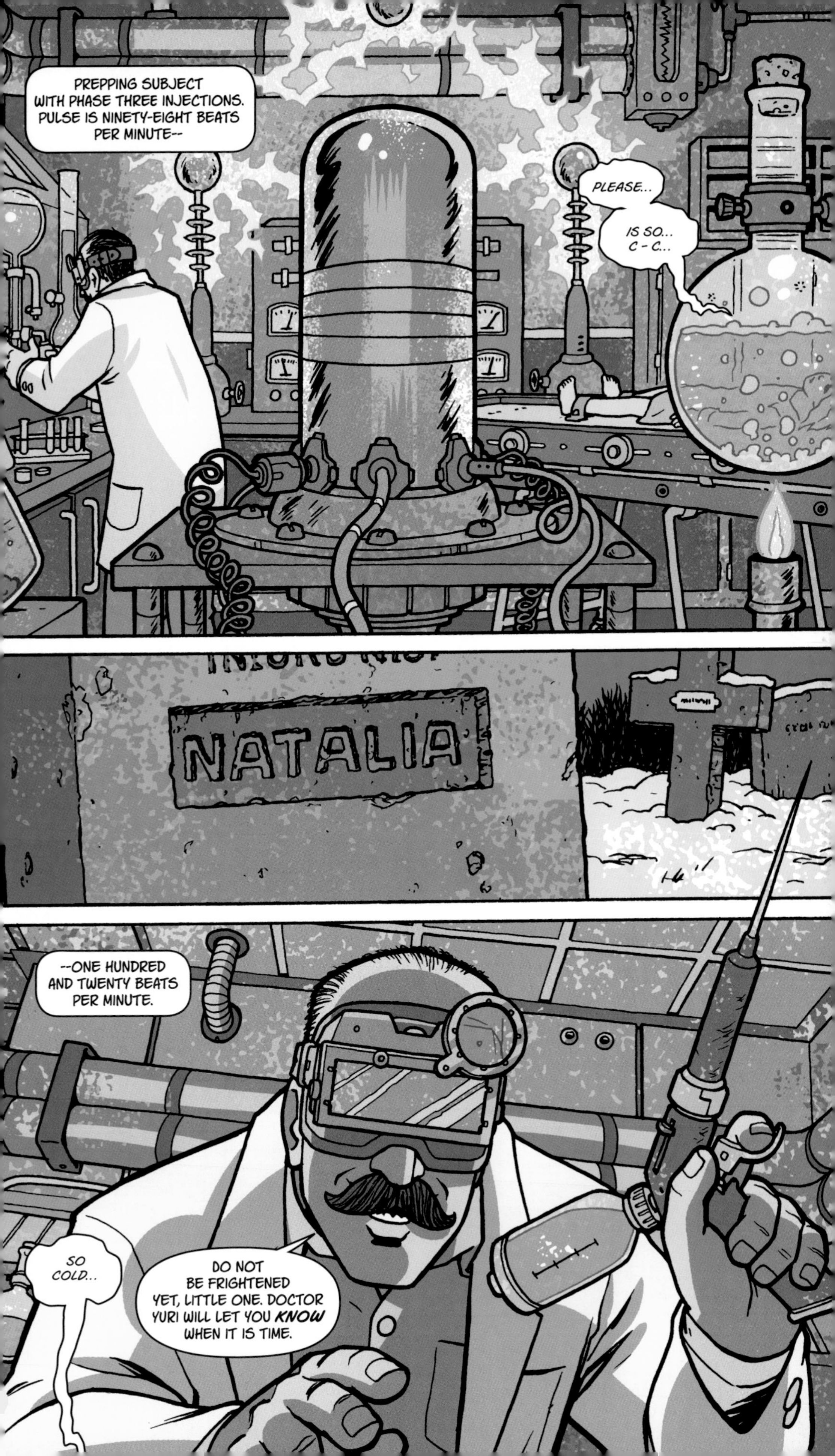
PREPPING SUBJECT WITH PHASE THREE INJECTIONS. PULSE IS NINETY-EIGHT BEATS PER MINUTE--
PLEASE...
IS SO... C - C...
NATALIA
--ONE HUNDRED AND TWENTY BEATS PER MINUTE.
SO COLD...
DO NOT BE FRIGHTENED YET, LITTLE ONE. DOCTOR YURI WILL LET YOU KNOW WHEN IT IS TIME.

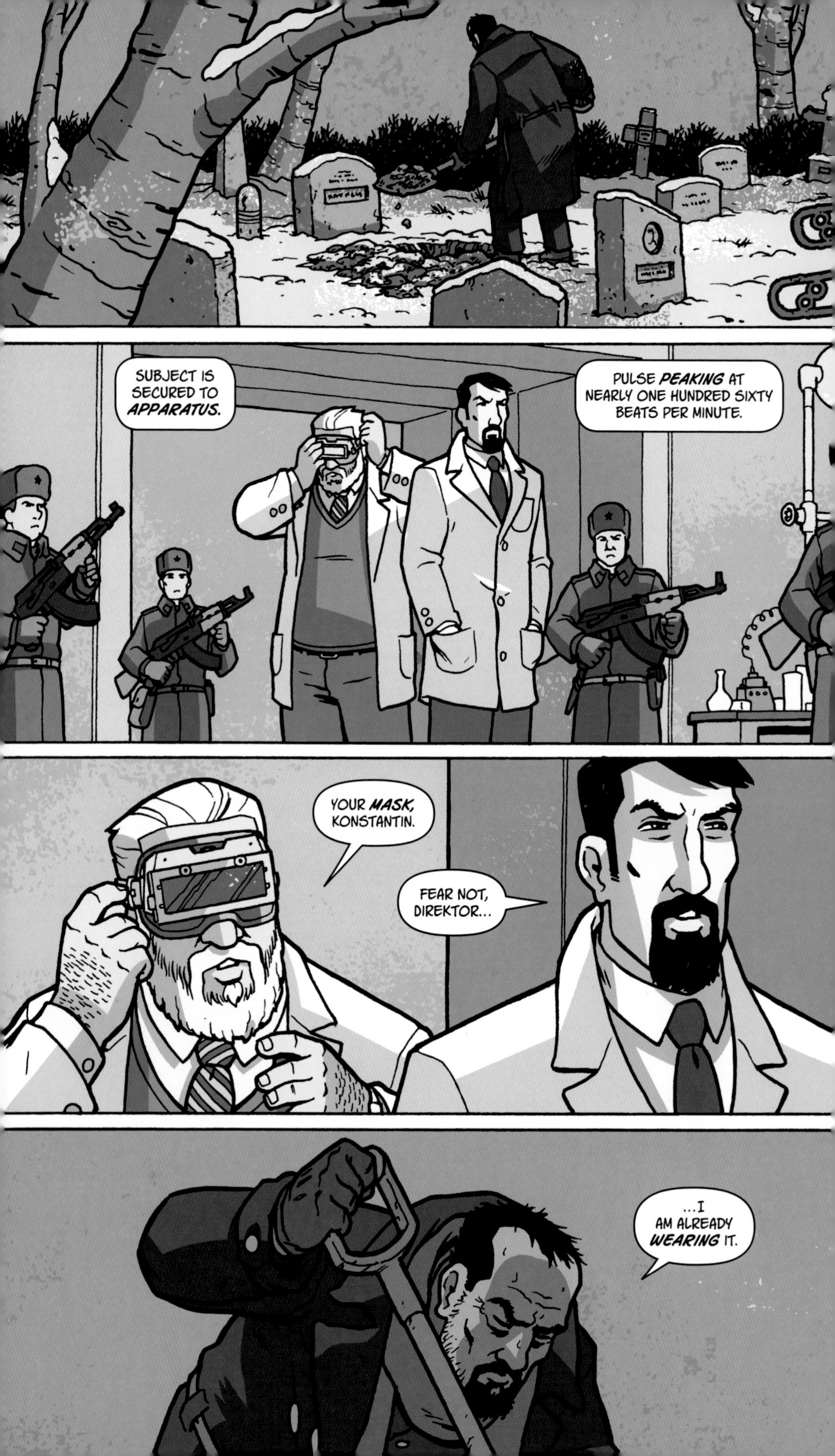
SUBJECT IS SECURED TO APPARATUS.
PULSE PEAKING AT NEARLY ONE HUNDRED SIXTY BEATS PER MINUTE.
YOUR MASK, KONSTANTIN.
FEAR NOT, DIREKTOR...
...I AM ALREADY WEARING IT.

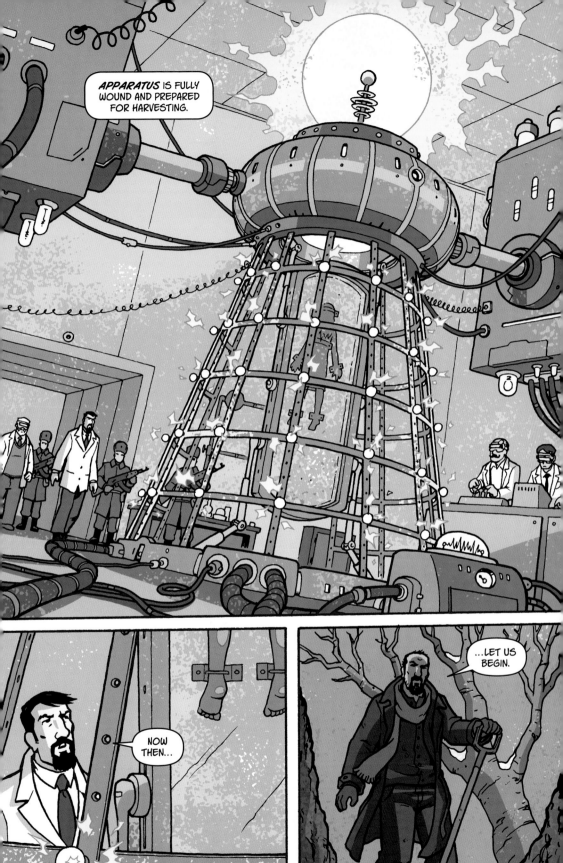

APPARATUS IS FULLY WOUND AND PREPARED FOR HARVESTING.

NOW THEN...

...LET US BEGIN.

THE LIST OF *DOSVIDANYA* MURDERS STARTED AFTER THE THEFT AT THE PROJEKT FACILITY. BUT IT WASN'T *KONSTANTIN* WHO WAS BEHIND ANY OF IT.

HE'S ON THE *RUN* BECAUSE HE KNOWS HE'S NEXT. IT'S ALWAYS BEEN THAT WAY. HE'S ALWAYS KNOWN THIS WAS COMING.

HE'S ALWAYS KNOWN *NATALIA* WAS COMING FOR *HIM.*

RECORDS FOUND AT GREGORI ULUNOV'S RESIDENCE MENTION BIRTH OF BABY GIRL NAMED *NATALIA* AT DOSVIDANYA PROJEKT FACILITY IN 1978.

THAT'S WHAT THEY MUST HAVE STARTED DOING ONCE THEY FOUND OUT THE GODDAMN *MONGOL HORDE* MIGHT BE BEYOND THEIR CONTROL!

KONSTANTIN *CONDITIONED* NATALIA TO THINK ONE OF THESE *DOLLS* WAS OUT TO GET HER. HE CREATED A *FA SAFE* SO HE COULD HOLD HER OFF THINGS EVER WENT SOUTH AGAIN.

SHE WAS TAUGHT THINGS, CONTROLLED, MADE INTO SOMETHING THAT DIDN'T QUESTION OR RESIST. THEN SHE WAS *EXECUTED* AND HER SPIRIT WAS *IMPRISONED* IN ONE OF THOSE CONTAINERS AT THE DOSVIDANYA COMPLEX.

NOW SHE'S FREE AND SHE'S GETTING HER *REVENGE* ON EACH OF THE SONSOFBITCHES RESPONSIBLE. THERE'S A LINE OF DEAD BASTARDS OUT THERE WITH A *DOSVIDANYA PROJEKT* RESUME.

THAT LINE LEADS RIGHT TO *KONSTANTIN.*

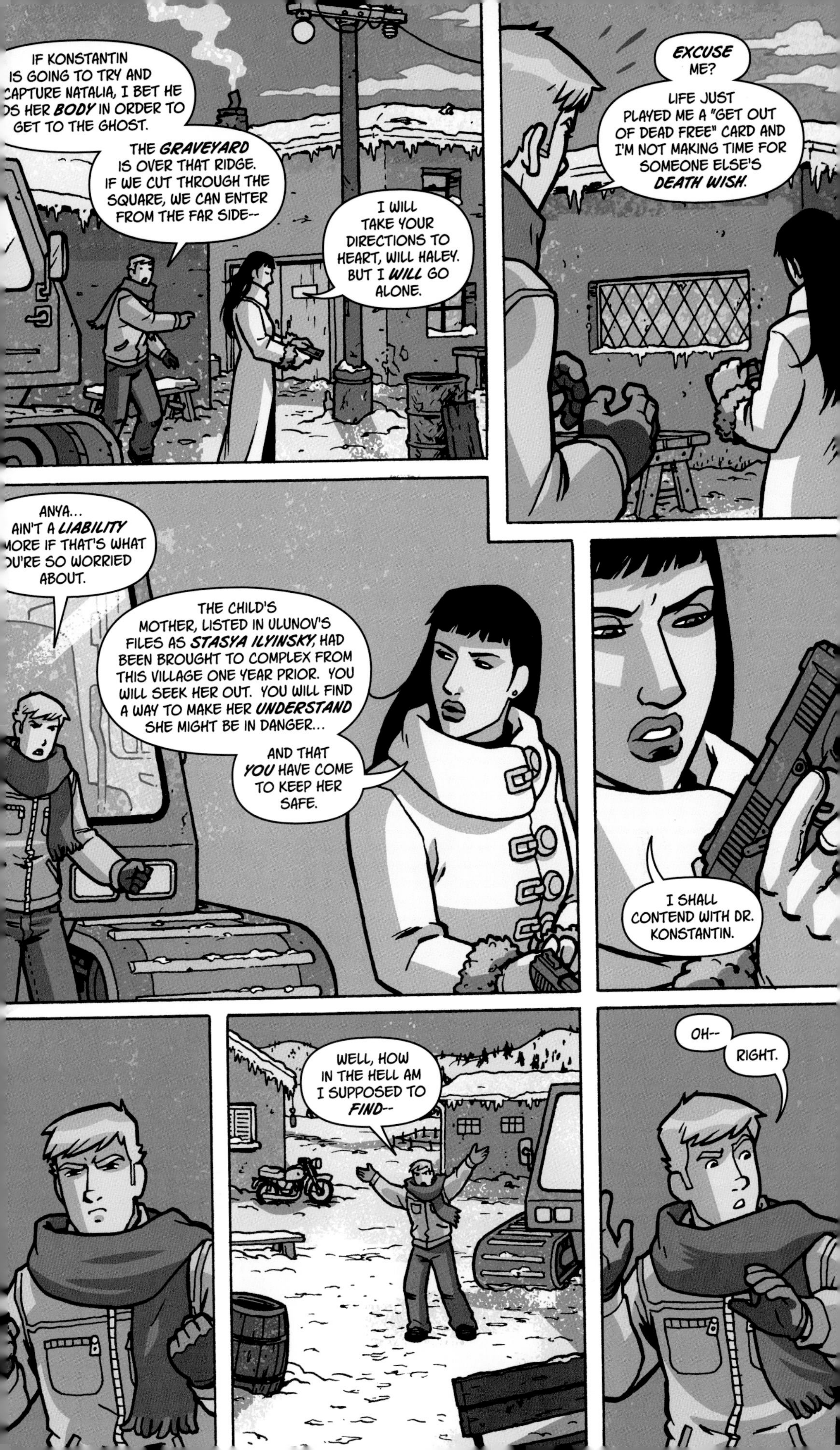
IF KONSTANTIN IS GOING TO TRY AND CAPTURE NATALIA, I BET HE NEEDS HER BODY IN ORDER TO GET TO THE GHOST.
THE GRAVEYARD IS OVER THAT RIDGE. IF WE CUT THROUGH THE SQUARE, WE CAN ENTER FROM THE FAR SIDE--
I WILL TAKE YOUR DIRECTIONS TO HEART, WILL HALEY. BUT I WILL GO ALONE.
EXCUSE ME?
LIFE JUST PLAYED ME A "GET OUT OF DEAD FREE" CARD AND I'M NOT MAKING TIME FOR SOMEONE ELSE'S DEATH WISH.
ANYA... AIN'T A LIABILITY ANYMORE IF THAT'S WHAT YOU'RE SO WORRIED ABOUT.
THE CHILD'S MOTHER, LISTED IN ULUNOV'S FILES AS STASYA ILYINSKY, HAD BEEN BROUGHT TO COMPLEX FROM THIS VILLAGE ONE YEAR PRIOR. YOU WILL SEEK HER OUT. YOU WILL FIND A WAY TO MAKE HER UNDERSTAND SHE MIGHT BE IN DANGER...
AND THAT YOU HAVE COME TO KEEP HER SAFE.
I SHALL CONTEND WITH DR. KONSTANTIN.
WELL, HOW IN THE HELL AM I SUPPOSED TO FIND--
OH--
RIGHT.

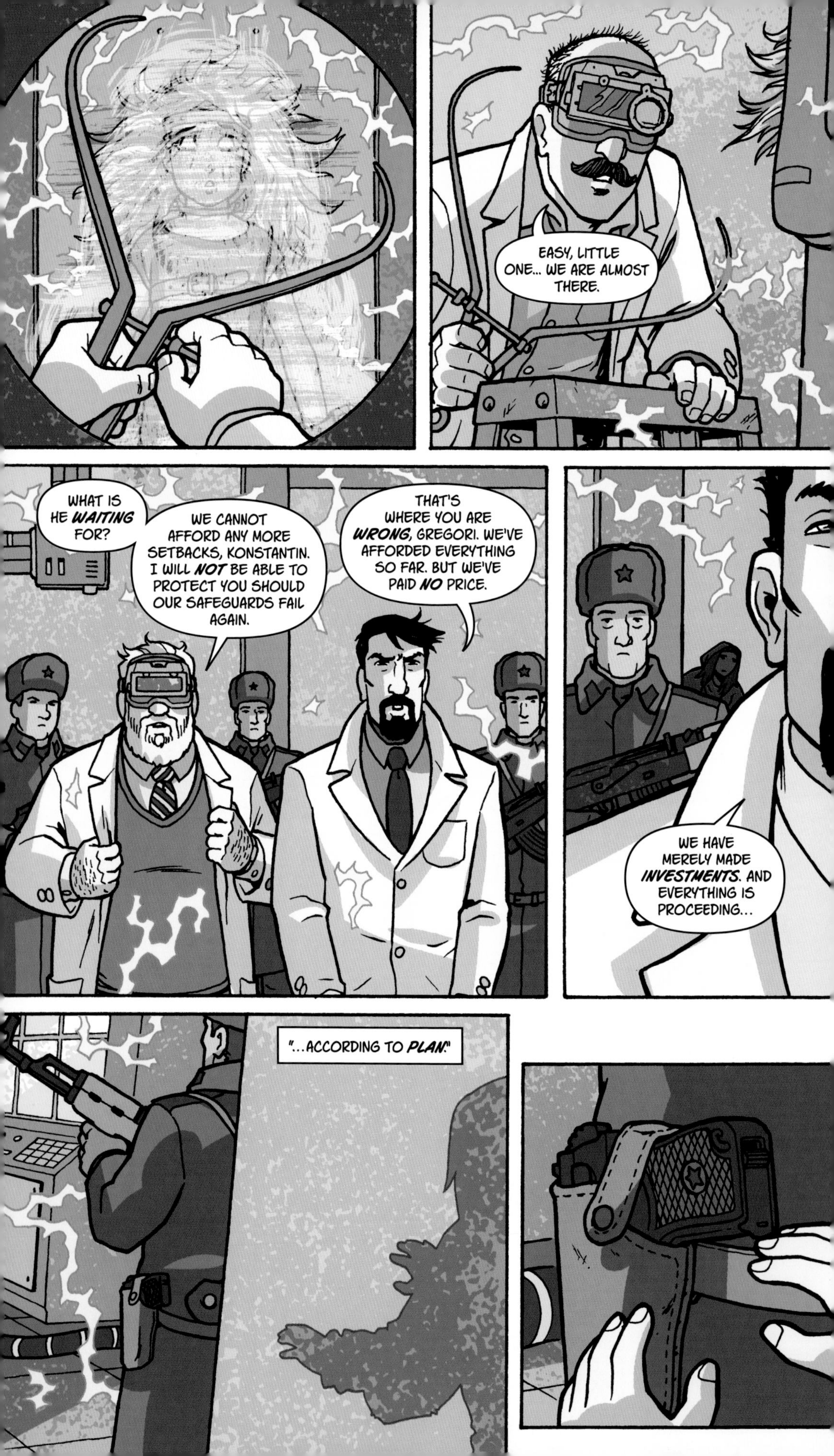

EASY, LITTLE ONE... WE ARE ALMOST THERE.
WHAT IS HE *WAITING* FOR?
WE CANNOT AFFORD ANY MORE SETBACKS, KONSTANTIN. I WILL *NOT* BE ABLE TO PROTECT YOU SHOULD OUR SAFEGUARDS FAIL AGAIN.
THAT'S WHERE YOU ARE *WRONG*, GREGORI. WE'VE AFFORDED EVERYTHING SO FAR. BUT WE'VE PAID *NO* PRICE.
WE HAVE MERELY MADE *INVESTMENTS*. AND EVERYTHING IS PROCEEDING...
"...ACCORDING TO *PLAN*."

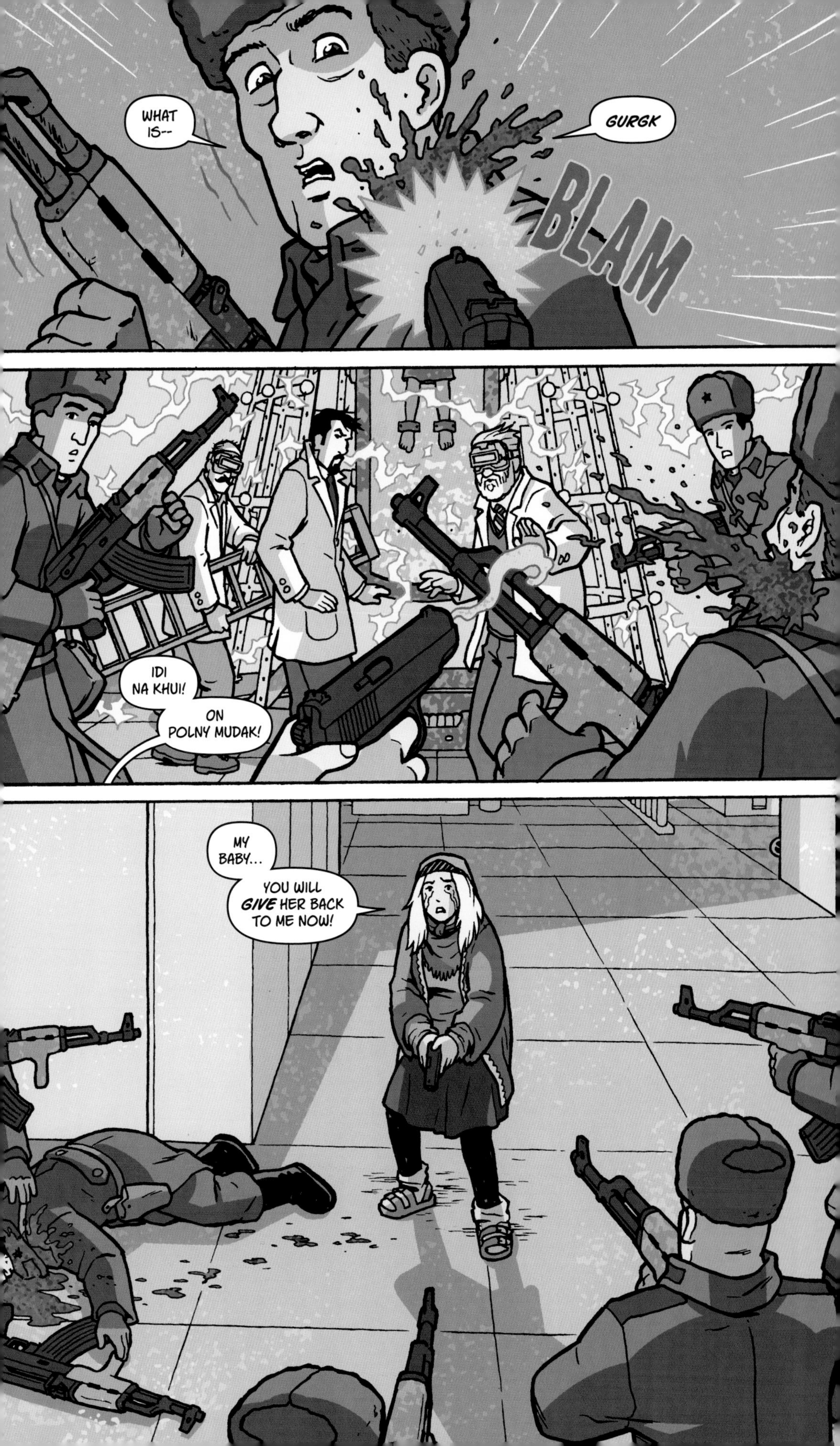
WHAT IS--
GURGK
BLAM
IDI NA KHUI!
ON POLNY MUDAK!
MY BABY...
YOU WILL *GIVE* HER BACK TO ME NOW!

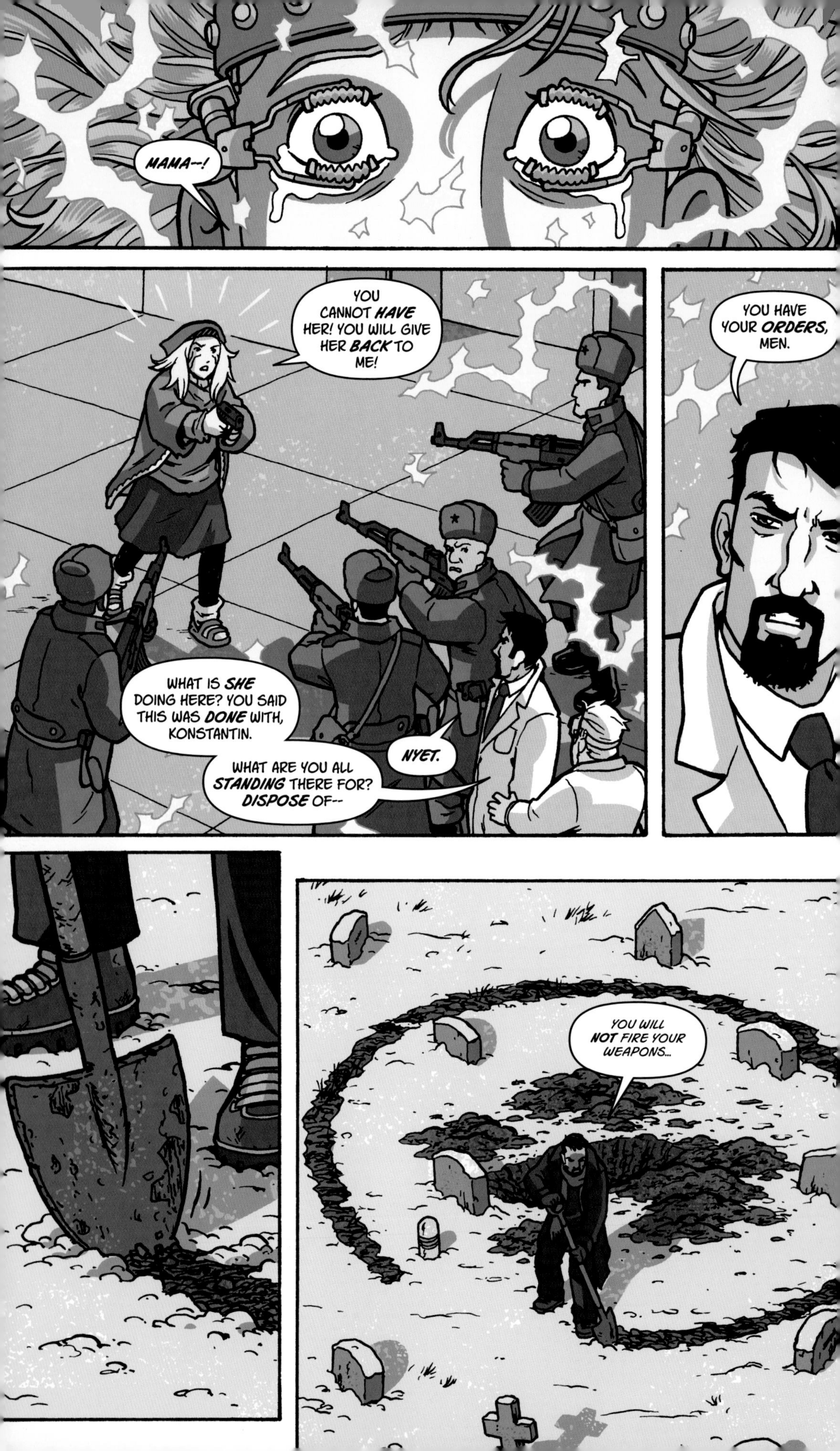
MAMA--!
YOU CANNOT HAVE HER! YOU WILL GIVE HER BACK TO ME!
YOU HAVE YOUR ORDERS, MEN.
WHAT IS SHE DOING HERE? YOU SAID THIS WAS DONE WITH, KONSTANTIN.
NYET.
WHAT ARE YOU ALL STANDING THERE FOR? DISPOSE OF--
YOU WILL NOT FIRE YOUR WEAPONS...

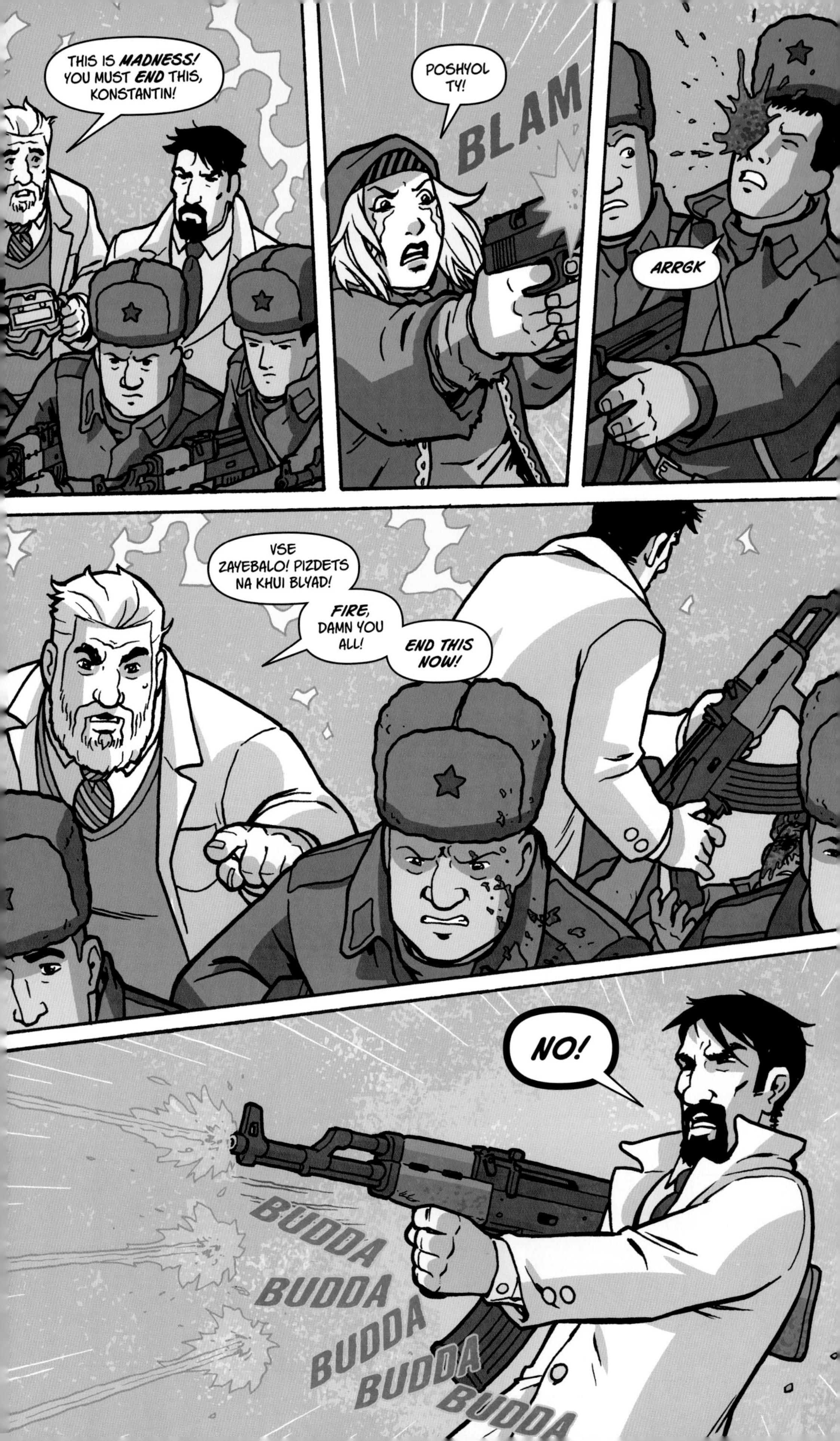
THIS IS MADNESS! YOU MUST END THIS, KONSTANTIN!
POSHYOL TY!
BLAM
ARRGK
VSE ZAYEBALO! PIZDETS NA KHUI BLYAD!
FIRE, DAMN YOU ALL!
END THIS NOW!
NO!
BUDDA
BUDDA
BUDDA
BUDDA
BUDDA

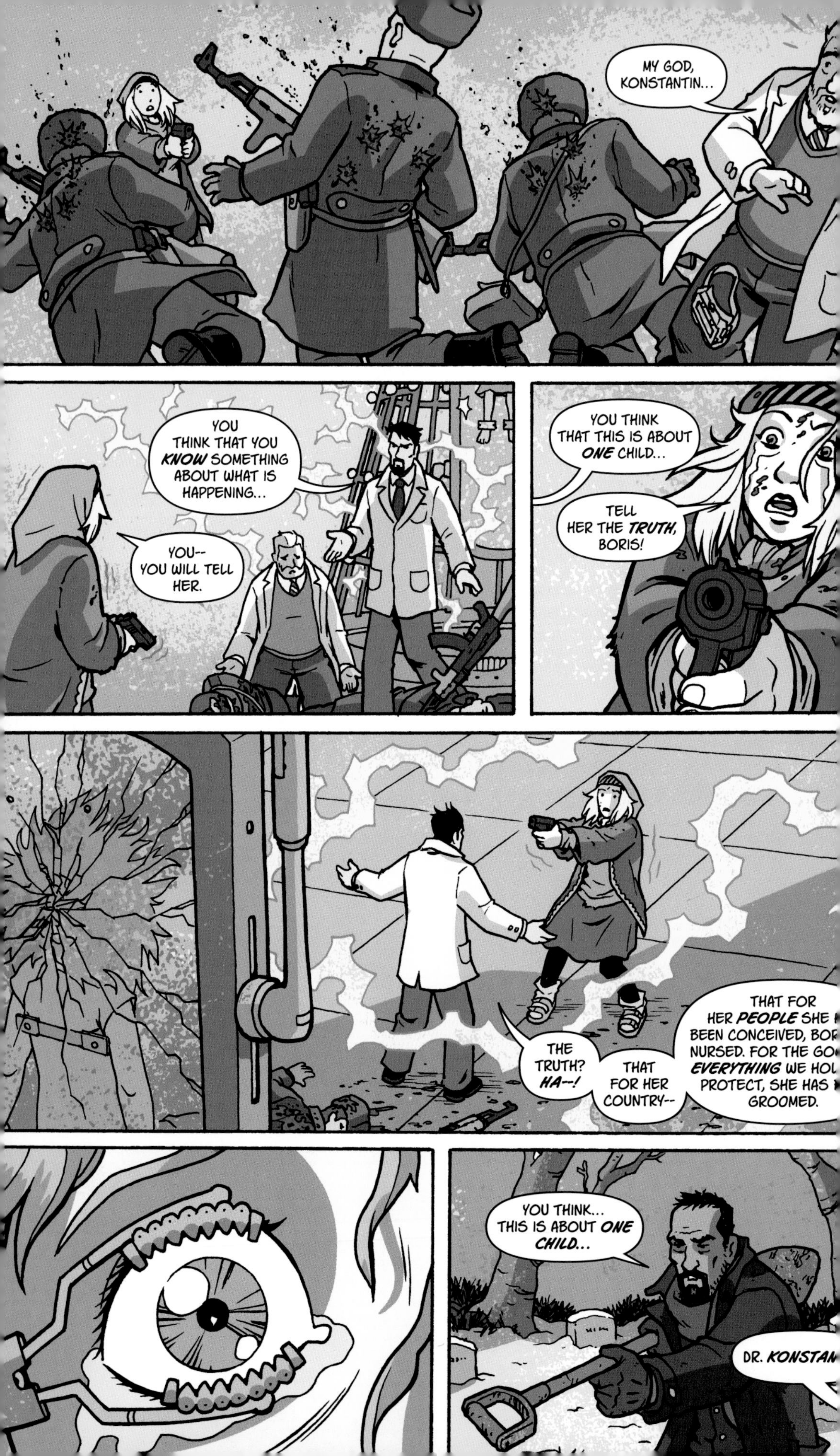
MY GOD, KONSTANTIN...
YOU THINK THAT YOU *KNOW* SOMETHING ABOUT WHAT IS HAPPENING...
YOU-- YOU WILL TELL HER.
YOU THINK THAT THIS IS ABOUT *ONE* CHILD...
TELL HER THE *TRUTH,* BORIS!
THE TRUTH? *HA--!*
THAT FOR HER COUNTRY--
THAT FOR HER *PEOPLE* SHE BEEN CONCEIVED, BOR NURSED. FOR THE GO *EVERYTHING* WE HOL PROTECT, SHE HAS GROOMED.
YOU THINK... THIS IS ABOUT *ONE* *CHILD...*
DR. *KONSTAN*

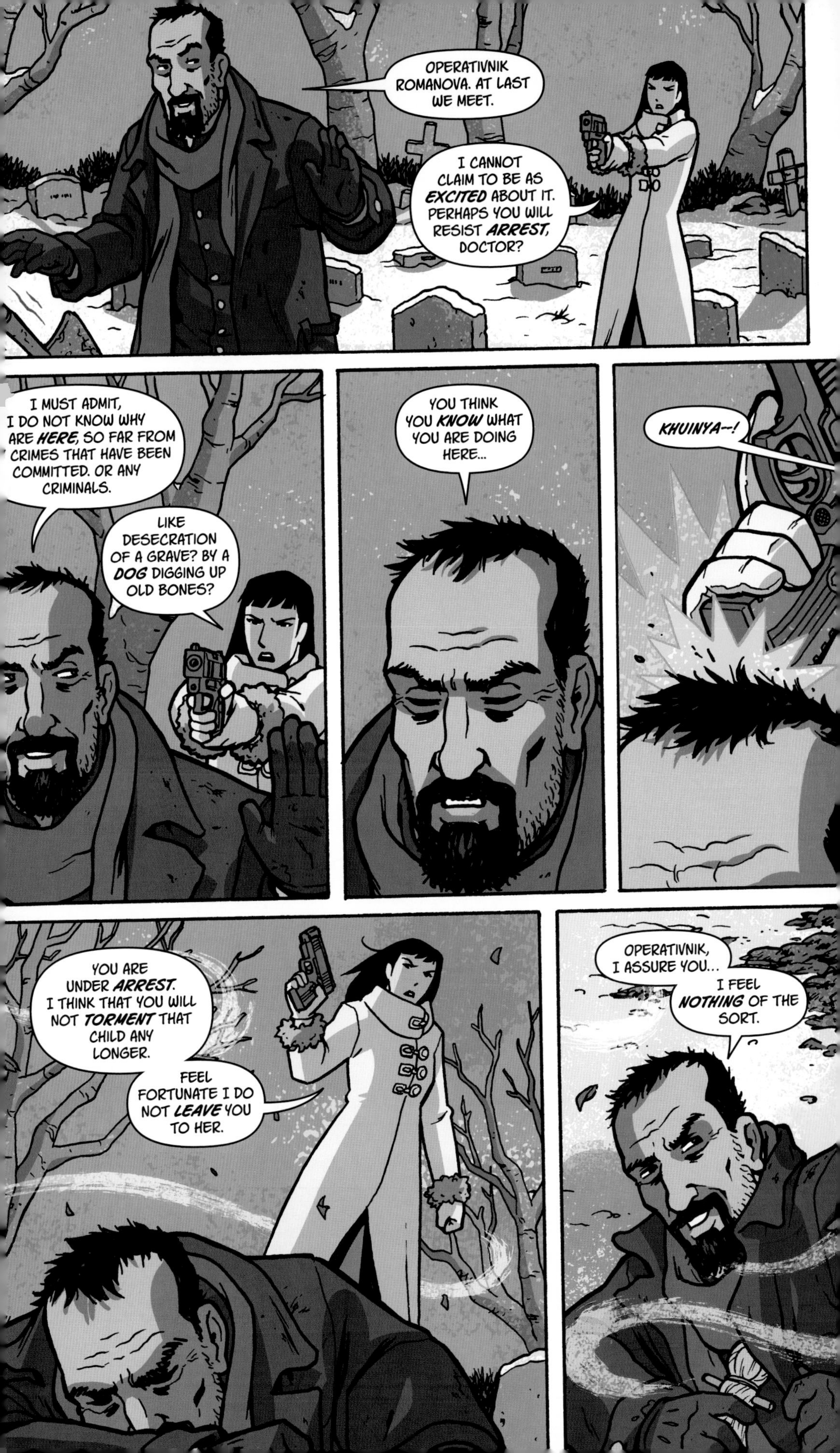
OPERATIVNIK ROMANOVA. AT LAST WE MEET.
I CANNOT CLAIM TO BE AS *EXCITED* ABOUT IT. PERHAPS YOU WILL RESIST *ARREST*, DOCTOR?
I MUST ADMIT, I DO NOT KNOW WHY ARE *HERE*, SO FAR FROM CRIMES THAT HAVE BEEN COMMITTED. OR ANY CRIMINALS.
LIKE DESECRATION OF A GRAVE? BY A *DOG* DIGGING UP OLD BONES?
YOU THINK YOU *KNOW* WHAT YOU ARE DOING HERE...
KHUINYA--!
YOU ARE UNDER *ARREST*. I THINK THAT YOU WILL NOT *TORMENT* THAT CHILD ANY LONGER.
FEEL FORTUNATE I DO NOT *LEAVE* YOU TO HER.
OPERATIVNIK, I ASSURE YOU...
I FEEL *NOTHING* OF THE SORT.

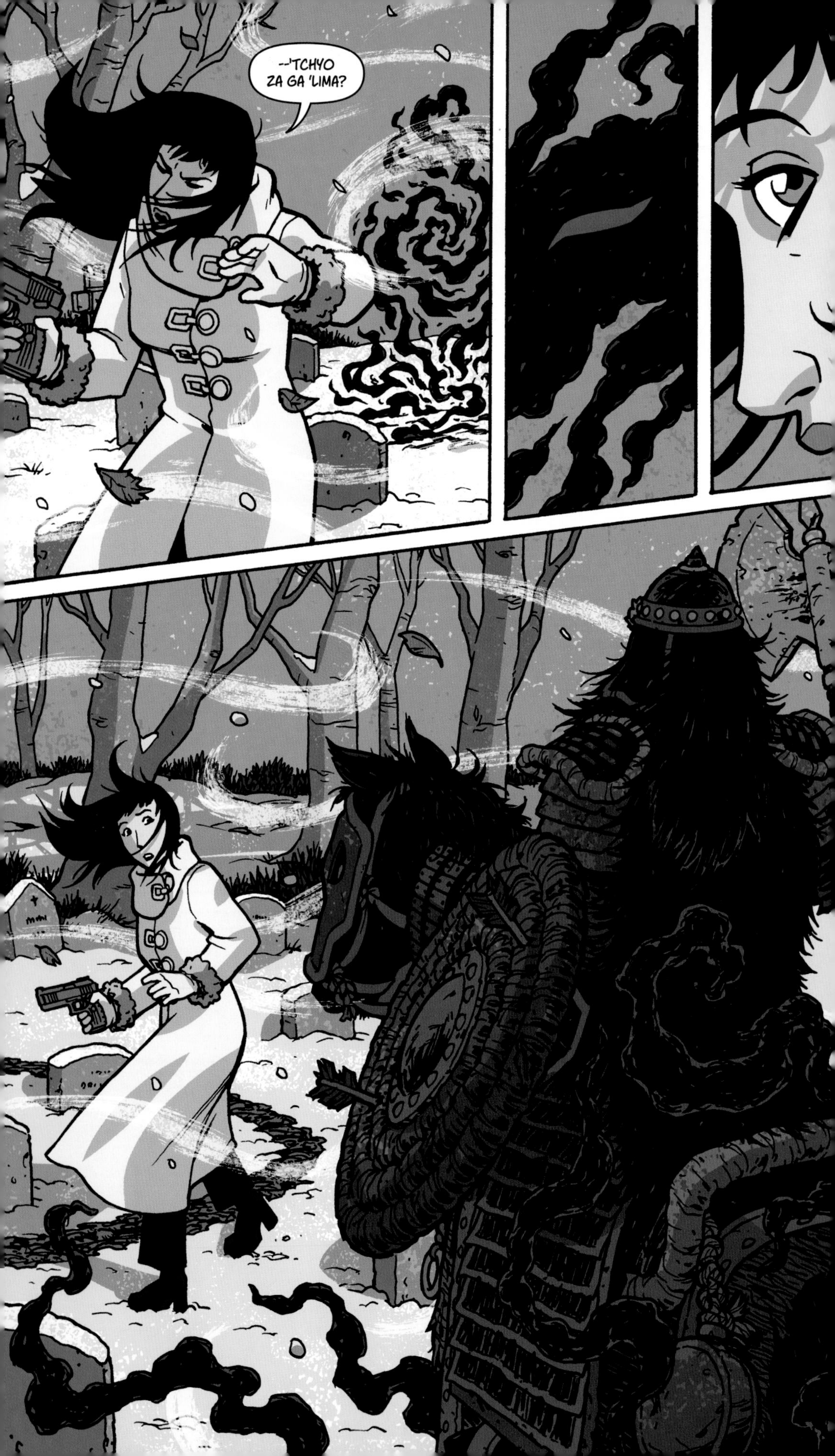
--'TCHYO ZA GA 'LIMA?

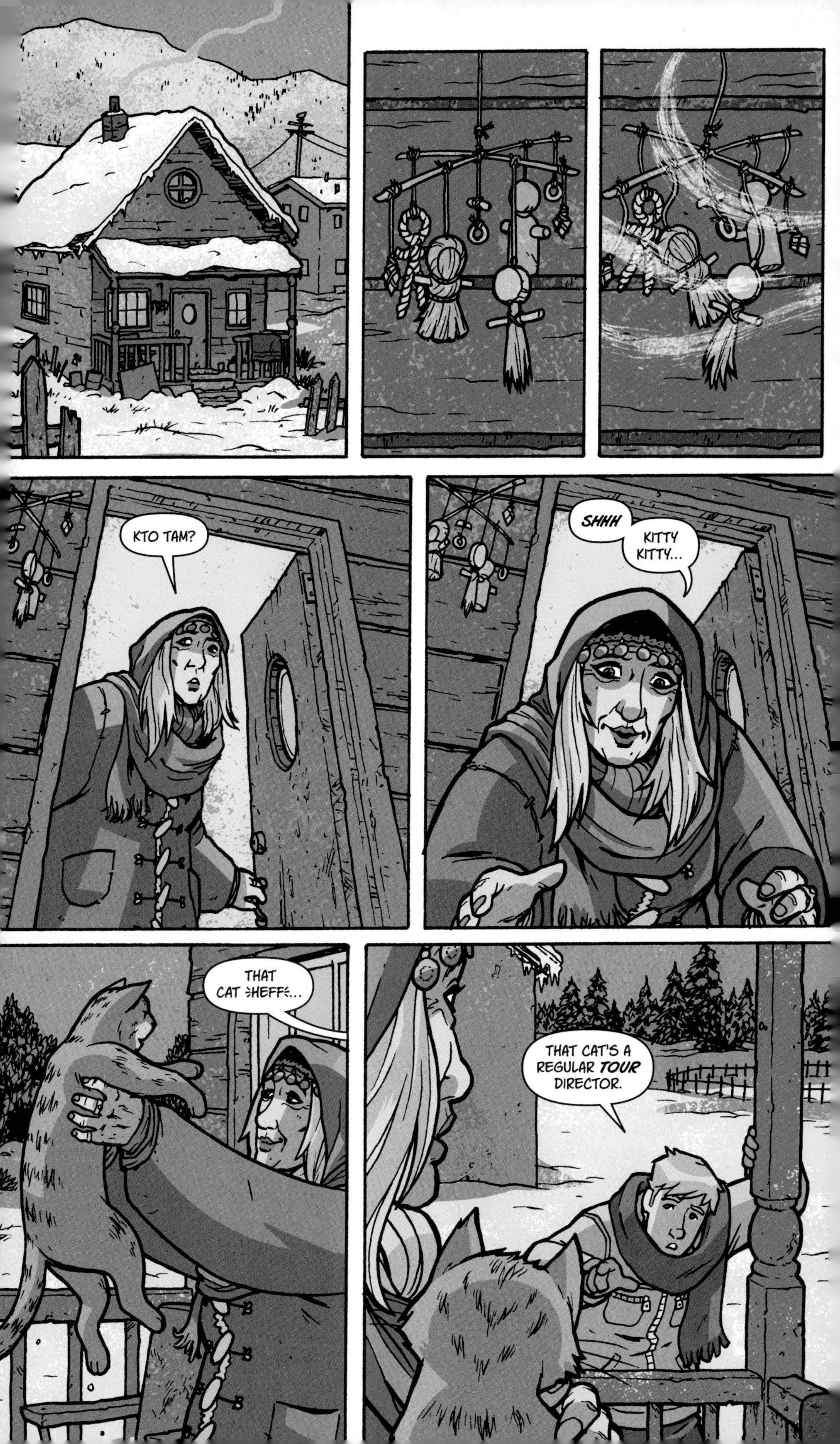
KTO TAM?
SHHH
KITTY KITTY...
THAT CAT HEFF...
THAT CAT'S A REGULAR *TOUR* DIRECTOR.

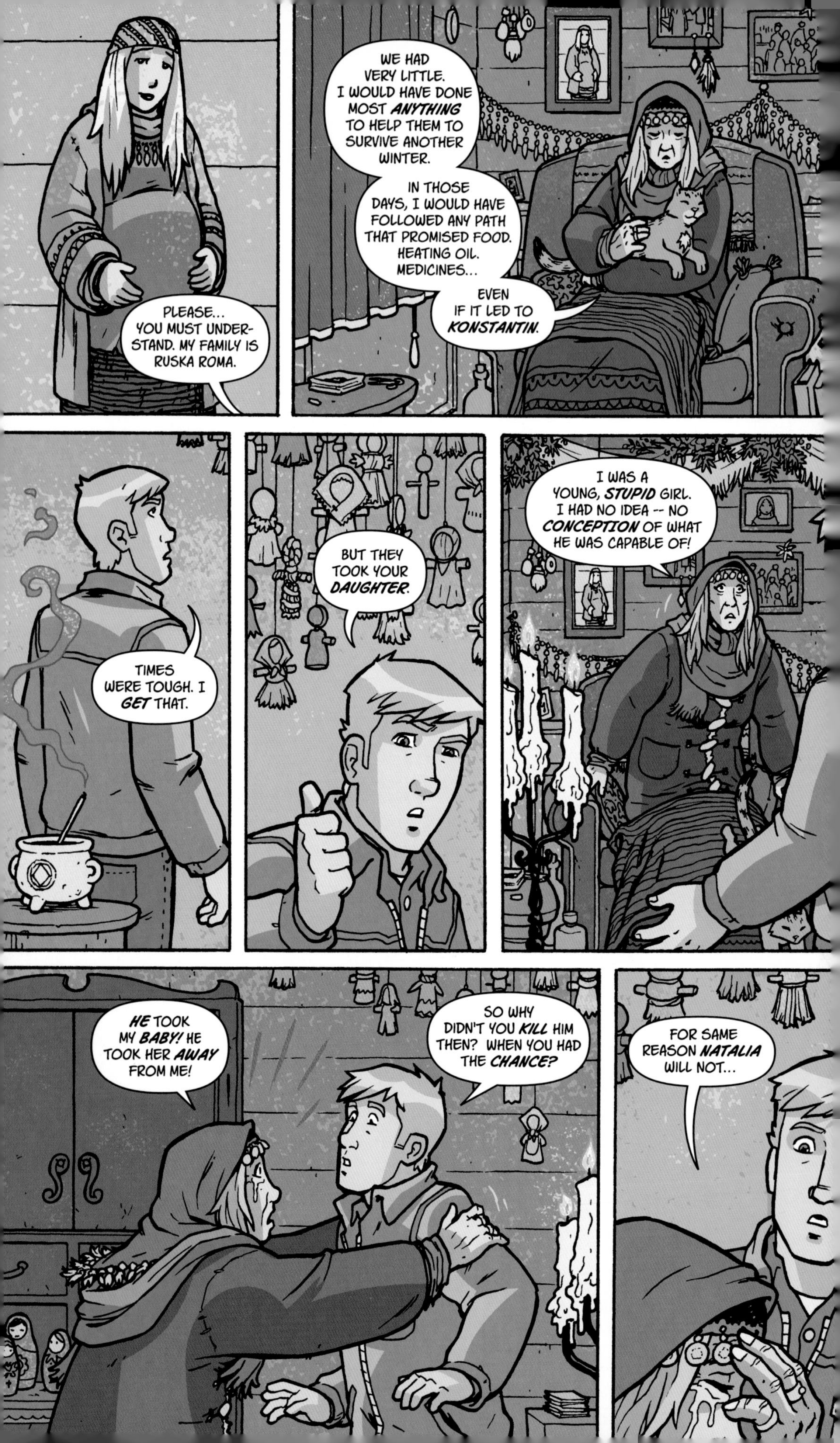
PLEASE... YOU MUST UNDER-STAND. MY FAMILY IS RUSKA ROMA.
WE HAD VERY LITTLE. I WOULD HAVE DONE MOST *ANYTHING* TO HELP THEM TO SURVIVE ANOTHER WINTER.
IN THOSE DAYS, I WOULD HAVE FOLLOWED ANY PATH THAT PROMISED FOOD. HEATING OIL. MEDICINES...
EVEN IF IT LED TO *KONSTANTIN*.
TIMES WERE TOUGH. I *GET* THAT.
BUT THEY TOOK YOUR *DAUGHTER*.
I WAS A YOUNG, *STUPID* GIRL. I HAD NO IDEA -- NO *CONCEPTION* OF WHAT HE WAS CAPABLE OF!
HE TOOK MY *BABY!* HE TOOK HER *AWAY* FROM ME!
SO WHY DIDN'T YOU *KILL* HIM THEN? WHEN YOU HAD THE *CHANCE?*
FOR SAME REASON *NATALIA* WILL NOT...

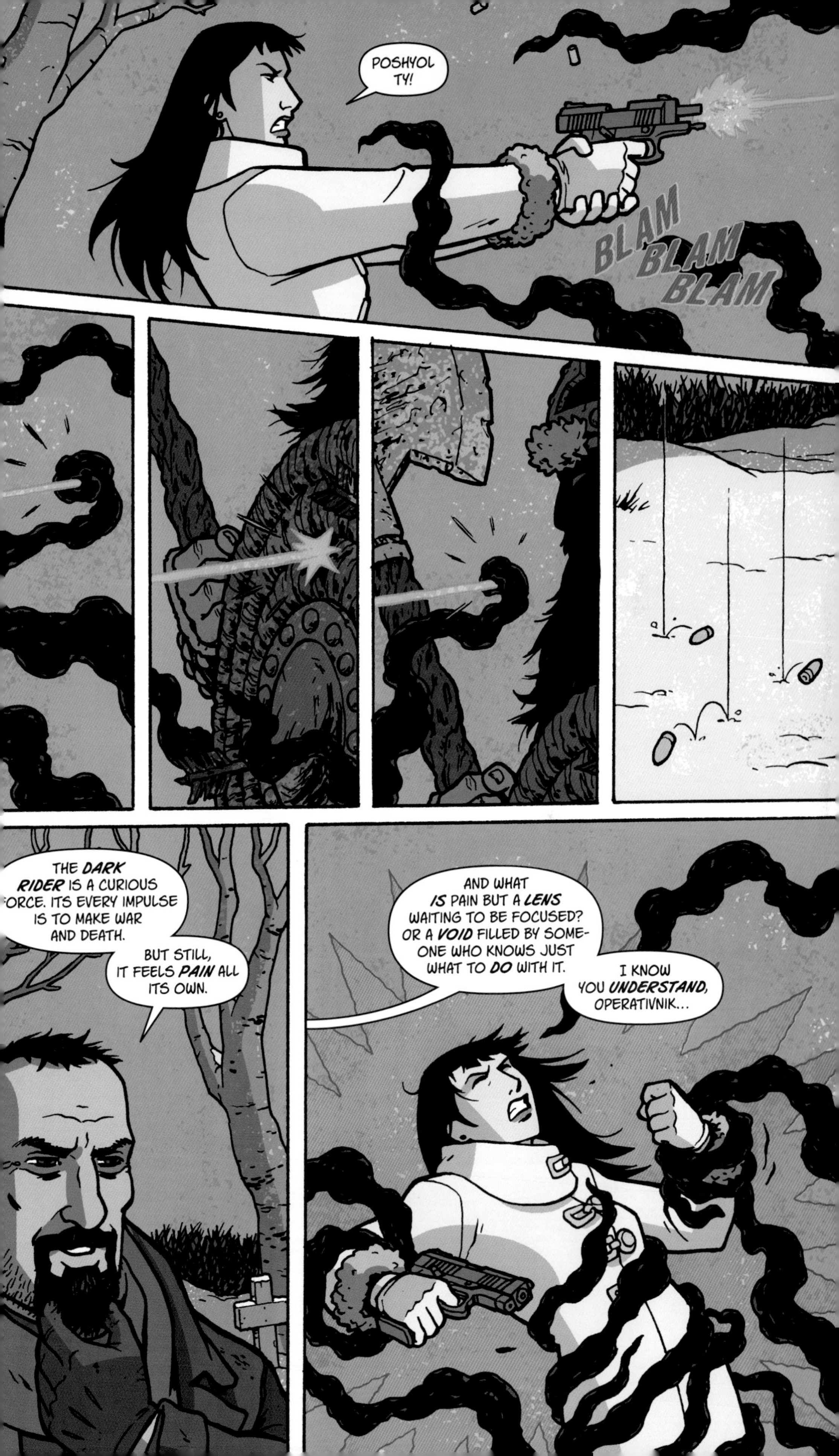

POSHYOL TY!
BLAM BLAM BLAM
THE DARK RIDER IS A CURIOUS FORCE. ITS EVERY IMPULSE IS TO MAKE WAR AND DEATH.
BUT STILL, IT FEELS PAIN ALL ITS OWN.
AND WHAT IS PAIN BUT A LENS WAITING TO BE FOCUSED? OR A VOID FILLED BY SOME-ONE WHO KNOWS JUST WHAT TO DO WITH IT.
I KNOW YOU UNDERSTAND, OPERATIVNIK...

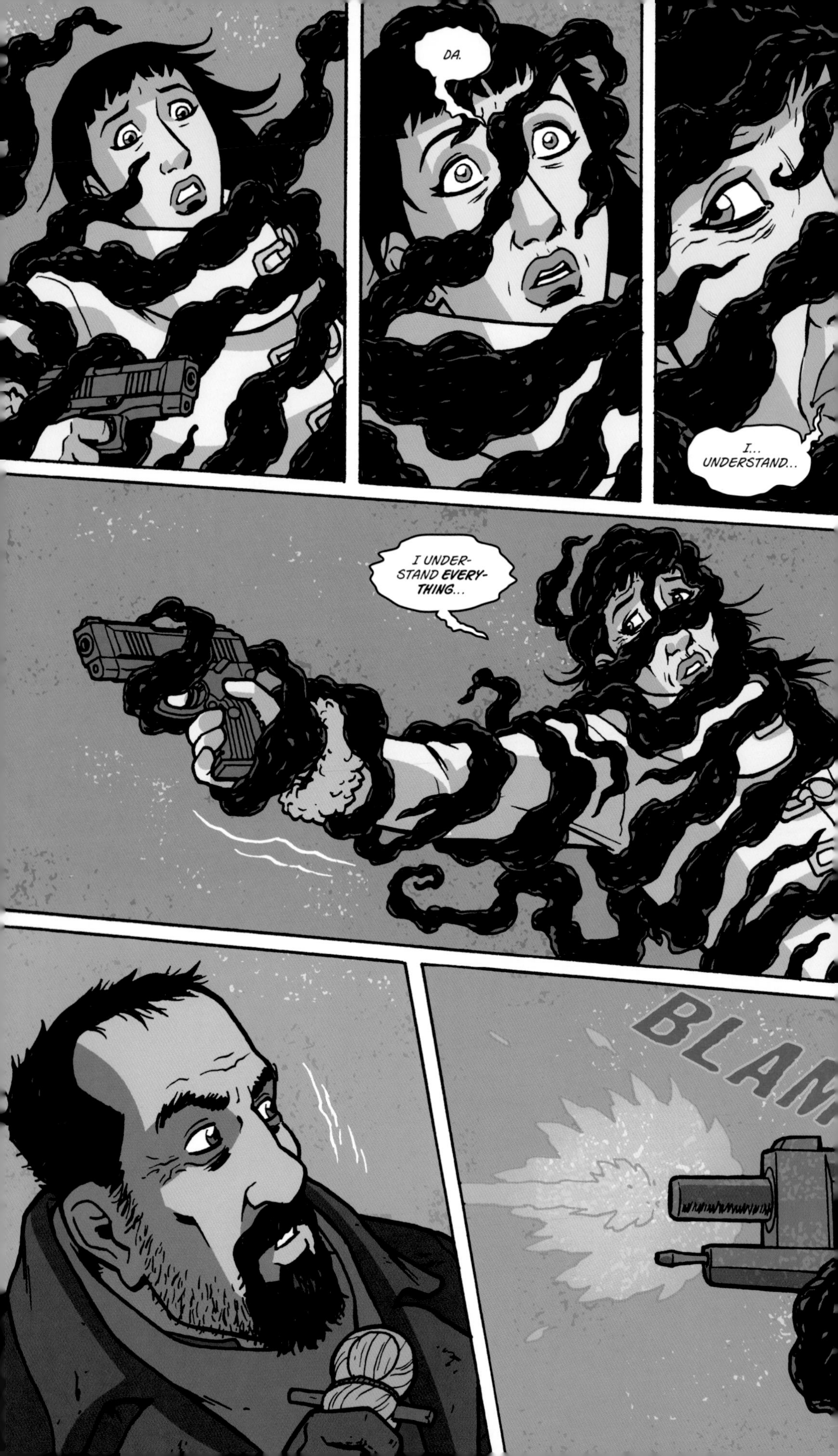
DA.
I... UNDERSTAND...
I UNDER-STAND EVERY-THING...
BLAM

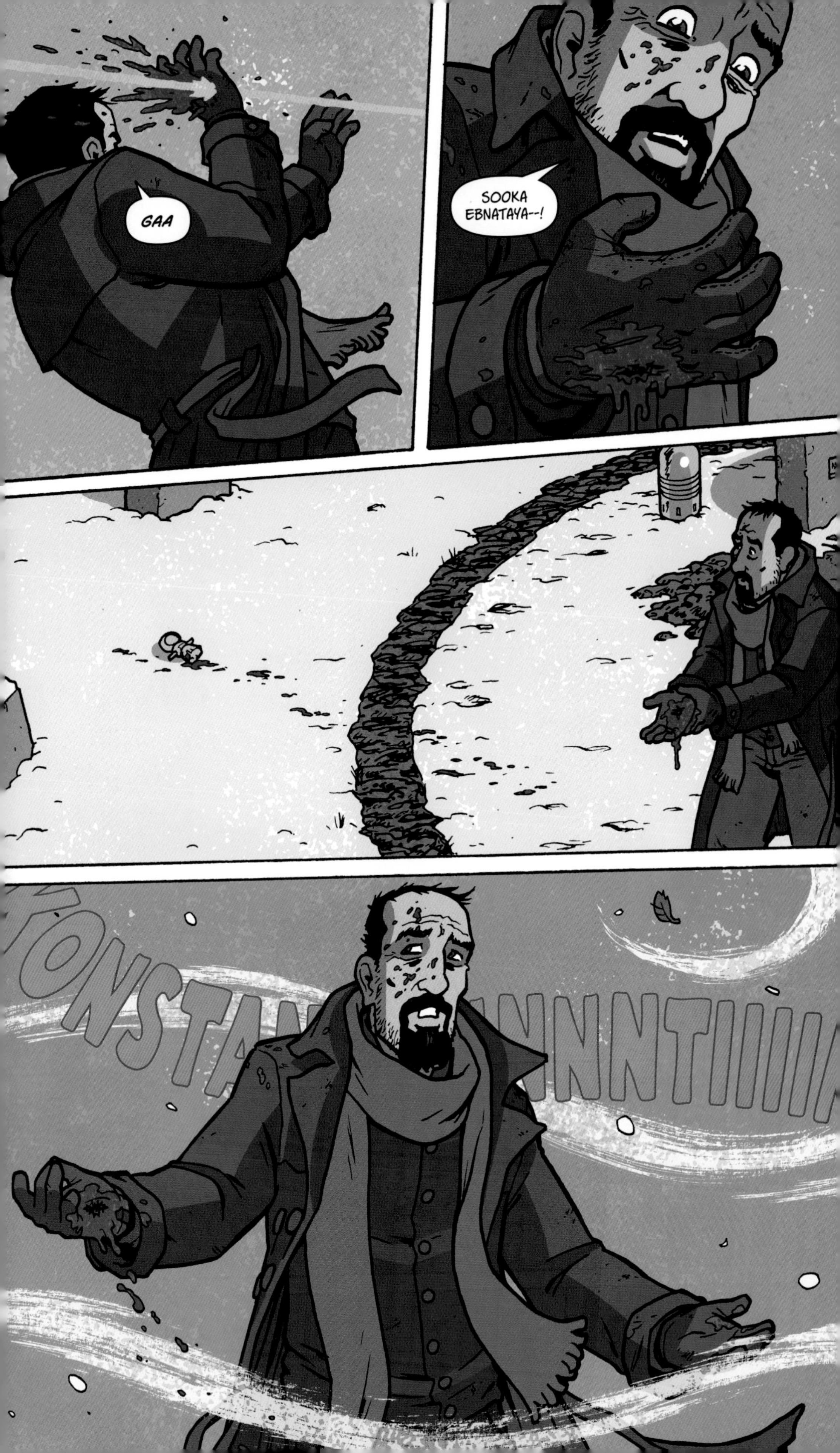
GAA
SOOKA EBNATAYA--!

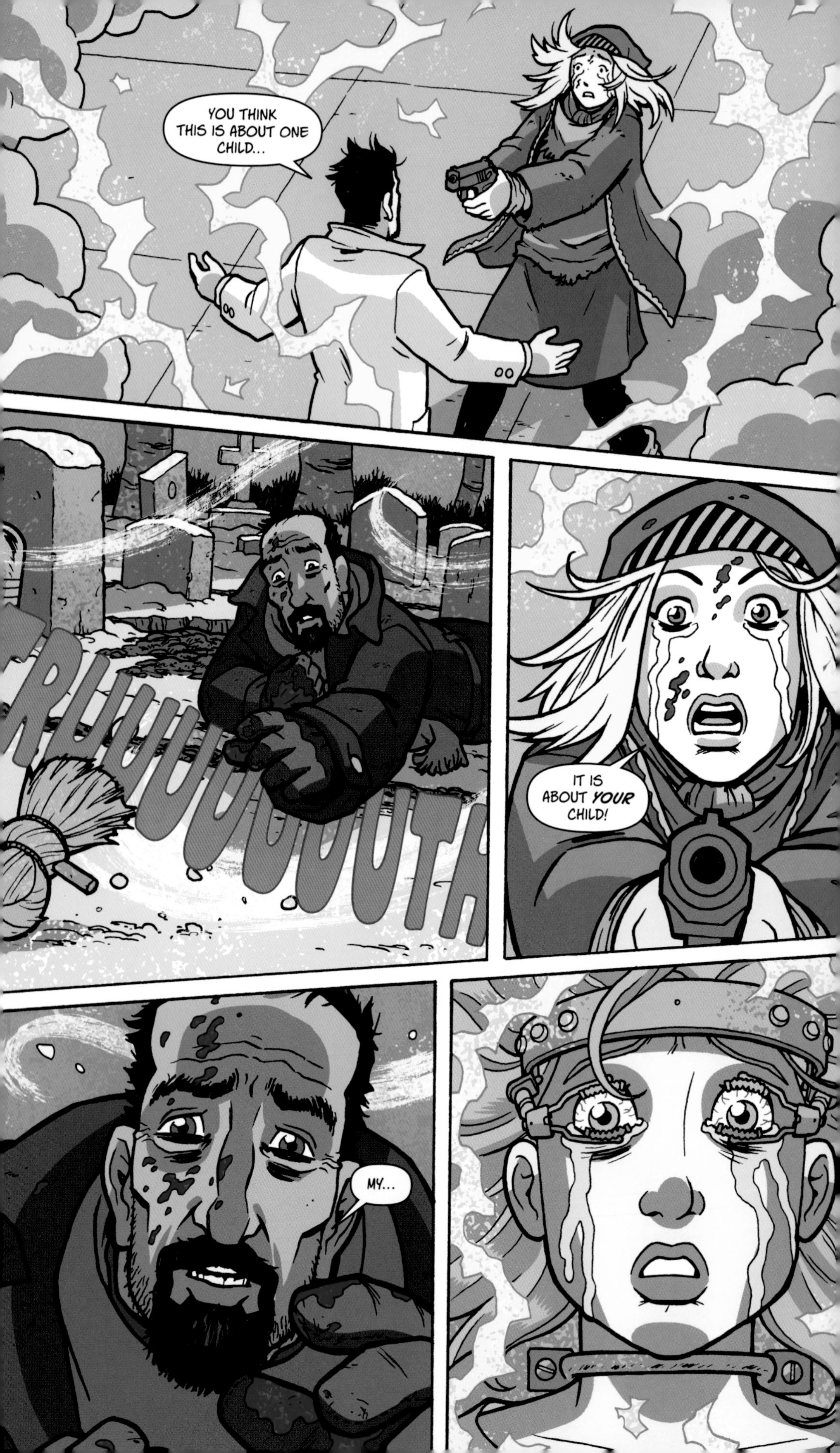
YOU THINK THIS IS ABOUT ONE CHILD...
RUUUUUUUUTH
IT IS ABOUT *YOUR* CHILD!
MY...

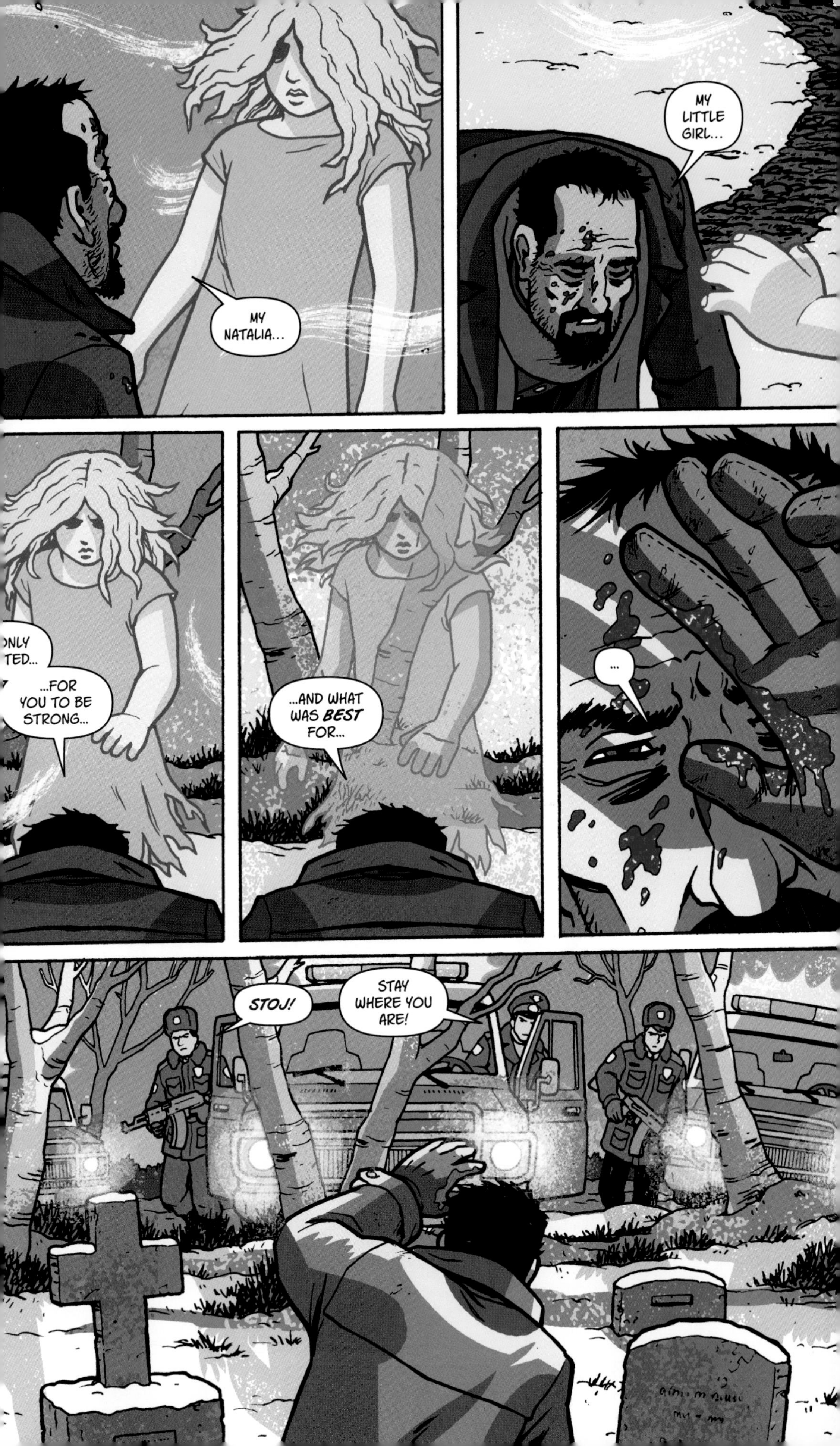
MY NATALIA...
MY LITTLE GIRL...
ONLY ...TED...
...FOR YOU TO BE STRONG...
...AND WHAT WAS *BEST* FOR...
...
STOJ!
STAY WHERE YOU ARE!

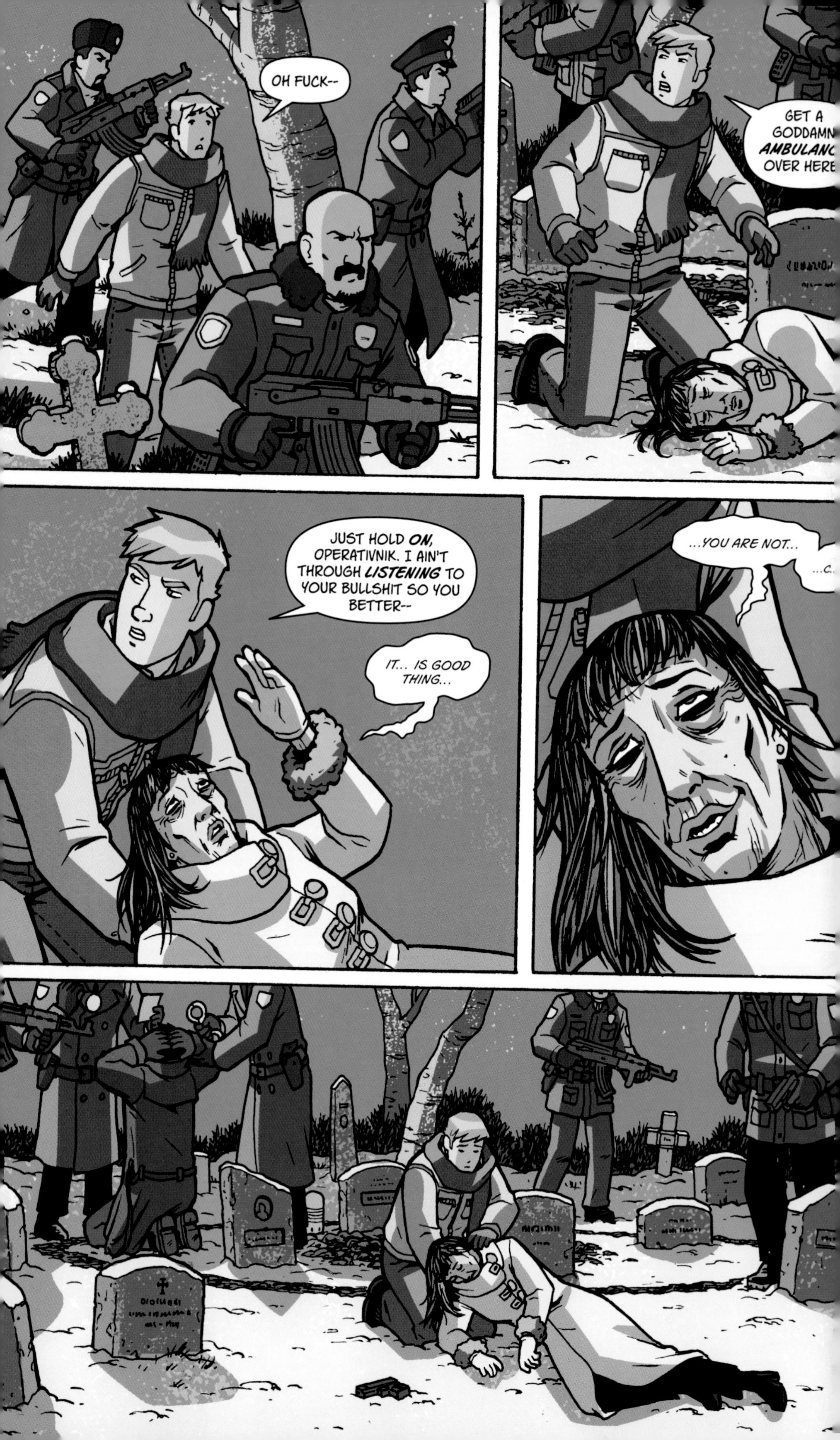
OH FUCK--
GET A GODDAMN AMBULANC OVER HERE
JUST HOLD ON, OPERATIVNIK. I AIN'T THROUGH LISTENING TO YOUR BULLSHIT SO YOU BETTER--
IT... IS GOOD THING...
...YOU ARE NOT...
...C...

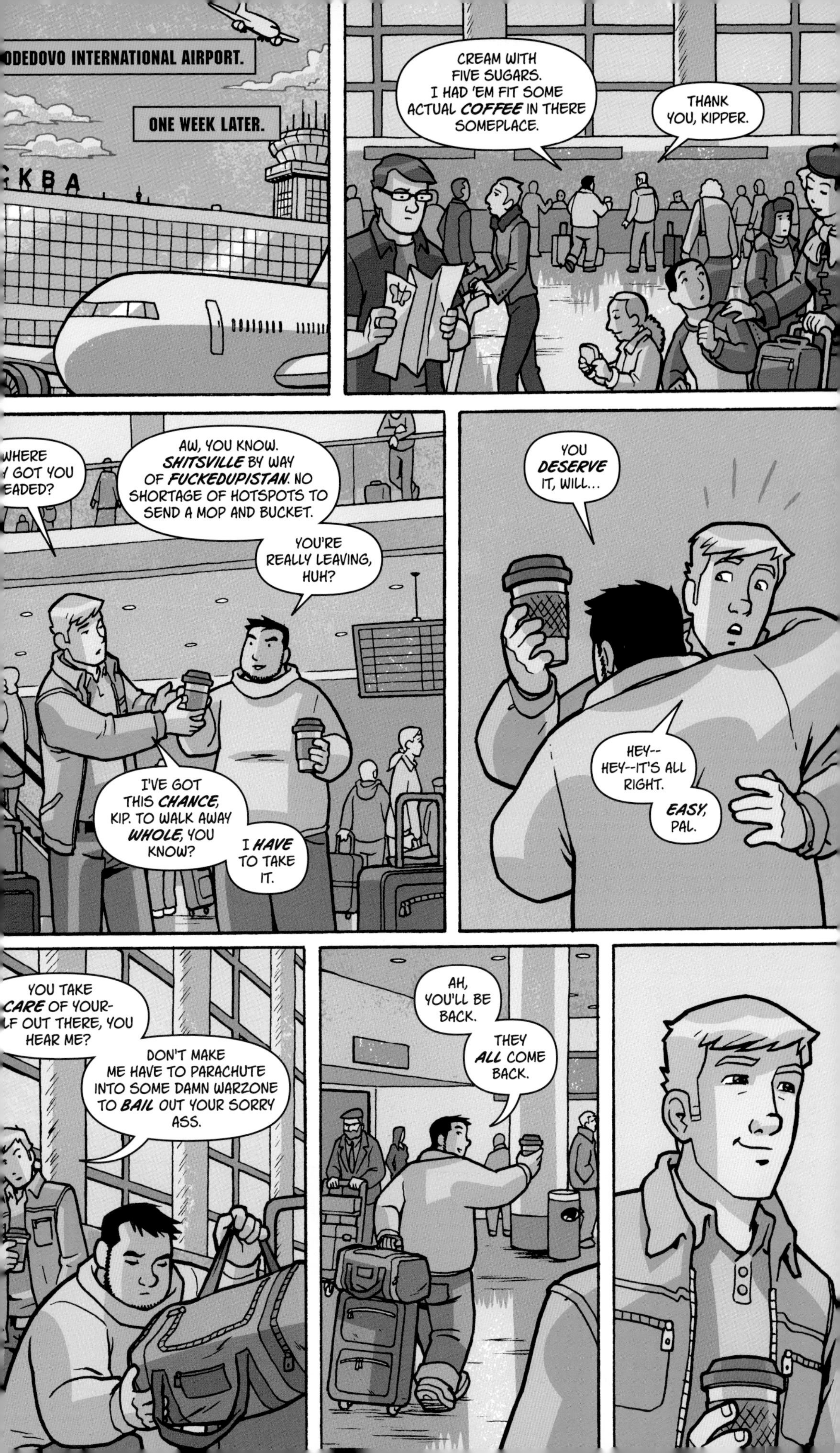
ODEDOVO INTERNATIONAL AIRPORT.
ONE WEEK LATER.
CREAM WITH FIVE SUGARS. I HAD 'EM FIT SOME ACTUAL COFFEE IN THERE SOMEPLACE.
THANK YOU, KIPPER.
WHERE GOT YOU EADED?
AW, YOU KNOW. SHITSVILLE BY WAY OF FUCKEDUPISTAN. NO SHORTAGE OF HOTSPOTS TO SEND A MOP AND BUCKET.
YOU'RE REALLY LEAVING, HUH?
I'VE GOT THIS CHANCE, KIP. TO WALK AWAY WHOLE, YOU KNOW?
I HAVE TO TAKE IT.
YOU DESERVE IT, WILL...
HEY-- HEY--IT'S ALL RIGHT.
EASY, PAL.
YOU TAKE CARE OF YOUR- LF OUT THERE, YOU HEAR ME?
DON'T MAKE ME HAVE TO PARACHUTE INTO SOME DAMN WARZONE TO BAIL OUT YOUR SORRY ASS.
AH, YOU'LL BE BACK.
THEY ALL COME BACK.

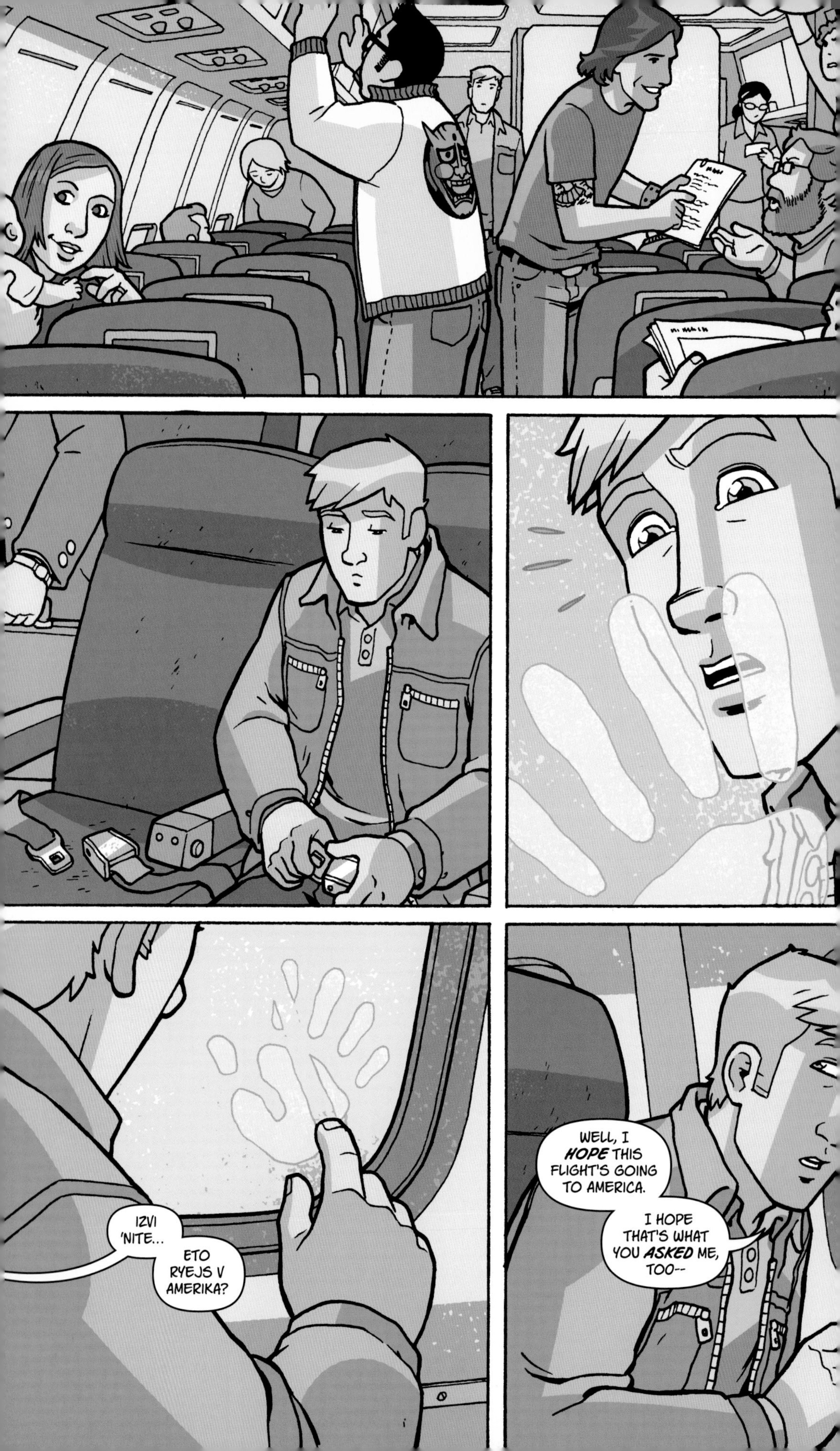
IZVI 'NITE...
ETO RYEJS V AMERIKA?
WELL, I *HOPE* THIS FLIGHT'S GOING TO AMERICA.
I HOPE THAT'S WHAT YOU *ASKED* ME, TOO--

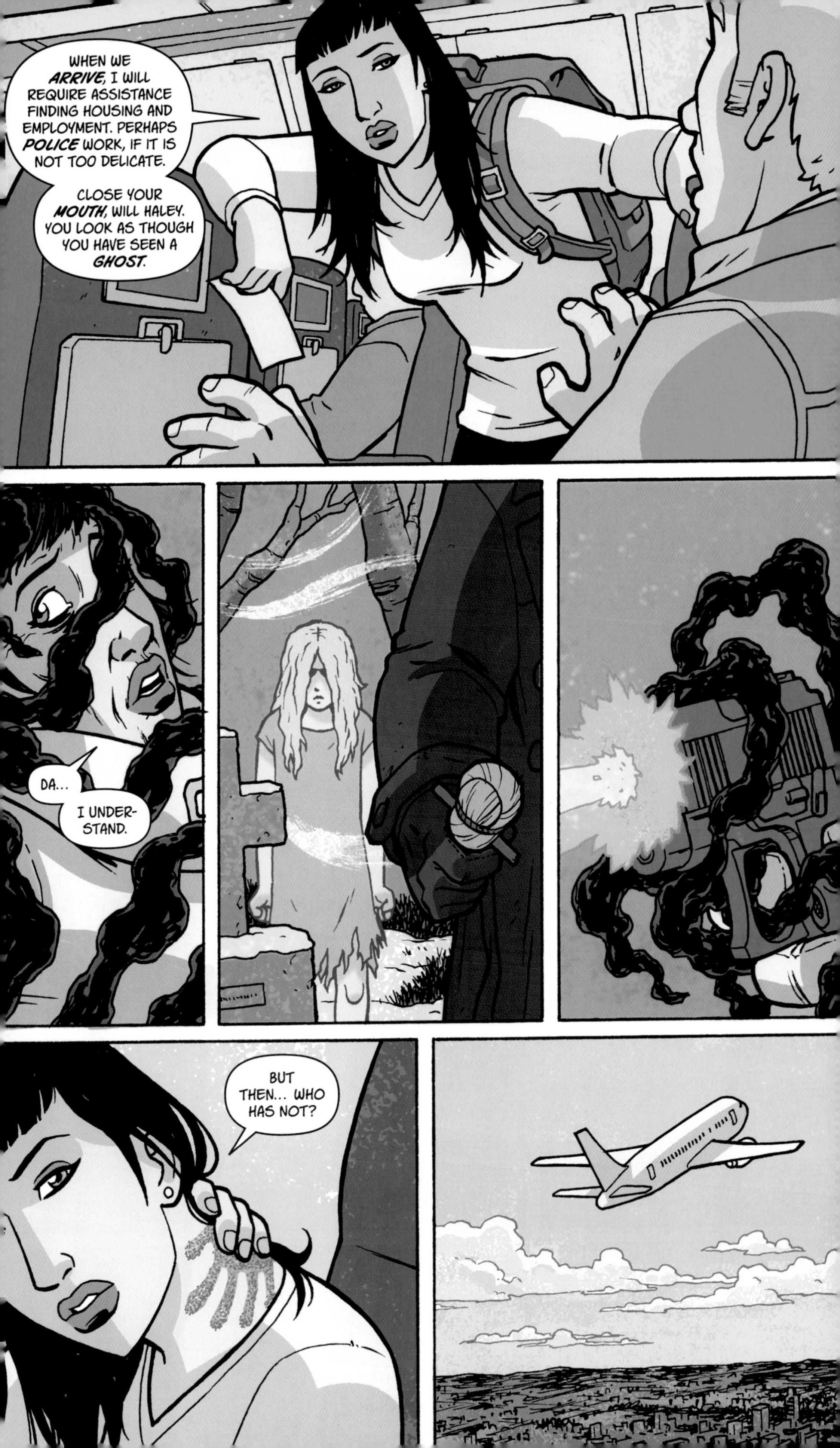

WHEN WE ARRIVE, I WILL REQUIRE ASSISTANCE FINDING HOUSING AND EMPLOYMENT. PERHAPS POLICE WORK, IF IT IS NOT TOO DELICATE.
CLOSE YOUR MOUTH, WILL HALEY. YOU LOOK AS THOUGH YOU HAVE SEEN A GHOST.
DA...
I UNDER-STAND.
BUT THEN... WHO HAS NOT?

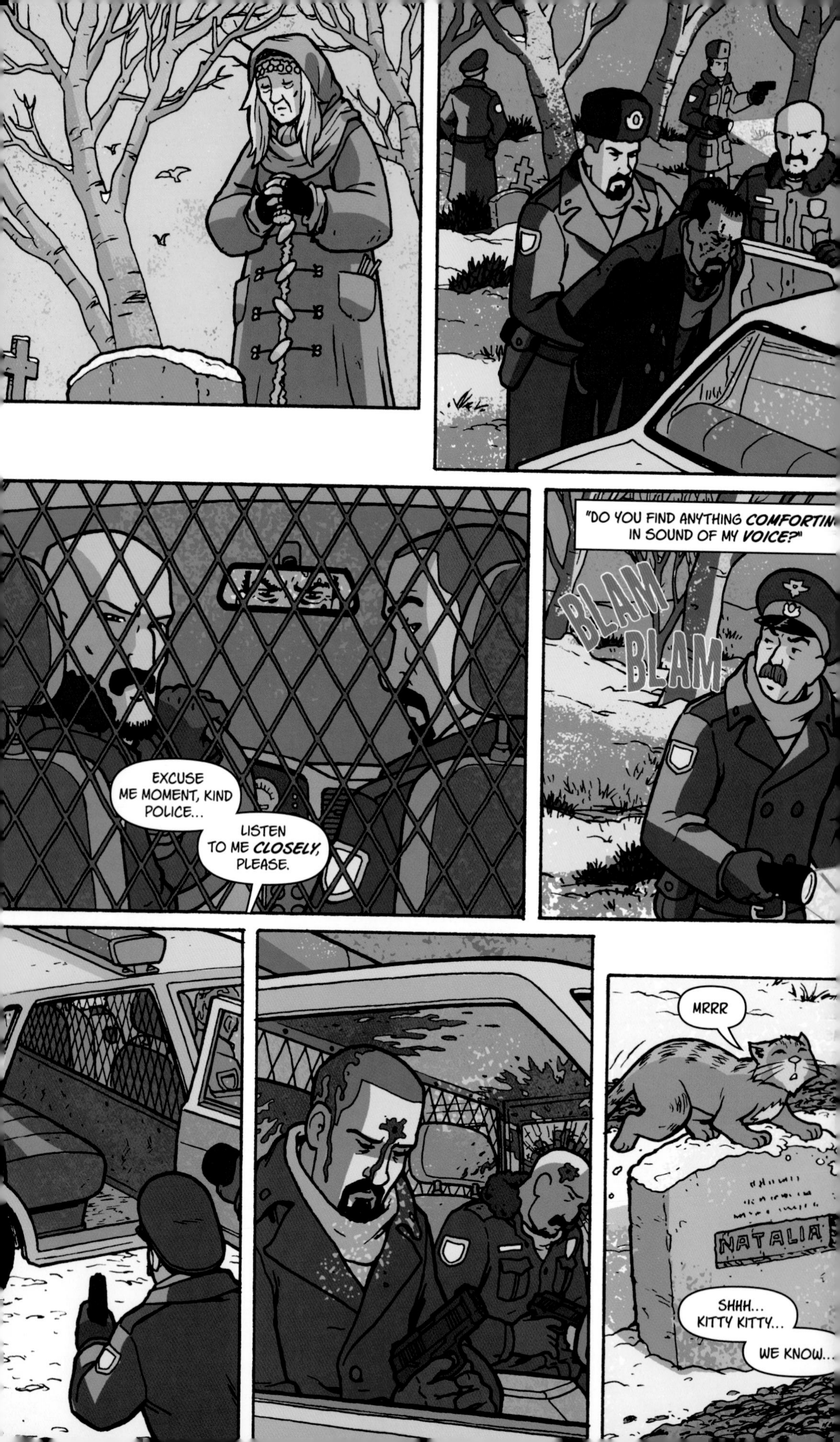
EXCUSE ME MOMENT, KIND POLICE...
LISTEN TO ME CLOSELY, PLEASE.
"DO YOU FIND ANYTHING COMFORTIN
IN SOUND OF MY VOICE?"
BLAM
BLAM
MRRR
NATALIA
SHHH... KITTY KITTY...
WE KNOW...

"NOW I'M NOT, PERSONALLY, PERMITTED TO OFFER YOU ANY SORT OF *DEAL* BEYOND THE TERMS OF YOUR ASYLUM ARRANGEMENTS WITH THE U.S. STATE DEPARTMENT..."

BUT I *AM* HERE TO TELL YOU THAT IF YOU PLAY BALL WITH US, WE'LL PLAY WITH YOU.

"THIS PROPOSAL COMES DIRECTLY FROM THE SECRETARY OF DEFENSE. YOU CAN... REASONABLY ASSUME THE *PRESIDENT* WILL BE BRIEFED ON THESE DEVELOPMENTS IN TIME."

YOU MAY TELL THEM BOTH THEY HAVE MY *UNDYING* LOYALTY.

\S WELL AS MY *GRATITUDE*."

EPT OF DEFENSE
JHSR-608D3

PT OF DEFENSE
HSR-6080

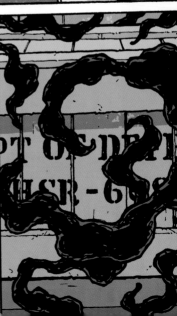

PT OF DEF
HSR-6

TING
DLING

EH?

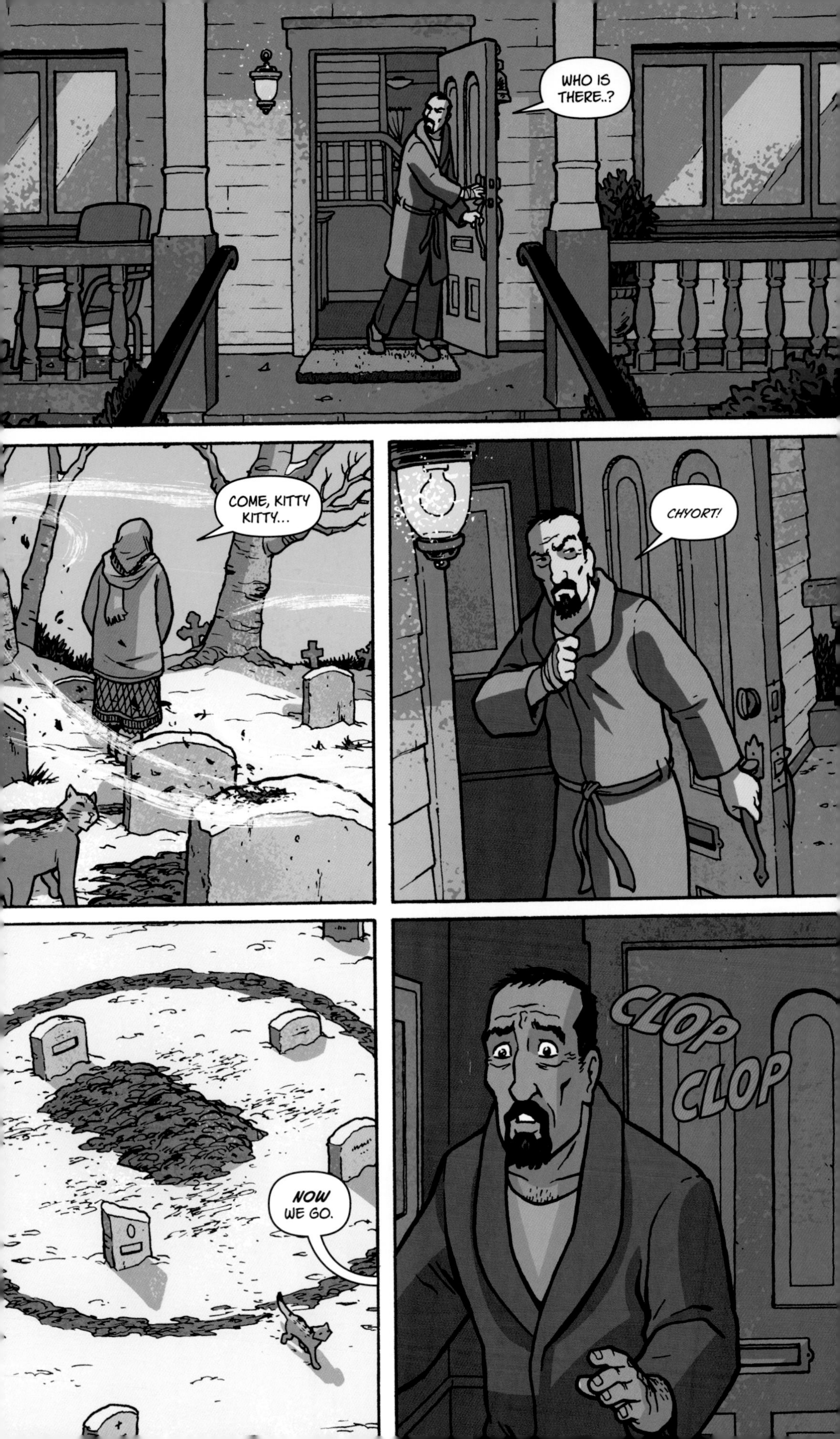
WHO IS THERE..?
COME, KITTY KITTY...
CHYORT!
NOW WE GO.
CLOP CLOP

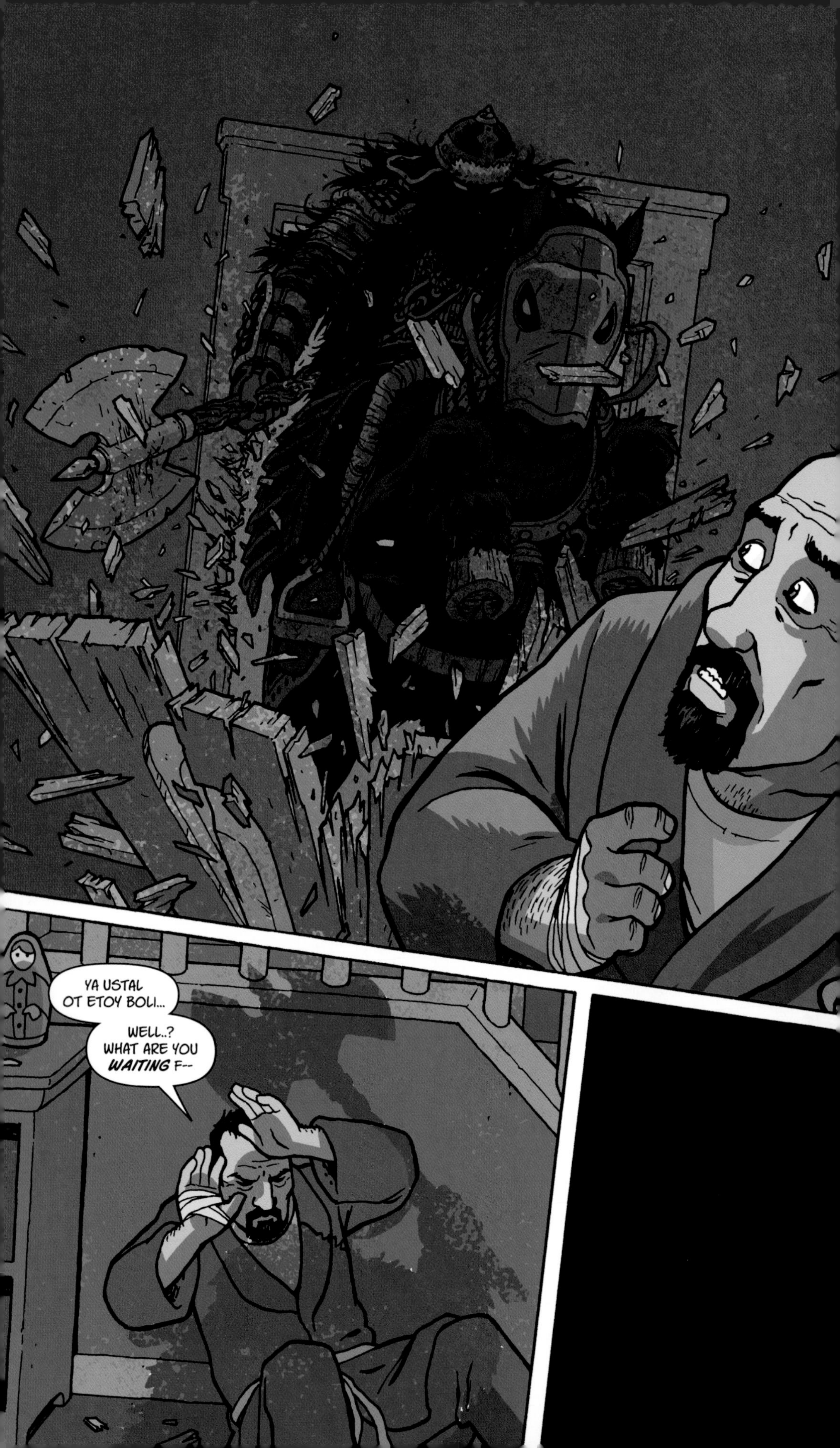
YA USTAL OT ETOY BOLI...
WELL..? WHAT ARE YOU ***WAITING*** F--

FROM THE SCRIPT
TO THE PAGE

The following section illustrates how a comic book page is born, from the script through to the printed page. In taking a closer look at page 23 and 24 of issue #2, the ruminations of everyone involved provide a glimpse into the collaborative nature of the work.

(five panels)

Note: *I had envisioned this layout as having five wide panels down the page, with panel one a bit larger than the next four to further transition us inside the storage facility. But I get ahead of myself...*

Panel 1:

Will and Kip are ready, suits on and lanterns lit. They stand before a large, rusted garage door. Coordinates are screened in big, faded characters above—

ON WALL: C-9

KIP: So what are you THINKING? This Konstantin killer guy. He's using something CHEMICAL, not biological, then. I mean, why ELSE would he send you all the way out to this place?

KIP: You think he's using VX? Sarin gas? Something WORSE, even?

WILL: I think he wants to SHOW us. Beyond that, I have NO idea.

Panel 2:

We're in a dark room. Nothing but pitch black.

WILL (OS; no pointer): All right. Let's hit it.

Panel 3:

Same shot. LIGHT from two flashlight beams seeps into what appears to be a dusty old storage area as the garage door is raised. Will and Kip are holding those flashlights, but we don't have to see much more than their feet/legs at this point as they crouch down and get ready to enter.

KIP: Well, Will... you keep making FRIENDS like these, I'm liable to get a little jealous.

WILL: I keep making friends like THESE...

Panel 4:

Looking up from their POV. We're really tight on what looks like a FACE almost completely lost in shadow. The light source is from a flashlight beam shining from below. It looks like a SKULL in some sort of head dress... only it isn't detailed or clear. Merely lost in scary shadows. Just a hint of what we're going to reveal next page. Something's looming there, in the darkness of this garage.

WILL (OS): ...and my CANCER is gonna be the least of my--

Panel 5:

Looking down on Will (from the skull's POV) as he shines his flashlight up toward our camera. He

looks stunned by what he's discovered. Kip is startled and starts to turn as Will notices something and exclaims, getting his attention.

WILL: Holy shit, Kip.

(one panel)

Panel 1:

FULL PAGE SPLASH. Standing in the darkness, and now revealed by the pooled power of their lanterns, is a MASSIVE TARTAR SKELETON. Reassembled like a museum dinosaur exhibit and mounted on the skeletal remains of his war horse, arm raised like a menacing club. This should be a startling, frightening image. I think we might want to include Will and Kip in the foreground, for scale as much as anything else. This... thing towers over them both!

This is one of my favorite moments in the entire book. The discovery of the Tartar Warrior skeleton was not part of my original story outline at all. We were always going to introduce one of these things—the Dark Rider—later on, teasing them first in the flashback to the Dosvidanya facility circa 1972 as a frightening precursor to having one of them eventually freed from captivity in Red Square.

But as I continued scripting the series, I felt like the reveal of just what the Dosvidanya Projekt was about needed an even slower, more methodical roll out. And that towering skeletal image of an ancient badass warrior, still mounted on his armored horse, still majestic and even more horrifying as an assembled fossil of his former self, just hit me.

It reminds me of the Tyrannosaurus Rex skeleton I'd sit under for hours after running off on my own from school field trips to New York City's Museum of Natural History when I was a little kid. The sort of stuff that really inspired my imagination at an early age. The whole reveal when they pry that garage door open and shine their flashlights into the darkness feels like a Hardy Boys mystery, just with cussing... and less Shaun Cassidy.

It was also a great place for more Will and Kip banter, which was some of the most fun and disarming stuff to write. The joking around before they open the door and let the light spill in is gallows humor, really, which I'd imagine one has to have in this line of work.

The scene takes place in a town called Dzerzhinsk, which is about 400 KM outside of Moscow and one of the most polluted places on earth. Home to countless chemical weapons dumps and decaying industrial complexes, it seemed the perfect place to stash any number of Cold War-era secrets.

☆ JOE HARRIS

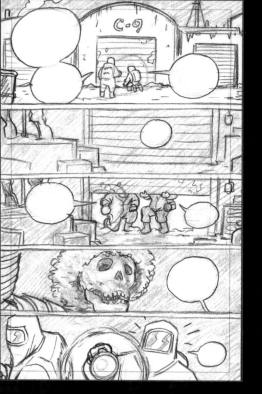

Here's a look at my thumbnail sketches for this scene. I put a decent amount of effort into these five-inch-tall drawings because I like to nail down all the major components before committing to a page layout. It's common for me to go through several versions of a panel before I find one where the shape, camera angle, composition, poses, dialogue flow and everything else fit together just right. I'd rather find out I'm not happy with a page at this stage rather than after I've drawn it on a nice big sheet of bristol board.

I'm also able to show these thumbnails to the writer so I can be confident I captured the moment that he had in mind. Once I get Joe's blessing, I print out an enlarged version of the thumbnail that I can trace onto a piece of Bristol, using a lightbox my dad built me years ago (thanks Dad!).

I don't have any penciled versions of my pages to show off because I've started inking while I'm still on the lightbox. Sometimes I still need to tighten up my drawings in pencil to make sure the anatomy, perspective and details are right. But, if possible, I'll grab my pens and go straight to ink.

As for this scene in particular... well, I always knew horses were tough to draw. This big reveal taught me that horse skeletons are even trickier! Have you ever looked at the neck of a horse skeleton? I partly covered this one with armor for a good reason (aside from the obvious reason of it being a battle horse).

Thankfully I had the Internet on my side. I was able to track down over a dozen good photos of horse skel-

etons from various angles. Having multiple angles to study was key. That allowed me to understand the structure of the bones and adjust the angle to suit the shot I wanted, not being forced to copy a pose directly from the photo reference.

The same goes for a lot of things in this book and is my justification for spending so many hours hunting for images of Red Square and the various weapons and uniforms seen throughout. And, of course, the Tartar/Mongol clothing and armor you see here.

If you have a keen eye for detail, you may have noticed that this skeleton is not dressed like the Dark Rider we saw unleashed later in the book. Well, at last count, there were still four unopened canisters. I'm betting this guy will be just as angry when he gets out!

☆ STEVE ROLSTON

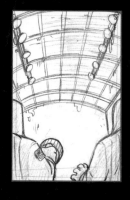

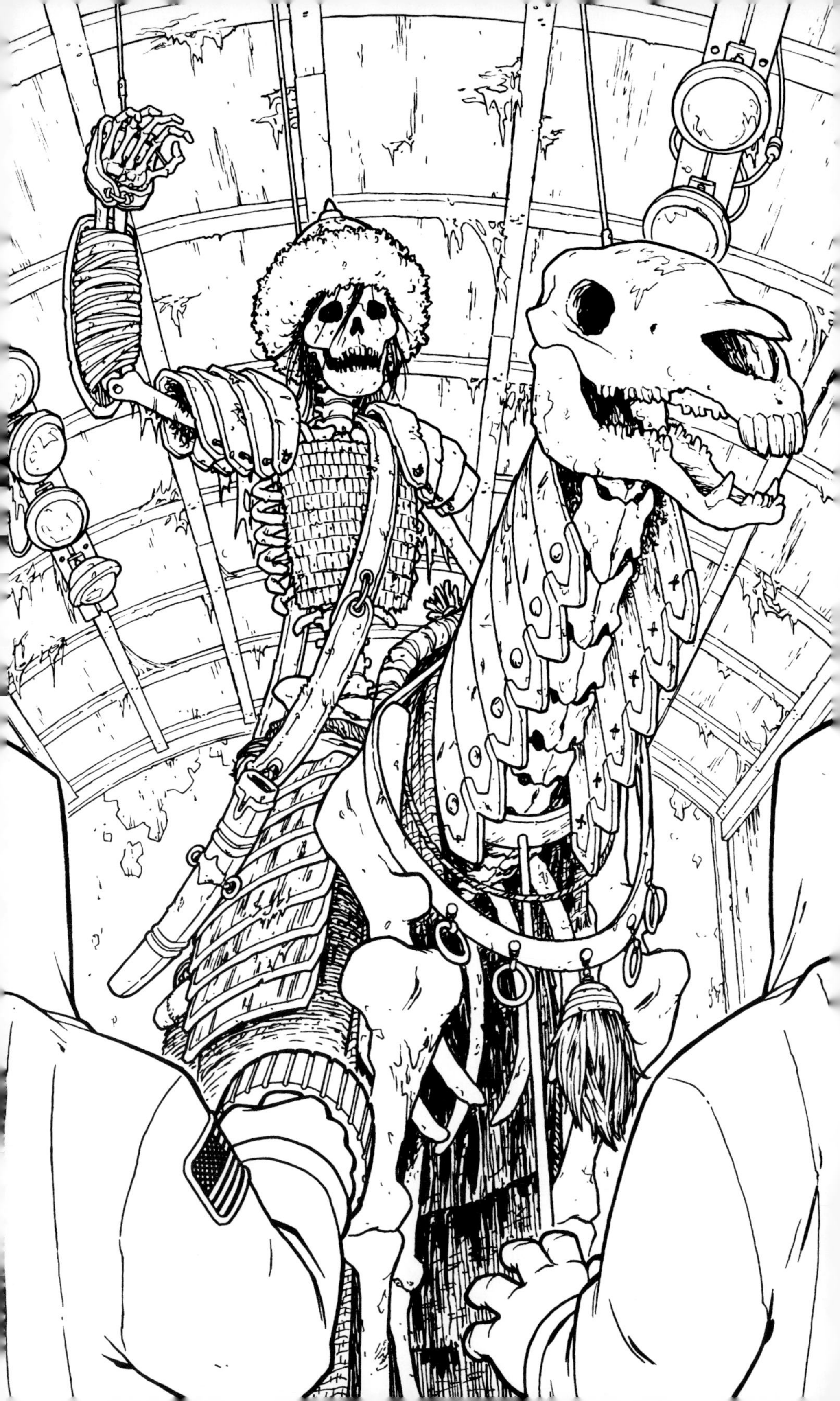

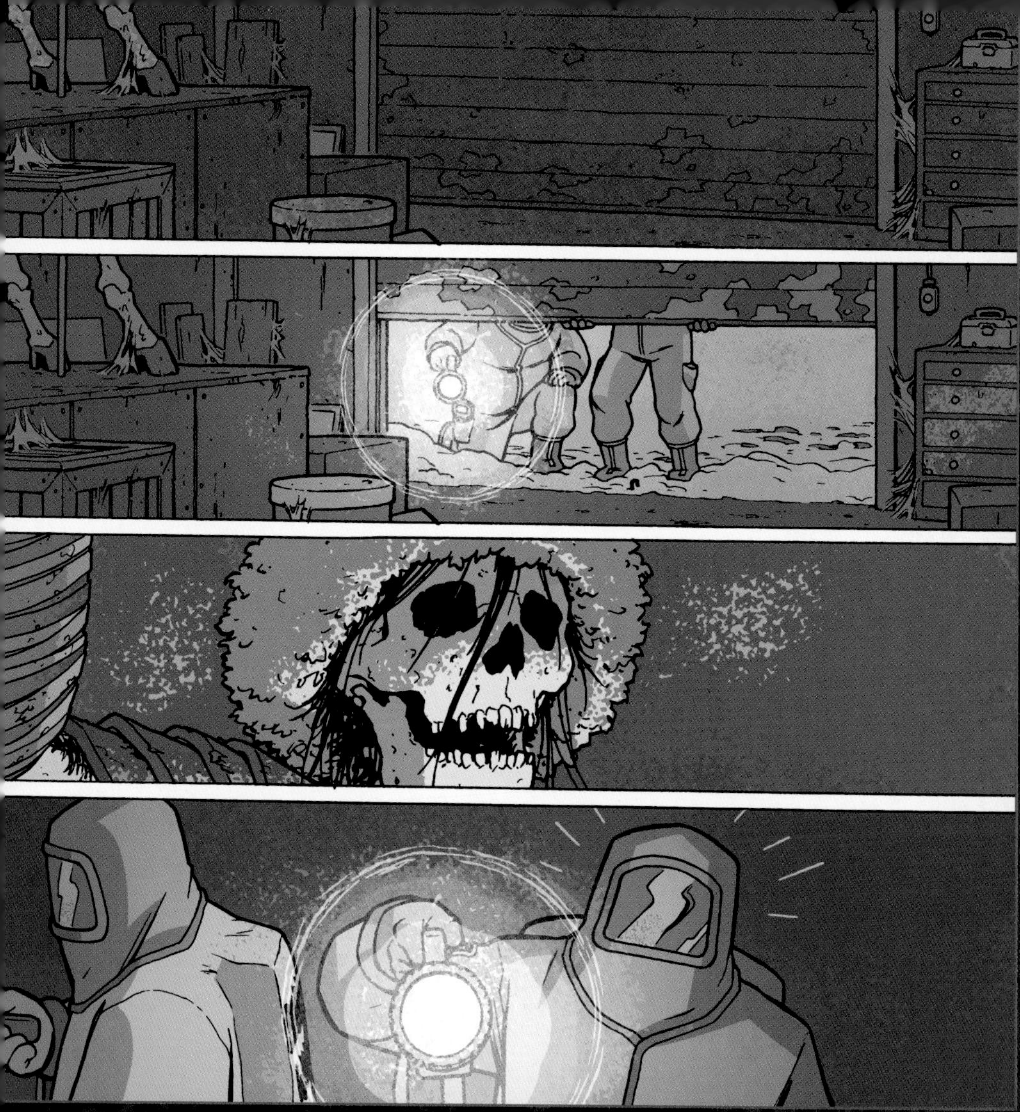

As the colorist for Ghost Projekt, I worked closely with artist Steve Rolston to create the finished color artwork, often using his notes ınd suggestions. For my part, I tried to accentuate he dramatic tensions and scene breaks with lighting.

For the series' recurring wind gusts and lighting efects, like the flashlight's glare here, Steve would send an additional page of just that one element, o be laid down over the regular artwork using my own color choices. This collaborative effort helped make the final artwork appear very cohesive. Also, often "dropped lines out," or turned certain lines originally inked in black by Steve into color lines, ike the excitement marks in this scene. Again, this effect was intended to make the finished art seem completely unified.

To help Steve's characters really pop, I used a clean, one-cut" shading style for most of the characters ınd foreground objects in the series. For Steve's simlified, consistent drawing style, I find this method of coloring works better than excessive rendering, matching the confident linework with equally bold cuts of shadow and light. Not surprisingly, this kind of simplification works great in comics, where the reader's mind creates the closure necessary to perceive the images as active, mobile, and three-dimensional.

For the background elements, however, I wanted something with a bit more depth and variety, so I used a dry-brush style to complete the "animated series" vibe established with the characters. In this scene, I think the grainy, dry-dust texturing served the skeletal surprise especially well.

Throughout the series, I tried to use color to evoke more mystery, more excitement, and more danger than could've been implied in just black and white pages. As a longtime fan of Steve's work, it was an honor to join him and writer Joe Harris on this "Projekt!"

☆ DEAN TRIPPE

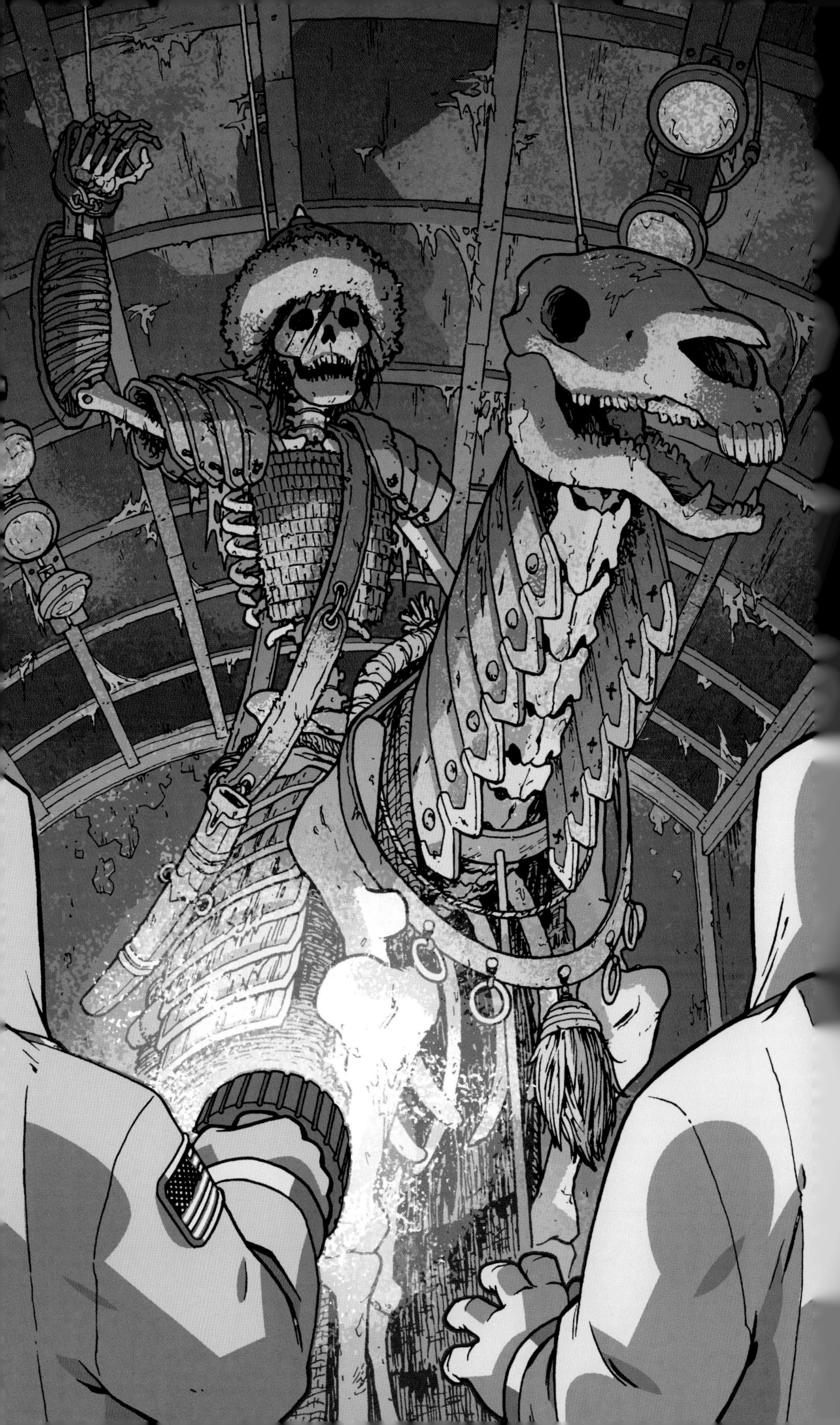

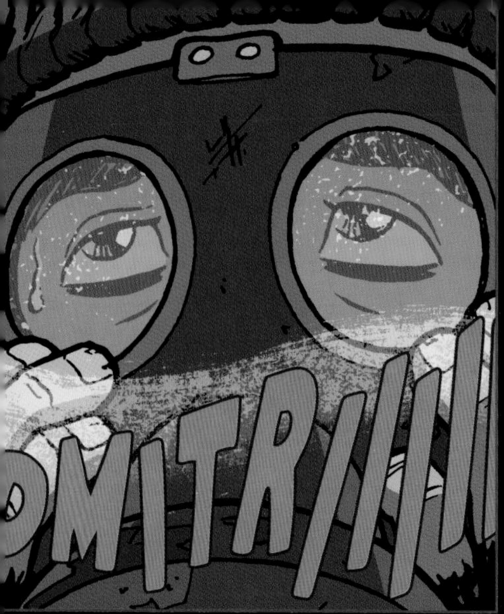
MITRIIII

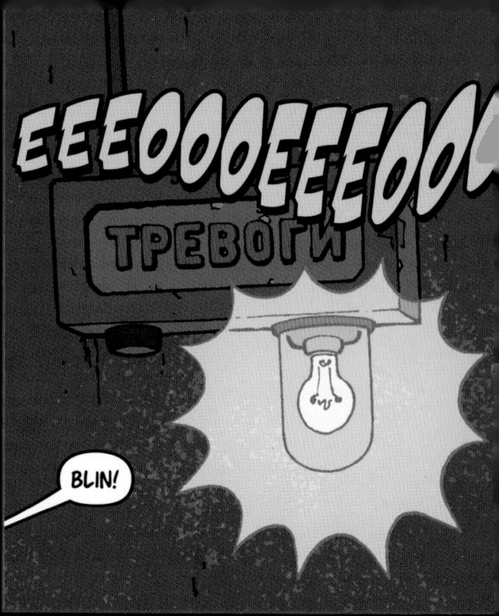
EEEOOOEEEOO
ТРЕВОГИ
BLIN!

Lettering this AWESOME series really gave me a chance to try out some new fun stuff with SFX and other creative lettering, such as the "swirl-ng ghost text." This scene in particular, however, lidn't require much work to letter. Just copy and paste the text on one layer, then draw some balloons and tails in Adobe InDesign on a layer below it and boom! Done.

_et me throw out some examples of the real fun I had working on this book.

Here are examples of scenes using the "swirling ghost text," as Joe calls it in his scripts. The idea is hat it represents the voice people hear when near he source of the ghost. Steve did a separate layer of brushy wind effects, which I would take and drop nto Adobe Illustrator . For most of them I tried my hardest to draw a line that is parallel to Steve's brush line, and then drop the text into that line. For a fev of them, I had to create my own line because the tex would get too distorted.

For the color, I pulled the red Dean used for th hand print on Dmitri's forehead at the end of issu one, and kept it consistent throughout the series. like doing this for dialogue caption boxes and SF whenever possible, so the reader can visually ti the dialogue or SFX. Here I tried to tie the sound ef fect text to the scene with color.

Once I'm done with all my lettering and sound ef fects, I send the issue off to the editors to proo then any corrections are made and the book get sent off to print!

☆ DOUGLAS E. SHERWOOD

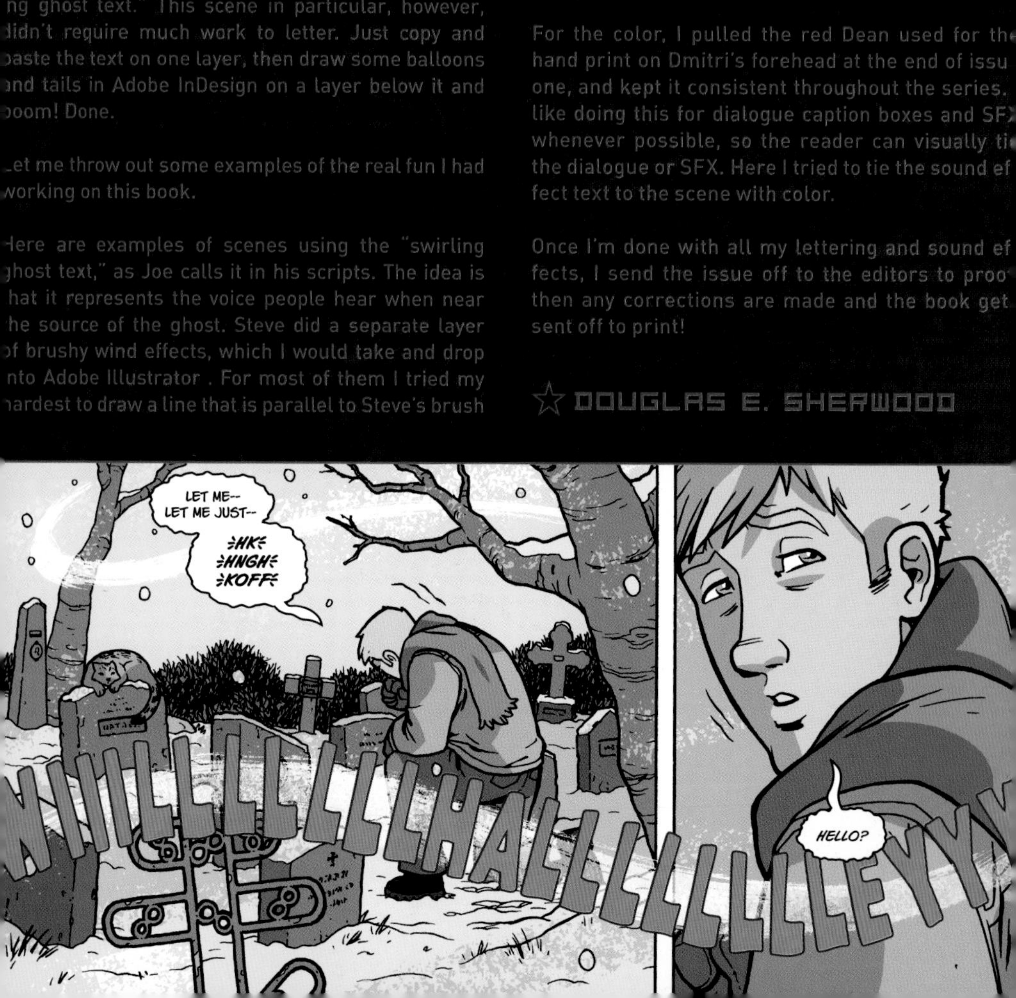
LET ME--
LET ME JUST--
HK
HNGH
KOFF
NIIILLLLLLLHALLLLLLLLEYY
HELLO?

ABOUT THE CREATORS

☆ **JOE HARRIS** is the acclaimed writer of numerous comics, graphic novels and movies.

As a young creator at Marvel Comics, Harris launched the cult classic *Spider-Man* series, *Slingers*, writing what Wizard Magazine described as "great teen angst." While at Marvel, Joe wrote myriad titles including *Bishop: The Last X-Man* and *X-Men: The Search For Cyclops*.

Harris made his screenwriting debut with Sony Pictures', *Darkness Falls*. Conceived and co-written by Joe, the hit movie was based on *Tooth Fairy*, a short horror film he both wrote and directed which offered a dark twist on the children's bedtime myth. He also co-wrote *The Tripper* with actor David Arquette. A Twentieth Century Fox release, it mixed politics and horror into an outrageous tale of murder, mayhem and the American Way.

Upcoming Oni Press projects include the supernatural thriller, *Spontaneous*, the dark children's fantasy collaboration with Adam Pollina, *Wars In Toyland* and the original graphic novel mixing action, drug humor and politics, *The Hashishian*.

His environmental disaster and survival adventure series, *Great Pacific* is forthcoming from Image Comics and *Bastardized*, the new horror series co-created with Ethan Van Sciver, is due from DC Comics in 2011.

Joe resides in New York City, where he was born and raised. For more information about his projects, please visit joeharris.net.

☆ **STEVE ROLSTON** can be found drawing comics under the floorboards of an abandoned weapons facility in Vancouver, Canada. According to declassified documents, his first official mission was as the original artist on the Eisner Award winning spy comic *Queen & Country*. In the decade that followed, his art skills were deployed on a variety of comics such as *Pounded*, *Mek*, *The Escapists*, *Degrassi*, *Emiko Superstar* and his own graphic novel *One Bad Day*. Further data can be acquired online at steverolston.com.

☆ **DEAN TRIPPE** is a freelance comics creator who lives with his wife and son in Austin, TX. He is the creator of the superhero parody webcomic, *Butterfly*, the founder and editor of the superhero fashion blog, *Project: Rooftop*, and was a contributing artist to the Eisner and Harvey award-winning graphic anthology, *Comic Book Tattoo*. Dean is a former comic shop manager, a lifelong superheroes fan, and has an actual degree in comic books. For more of his work, visit deantrippe.com

OTHER BOOKS FROM ONI PRESS...

DAMNED, VOLUME 1: THREE DAYS DEAD
By Cullen Bunn & Brian Hurtt
160 pages • 6"x9" Trade Paperback
Black-and-White
$14.99 US
ISBN 978-1-932664-6-38

QUEEN & COUNTRY:
DEFINITIVE EDITION, VOLUME 1
By Greg Rucka, Steve Rolston, Brian Hurtt
& Leandro Fernandez
376 pages • 6"x9" Trade Paperback
Black-and-White
$19.99 US
ISBN 978-1-932664-87-4

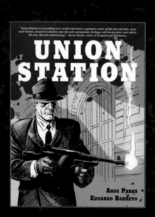

RESURRECTION:
VOLUME 1
By Marc Guggenheim, David Dumeer &
Justin Greenwood
384 pages • Standard
Black-and-White and Full Color
$24.99 US
ISBN 978-1-934964-28-6

UNION STATION
By Ande Parks & Eduardo Barreto
128 pages, 6"x9" Trade Paperback
Black-and-White
$11.95 US
ISBN 978-1-934964-27-9

WASTELAND:
THE APOCALYPTIC EDITION, VOLUME 1
By Antony Johnston & Christopher Mitten
384 pages • Hardcover
Black-and-White
$34.99 US
ISBN 978-1-934964-19-4

WHITEOUT:
DEFINITIVE EDITION, VOLUME 1:
By Greg Rucka & Steve Lieber
128 pages, 6"x9" Trade Paperback
Black-and-White
$13.95 US
ISBN 978-1-932664-70-6

 **ONI PRESS**

For more information on these and other fine Oni Press comic books and graphic novels visit www.onipress.com. To find a comic specialty store in your area visit www.comicshops.us.